IN THE LATE 1980S ON THE JERSEY SHORE, Jane Wong watches her mother shake ants from an MSG bin behind the family's Chinese restaurant. She is a hungry daughter frying crab rangoon for lunch, a child sneaking naps on bags of rice, a playful sister scheming to trap her brother in the freezer before he traps her first. Jane is part of a family staking their claim to the American dream, even as this dream crumbles. Beneath Atlantic City's promise lies her father's gambling addiction, an addiction that causes him to disappear for days and ultimately leads to the loss of the restaurant.

In her debut memoir, Jane Wong tells a new story about Atlantic City, one that resists a single identity, a single story as she writes about making do with what you have—and what you don't. What does it mean, she asks, to be both tender and angry? What is strength without vulnerability—and humor? Filled with beauty found in unexpected places, *Meet Me Tonight in Atlantic City* is a resounding love song of the Asian American working class, a portrait of how we become who we are, and a story of lyric wisdom to hold and to share.

"In *Meet Me Tonight in Atlantic City*, Jane Wong mines her life with a poet's comb, examining even its frayed, messy edges in breathtaking detail, and shining light on its most intimately vulnerable questions. A thoughtful, vivid storyteller with formidable lyricism, Wong has written a spectacular ode to the words and women that raised her."

—**MORGAN PARKER**,
author of *You Get What You Pay For*

"To borrow Jane Wong's own words, there are sparks coming off Wong's blade of language. The spunky voice in this memoir shines through. I'm so grateful to Wong for telling her unique story in only the way she can, and in the process, expanding the possibilities of Asian American stories. There's so much heart in these stories that explore race, class, and family history, that we can't help but root for the protagonist. This is a big-hearted coming-of-age book that simultaneously asks hard questions."

—**VICTORIA CHANG**,
author of *With My Back to the World*

"My favorite aphorism about New Jersey is that only the strong survive it. I see that place here in all its chaotic splendor and that strength in the carving marks on each finely cut image. This is a perfect and glimmering book that could only have been forged in Jane Wong's bloody and beautiful heart."

—**ELISSA WASHUTA**,
author of *White Magic*

"Jane Wong, with her poet's eye for precise and delightful detail, carves out a quintessential story of family, gambling, loss, heartaches, toothaches, and above all, love. *Meet Me Tonight in*

Atlantic City takes a father's addiction to the prismatic casinos of Atlantic City and places it against a mother's fierce, unsparing devotion and a daughter's struggle to make sense of loss. I love the tenderness and ferocity of her prose, unsentimental and wrenching, that refuses easy triumph in its immigrant story and isn't afraid of uncovering both beauty and brutality. *Meet Me Tonight in Atlantic City* is, at heart, a love story between Wong and her mother, Wong and herself."

—SALLY WEN MAO,
author of *Ninetails*

"Filled with wisdom, wit, and wonder, Jane Wong's sumptuous and soulful *Meet Me Tonight in Atlantic City* is a bold, joyous ballad to all the unseen and unsung parts of life, and dares to find beauty and strength in them. Rendered in gorgeous, evocative prose, this is a book that shimmers, swings, and soars on every page." —GINA CHUNG,
author of *Green Frog*

"Searing, stunning, and singular." —KYLE LUCIA WU,
author of *Win Me Something*

"In *Meet Me Tonight in Atlantic City*, Wong sinks her nails into the glimmering illusions of the American Dream and does not stop until she draws blood. Lofting her words in loyal fury, Wong demands acknowledgement for her family and community, and for all the immigrants invisibly drawn to the shining promises of a future never built for them. With rage and generosity, Wong draws a line in the sand, calling out a lyrical refusal to be defined by anything but herself." —TESSA HULLS,
author of *Feeding Ghosts*

MEET ME TONIGHT IN ATLANTIC CITY

A Memoir

JANE WONG

TIN HOUSE / PORTLAND, OREGON

This is a work of nonfiction, except for a handful of names and
identifying details changed to respect individuals' privacy.

CREDITS: Gwendolyn Brooks, excerpt from "Speech to the Young: Speech to the Progress-Toward
(among Them Nora and Henry III)," from *Blacks* (Chicago: Third World Press,1991). Reprinted By
Consent of Brooks Permissions. | Marilyn Chin, excerpt from "How I Got That Name" from *The
Phoenix Gone, the Terrace Empty*. Copyright © 1994 by Marilyn Chin. Reprinted with the permission
of The Permissions Company, LLC on behalf of Milkweed Editions, www.milkweed.org. | Lucille
Clifton, excerpt from "why some people be mad at me sometimes" from *How to Carry Water: Selected
Poems*. Copyright © 1987 by Lucille Clifton. Reprinted with the permission of The Permissions
Company, LLC on behalf of BOA Editions Ltd., boaeditions.org. | Lucille Clifton, excerpt from "*won't
you celebrate with me*" from *The Book of Light*. Copyright © 1993 by Lucille Clifton. Reprinted with the
permission of The Permissions Company, LLC on behalf of Copper Canyon Press, coppercanyonpress.
org. | bell hooks, excerpts from *All About Love: New Visions* (New York: HarperCollins Publishers,
2018). Copyright © 2001 by Gloria Watkins. | "Final Curve" from THE COLLECTED POEMS OF
LANGSTON HUGHES by Langston Hughes, edited by Arnold Rampersad with David Roessel,
Associate Editor, copyright © 1994 by the Estate of Langston Hughes. Used by permission of Alfred A.
Knopf, an imprint of the Knopf Doubleday Publishing Group, a division of Penguin Random House
LLC. All rights reserved. | Audre Lorde, excerpt from "Poetry Is Not a Luxury" from *The Selected
Works of Audre Lorde*, edited and with an introduction by Roxane Gay (New York: W. W. Norton &
Company, 2020). Copyright © 2020 by Roxane Gay. Copyright © 2009, 2007, 2006, 1993 by the Estate
of Audre Lorde. Copyright © 1988, 1986, 1984, 1982, 1978, 1976, 1974, 1973, 1970, 1968 by Audre Lorde.

First US Edition 2023
Printed in the United States of America
First paperback edition 2024

Manufacturing by Sheridan | Interior design by Beth Steidle

Library of Congress Cataloging-in-Publication Data
Names: Wong, Jane, author.
Title: Meet me tonight in Atlantic City : a memoir / Jane Wong.
Description: Portland, Oregon : Tin House, [2023]
Identifiers: LCCN 2022060779 | ISBN 9781953534675 (hardcover) | ISBN 9781953534743 (ebook)
Subjects: LCSH: Wong, Jane—Family. | Chinese American women—New Jersey—
Atlantic City--Biography. | Chinese Americans—New Jersey--Atlantic City—Biography.
| Women poets—Washington (State)—Seattle—Biography. | Poets—Washington
(State—Seattle—Biography. | Atlantic City (N.J.)—Biography. | Seattle (Wash.)—Biography.
Classification: LCC F144.A8 W66 2023 | DDC 974.9/850092
[B]—dc23/eng/20221229
LC record available at https://lccn.loc.gov/2022060779

Paperback ISBN 9781959030393

Tin House | 2617 NW Thurman Street, Portland, OR 97210 | www.tinhouse.com

Distributed by W. W. Norton & Company

1 2 3 4 5 6 7 8 9 0

For my mother and brother, my everything.
Let's get pizza, you know where!

TABLE OF CONTENTS

MEET ME TONIGHT IN ATLANTIC CITY

DRAGON FRUIT

IN THE MURKY BROTH OF YET ANOTHER HEARTACHE, MY mother cuts me slices of dragon fruit. I'm home in Jersey and slumped at the kitchen table. My hair is dip-dyed in snot, tears, and hot mascara. She hands me a slice, the white interior flecked with black seeds like suspended ants. The slice dangles on her knife, the glinting steel close to my mouth. I eat it off the knife. I've always eaten fruit this way, right off the sparks of my mother's blade. I take it into my throat, still heaving from too much survival mode. The taste is mild, despite the fluorescent hot-pink flame. The seeds punctuate something I know must come. It slides down my throat like a sweet summer slug.

"Jane, you have to be strong. I need you to eat more," she tells me, cutting another slice.

But I tell her I'm so tired of being strong. Fuck strength, fuck resilience, fuck lessons to learn, fuck trying and trying and trying! I tell her I don't want to be strong. That I can't be strong anymore, even if I wanted to be. I want to be weak. I want to fall completely apart. I want all the atoms in my body to crumble, scree of the self. I want to lie down on this cold kitchen table forever. I want to be a-sloth-who-hasn't-shit-in-a-week weak. Cracked-ice, dish-soap-bubbles, mild-hot-sauce, rabbit-paralyzed-by-fear, my-breath-leaking-from-me-like-an-ellipsis weak.

I expect her to disagree, to demand strength, to tell me I have no choice. Did she have a choice, staring at the gaping pits my father left behind?

This time though, she doesn't fight me. "So be weak," she says, almost like a threat. Sticky fruit juice encircles her jade bracelet. Fruit flies rouse around us, dizzy stars. "But you have to eat more dragon fruit and clear your system."

She wants me to shit it out. This time, she hands me the knife.

1

MEET ME TONIGHT
IN ATLANTIC CITY

LET'S BEGIN HERE: ON THE GROUND. OR RATHER ON THE slabs of wood above the ground. In July, 1854, a New Jersey tourist train from Camden made its inaugural voyage to Atlantic City. Tourists came to stick their toes in the Atlantic Ocean—steel blue, the color of whales they'd never see. They came to lean against each other in the high dunes and make promises they couldn't keep. They let the wind lift those promises up, caught in the chandeliers of expensive hotels or the beaks of passing seagulls. The women who came held frilled umbrellas—jellyfish along the shore. And when they returned to their jobs and errands and thumb-sucking babies, they carried sand with them, making the train car a beach in and of itself. Glitter of the sea. This is how the boardwalk came to be: a frustrated railroad conductor and simply too much sand for his own sweeping sanity. On June 16, 1870, boards were erected, 10 feet wide and 12 feet long.

Just to be clear: this is not our story. Not yet. Our story moves across that steel-blue fantasy, onto another continent, toward a place where there is no such thing as "vacation." My ancestors will stare at that word, 假期, as if it were a cloud that could disappear at any point. On this continent, there are herds of oxen and lily pads the size of promises that can't be made. As a small child, I dreamt of this story. Of an ox and my mother riding its back, the hair on its hide so coarse, it makes your throat hurt. Our story, our history, is a different Atlantic City.

It is 1988 and my mother is still dreaming in Toisanese—not a single word of English worms its way through her open-mouth sleep world. My little brother, Steven, had just been born, howling like a wolf who knew he was a boy. Four years earlier, when the nurses placed me in my mother's arms, I stared at her silently. She held me up to the fluorescent hospital light and declared: "I'm afraid. She knows too much." By 1988, my father had been holding illegal mahjong gambling circles for five years, often in the basement. Cigarette smoke escaped like doves from underneath the floorboards. And the shuffling. The shuffling sound of mahjong tiles, a porcelain earthquake. I learned later that some of these tiles used to be made out of bone or bamboo. Now: Bakelite, plastic. My father always invited the same people to play with him: the Chicken Bone Man, City Uncle, and Balding Uncle. His friends always played with toothpicks dangling out of their mouths, moving the sticks from side to side in concentration. My brother and I named the crew the Toothpick Gang.

Just to be clear again: our story is not about small enterprises. Our story goes beyond the small batons of $20 bills passed around the mahjong table. Beyond the table's green felt, stained with cheap Tsingtao and sky-high piles of gnawed bones from the Chicken Bone Man's self-evident pastime.

Our story is Atlantic City. We are talking about the Taj Mahal, Caesars, Bally's. Casinos depicting worlds my father simply couldn't fathom. At Caesars, there were towering white columns so extravagant they held up nothing at all. There were white statues of horses braying, a ceiling painted like the sky with white clouds, the busts of white people we assumed were famous but were really just white. My parents didn't even know where Rome was on a map or that Rome existed. But Caesars was gleaming in its whiteness. Who could say no to the patina of wealth?

This is how we arrived: on that Chinese tourist bus where you have to fan yourself with your $10 gambling voucher and put your cigarette out in a Dixie cup. Or, if you hit it big like we once did, you can arrive in the dolphin-colored leather of your BMW, before you inevitably crash it into the Garden State Parkway median. No air-conditioning and the windows down, to save on gas mileage, of course. We arrived over a century later on a boardwalk full of non-white faces. Shoulder pads, pinstriped suits, and an amalgamation of languages punctuating the salty air. The poor, the working class, the hopeful in red-tag sequin dresses from Marshalls. Here we are! Yes, here, with self-serve wine and crab legs at the Palace Court Buffet—all of which we marveled at, but never touched.

* * *

DURING THE 1870S, THE boardwalk was broken apart after each summer came to a close and moved into storage for the cold season. Board by board. Stored like quilts, like pickled radishes, like a family who won't look each other in the eye.

For repeat patrons, i.e., patrons who threw enough money away, casinos offered free hotel stays for the whole family. Each Valentine's Day, Memorial Day, Fourth of July, Thanksgiving, and Christmas, my father disappeared into the red velvet of spinning roulette tables. We had other plans. Steven and I tested the structural soundness of hotel beds by jumping on them. Once, a cockroach flew out of the mattress, disturbed in its sleep. It somersaulted in the air, a perfect 10. "How is this fancy?" my mother bemoaned. She was used to crushing cockroaches and punched its antennae lights out. K.O. Game over.

Steven and I traded the remote back and forth like secrets, marveling over cable television. We spent hours watching channels we didn't have: Nickelodeon, MTV, Disney. We sang a dirge for basic television. *Rest in peace, you piece of shit. Rest in peace, you piece of shit.* In the afternoon, we walked the boardwalk back and forth with the other Chinese American kids who were never allowed to play that water-gun race. No stuffed dinosaurs for us, no Dippin' Dots. The game operators, home from college and tipsy on Pabst, were always shouting at my mother, words she didn't understand. "Hey gorgeous, lemme get your number while the brats play!" and "I'd let you play for free any day, baby!" and "Hey pretty lady, you speakee any Englishee?" At 26, my mother was all pink lipstick and confused by the attention, but she knew to accept gifts from white people: an ice-cold Coke pressed against her cheek, a stuffed orca whale for Steven.

Here is one scene, on a shore of many: on the way back to Caesars, my mother sits on a boardwalk bench, the dune grass behind her like the back of a throne. From her purse: stolen bread rolls from the Palace Court Buffet. She chews out all her anger on those bread rolls. Gnarls in the crust. Soft middles demolished along her patent leather heels, digging into boardwalk cracks. Seagulls swarm near her, in full praise. Glitter of the boardwalk.

"I'm tired, Mommy," I whine, pulling on her earrings with my sandy hands. Next year, her earlobes will split open from too-heavy earrings. The infection will heal and yield a scar I will grow jealous of.

"Tell that to Daddy."

The sky is all lavender and dragon fruit. Everywhere around us, people gawk at the swirling sky and take pictures. Later, when I ask my mother for baby pictures of me, she'll tell me we were too poor to afford a camera. She'll simply repeat: "I held you up. You didn't blink and had the biggest eyes I've ever seen." *I'm afraid. She knows too much.*

I lean my head against her sharp shoulders, which will always vacillate between sharpening and softening. Steven joins the seagulls and starts eating bread crumbs off the ground.

"What's it like in there? Where Daddy goes?" I ask her.

My mother stares at my brother. He has my father's eyes—big and shining like a dying flashlight. He will grow to be as tall as my father: six feet, to be exact. He will be a handsome man who has to shave, every day, stubble sprouting like fine bristles. But at this moment, his tongue is speckled with sand and gluten.

"Stop that right now," my mother screams at him. "Stop that, stop that!"

Soon, Steven is wailing, and that unrelenting sound answers all my questions. Meanwhile, an off-duty clown strolls down the boardwalk with his date for the night. She is holding one of his oversized bowling pins and laughing like something is stuck in her belly. Chilly wind cuts through the sand and the boardwalk shifts underneath our feet. Was winter coming? Yes, but not now: her hair is coiled cotton candy. "Show me that new trick," she sings in the dwindling light.

I did not know, at that time, what my mother thought of Atlantic City. What she thought of that fake blue sky at Caesars, of transparent lettuce with Russian dressing, of my father—a man she barely knew—throwing money on a table for something utterly intangible. Not long ago, she was a farm girl, sucking on sugarcane after hiking up the mountains to gather wood for the stove. This is before she was arranged to marry my father at 19. My father: a tall stranger who moved to a country where a piece of plastic could buy a car. My mother's name, because she's real: Jin Ai.

The scene continues for Jin Ai, but not for us: at 6:00 AM, my mother wakes up from a dream in a language she doesn't yet understand. *Hey gorgeous, hey pretty lady, hey baby.* She walks past our sleeping forms—consumed in white down feathers—and pulls on her heels. With purpose, she takes the elevator to the first floor. She walks into that red-velvet room and follows what her heart does not desire. My father is whiskey-eyed and half-asleep—a drowsy raccoon hunched over the blackjack table. His shirt is unbuttoned one too many and his empty wallet is an open window. My mother clenches her fists and imagines raising them to the fake sky above. Her eyes swirl like a whirlpool. No one will ever know if she's crying.

My father doesn't say her name or look up. "One more game."

Dozens of floors above, we are still dreaming. *K.O. K.O. K.O.*

* * *

REMEMBER: THIS STORY IS not about small enterprises. This story expands like an oil spill; it touches the fins of every faraway shore. This is a story poor immigrants share, like those packed bunk beds shared with false uncles and false aunts. Just to be clear: we are targeted. This is no mistake. This can't be boiled down to cultural proclivity for luck. Casino buses roll into Chinatowns across the country like ice cream trucks for a reason.

Cache Creek Casino, north of San Francisco, has a pet fish fittingly named Mr. Lucky: a two-foot-long dragonfish, also known as an Asian arowana. In an article on these fish, the *New York Post* likens their round scales to coins, and reveals that they can be worth up to $300,000. Cache Creek's vision: Chinese gamblers tapping the cool blue tank, hoping for luck. Wendy Waldorf, a spokesperson for Cache Creek, tells the *Los Angeles Times* that the casino caters to Asians, a significant market. In New York, NBC News reports, discount buses depart from Chinatown to take approximately 30,000 Chinese gamblers to casinos outside the metro area each week, including those in Atlantic City. In 2011, a bus on a return trip from the Mohegan Sun in Connecticut crashed and killed 14 passengers. With mangled limbs and empty pockets, whose grandmother was lost, whose father? In "How I Got That Name," Marilyn Chin writes of her own father's gambling addiction:

> While my father dithers,
> a tomcat in Hong Kong trash—
> a gambler, a petty thug,
> who bought a chain of chopsuey joints
> in Piss River, Oregon

In a 2012 *MELUS* interview with Chin about her gambling father, she speaks about her siblings and the necessity of humor: "We had to laugh deep from our guts to keep from crying."

Across the country, mirroring Chin's Piss River, Oregon, my father played all night in Atlantic City. He did not stop to eat or go to the bathroom or ask where his family was. My father owned a Chinese American takeout restaurant on the Jersey shore, and we would lose this one asset from his gambling. He did not dither in that red-velvet world of his. When we didn't go to Atlantic City with him, he'd disappear for days, sometimes a week. My mother ran the restaurant without him, her arms scraping the fryer, grime peeling like bark. Her anger: strips of wonton wrappers seething in that fryer, slow and dangerous. She was a motionless alligator ready to strike, and we avoided her gaze during those reptilian days.

When we'd drive home from Atlantic City together, my father would glow over his winnings. He'd flail an arm back in that poorly won BMW and toss a couple of $20 bills at us. "Liar," my mother would say, staring out the window. "You lost. You always lose." The new leather burned our thighs as we watched the Parkway smokestacks grow exponentially.

She was right. My father always lost in the end. Next year, he would ram the BMW into a median on his midnight way to Atlantic

City. What he would lose beyond money—his job, family, and sobriety, among other things—would not be clear to him until much later. Perhaps it's still not clear to him now; I wouldn't know. Underneath those boardwalk boards, there is so much rotting trash.

Gambling addiction rates among Asian Americans in the U.S. are notably high, according to psychiatrist Dr. Tim Fong at UCLA's Gambling Studies Program. In a 2007 article, Fong and his co-author Dr. John Tsuang speak about how factors such as shame, denial, guilt, language barriers, and help-seeking behaviors heighten pathological gambling within Asian American communities. Did my father seek a different future for all of us, or just for himself? One truth: the sky was always blue at Caesars. A director at the NICOS Chinese Health Coalition, Michael Liao explores the relationship between immigration, gambling, and social status. In his 2016 article "Asian Americans and Problem Gambling," he speaks about the impulse to gamble being tied to matters of control and decision-making processes. Among vulnerable communities who may feel powerless in their everyday lives, this is one way to take action. After we lost the restaurant, my father was unable to hold a steady job. He would spend a few days working for someone else as a cook, only to storm out shouting and hurling spatulas. His apron would be thrown in the trash, ties dangling in the wind like snakes. The same goes for that factory job, that A&P grocery job, that dim sum waiter job, that, and that. "I'm the boss," my father would snarl beneath a plume of cigarette smoke. His brown leather jacket slumped around his shoulders as if he were unable to shed his own hide. I always found it funny that his jacket's interior label read: *I Don't Want to Go to Work.* And so he didn't. My father rarely spoke to us, even more rarely in English, and this is what we remember him saying the most: *I'm the boss.* Translation: What can I hold onto?

Our shared story moves away from the past and into the future. In 2016, the Lucky Dragon Casino, proudly calling their casino Las Vegas's premier Asian-themed resort, opened. A 1.2-ton gold-plated dragon dangles from a chandelier. In its press release, the casino was clear about its target market: the larger Asian diaspora, particularly Chinese. Located inside the casino, Dragon's Alley is a restaurant modeled after night markets in China and Taiwan, with red chairs and napkins, a neon sign, lanterns, and even full-sized, decorative bicycles. It even has a brick wall flown in from a government-housing alley in Beijing. If you touch the wall, you can practically go home. David Jacoby, the Lucky Dragon's chief operating officer, reassures patrons via the *Los Angeles Times* that the casino is "heavily feng shui'ed." It's true: the kitchen is blessed in the glitter of the American dream. Cleansed in luck, in that steel-blue water we all traversed.

* * *

MY MOTHER TRIED TO leave many times. She woke up in the middle of the night and packed a suitcase, folding each dress like a present for no one in particular. And each time, she failed to get out the door. My brother wouldn't leave his dinosaur blanket behind and refused to pack it. I begged for us to walk past that door, into the blinding snow. I dreamt of the icicles stinging my cheeks: relief. Ngin Ngin, my paternal grandmother, crumpled like a poorly made bed by the front door. If she had to endure her arranged marriage, why couldn't my mother?

It was my father who ended up finally leaving. That day was like any other. I went to school. My mother slept, since she'd started working the night shift for the United States Postal Service. And there were lunches and recesses and leaves falling from trees and ants crawling through a maze in my brother's classroom. But he—my father—was gone. Just like that. Breaking down the boardwalk. Except it was perpetually winter and we were thankful for it. That week, my mother opened the windows of our house to let the cigarette smoke out. To air out each promise, each day my father disappeared in Atlantic City. She changed the locks. She surveyed the brilliant brass doorknobs in her hands and thought: *These would make beautiful earrings.* All three of us carried his dirty floral armchair replete with cigarette burns down to the basement. We shoved it into a cobwebbed corner we could all forget.

Disappearance is a strange choice. I'll grow to learn this later as an adult, when a parade of men will suddenly leave me. One strange attempt, in the months that followed: my father broke into the house through the basement window and left half a rotisserie chicken, a red packet with $5 in it, and a scribbled note: *Happy Birthday, Jane.* My birthday had been months ago. I thought of the Chicken Bone Man as I tore the salty, glistening skin from the leg; yes, I ate it. I was grateful, even for this. I ate that chicken down to the white bone, clean. With my father at six feet tall, I wondered how he climbed into that tiny basement window. He must have finally transformed into a raccoon.

One summer in Atlantic City, my mother bought us hermit crabs on the boardwalk. After trips with no ice cream or boardwalk games, which truly were a scam, this was a sign of utter generosity. We loved the crabs dearly. We kissed their shells and let them strut along the hotel room floor. In the morning, my father was passed out in bed, still in his cheap button-down and too-big slacks. He had been gambling again all night. My brother and I watched, our hands over each other's mouths, as one of the hermit crabs crawled all over his back. Manifest destiny.

Decades later, when I asked my mother why she bought us those hermit crabs, she talked about waiting. "I remember standing outside of the gambling floor, watching you both run all over the place. And I remember looking around me—at the other wives waiting with children. How I looked just like them. Tired. And thinking: Why? Why am I standing here?" She paused, removing the daggers from her eyes, thrown in the direction of my father. "I felt bad for you both. I bought you hermit crabs."

* * *

IN SEATTLE WHERE I live now, it's the Snoqualmie Casino. The casino buses are luxury coaches, with toilets and air-conditioning. They pick up patrons in the Chinatown-International District, right behind the Uwajimaya grocery store. When I'm grocery shopping for anything that reminds me of home—persimmons, sour dried plums, and Chinese pickled vegetables—I swear I see my father boarding that bus, loafers polished in kitchen grease. I take one step closer to see better, hugging my sagging grocery bag to my chest. But then: another. He looks like my father too, with his leather jacket and wet black eyes, as if he's been crying. In this gray and misty city, it's hard to tell. They're all my father. Do I care if they are? Regardless, I wish they'd look at me. This is what I think, as these aging Asian gamblers take the vouchers from the casino bus driver and hold them tightly in their hands. *Do you see me? Look at me!*

This is the story of lost enterprises. I was 31 when Ngin Ngin passed away. She had dementia for years and remembered only two people toward the end of her life: my father and me. She'd repeat the same story about taking me to the swing set at a park. Underneath this story is my father's story: his love for his mother, the only person he never left. When my father abandoned our family, he moved in with Ngin Ngin and stayed with her for as long as he could. He peeled her red grapes; he brushed her white hair; he clipped her softening toenails. Decades ago, my uncles and Yeh Yeh, my paternal grandfather, had left the village and moved to Hong Kong to make money in the big city. Ngin Ngin had remained and raised my father, the baby of the family, alone. When she died, I was on tour for my first book of poems, *Overpour*, in Shanghai. In Jersey, as she was lowered into the dirt, loose as coffee grounds, I was restless from jet lag and staying in a hotel that smelled like recycled air. She was a celebrity at her local Dunkin Donuts in Matawan. Every time she came in, they took a Polaroid of her and gave a free small cup of drip coffee and a Munchkin. She couldn't speak English, but the word for coffee in Toisanese sounds pretty similar: kaa fe. When they'd try to give her a coffee cup sleeve, she'd wave them away; her hands could handle the heat. Photos of her in a fleece vest covered the café wall like a shiny patchwork quilt. But her photo wall eventually stopped. I wondered if the baristas were worried, peeking their heads out the door to see if she was around the parking lot's corner.

A couple of months after Ngin Ngin passed away, when I returned to Jersey during my winter break in 2016, my father called my mother out of nowhere and asked if I was coming home. "I can't remember the last time he called. Something's not right," she said, half laughing, half suspicious. The absurdity of it all. "He said he wanted to see you. I told him it was up to you."

How the scene went, after all was lost: my father arrived through the garage door as if he'd lived here all along. No knock, no announcement. It'd been many, many years since I'd seen him. My father had grown old. He wasn't how I remembered him as a small child or teenager. All his rotten teeth had fallen out. One golden crown hung from his mouth like a cardboard crescent moon. He was in gray sweatpants and holding a gift of four giant oranges—the size of small planets. We sat awkwardly around the kitchen table. My brother weaved his hands together as if they were glued. My mother peeled her own orange— an orange she'd bought—and aimed for a slowly brewing growl. My father, in his flitting laughter, told us how he'd learned to make his own wine. That it tasted terrible, like dirty feet. He announced in mixed Toisanese and English: "I can do whatever I want now." We all silently wondered if he was drunk. My mother, finished with her orange, grabbed a cleaver and started beheading apples. Tart slices rolled across the counter. It was time for my father to go.

Steven, 28 and fully bearded, had bought a bottle of merlot when he heard that our father was coming. As our father pulled on his shoes—stained white sneakers covered in grass cuttings—I watched my brother offer him this gift. Steven laughed, deep from the gut, to stop himself from crying. He was sweating, and I hoped that the bottle would slip right out of his hands and break open in the hallway, sputtering like sweet pomegranate seeds everywhere. At least, then, our father wouldn't take it. Later, when I asked my brother why he gave him the bottle, he said in the gentlest voice: "To pass the time."

I think of my father drinking too much and watching the NBA playoffs as I watch the playoffs. Of drinking himself to sleep and dreaming about his mother, her purple jade bracelet shining deep within the earth. Of how he jolts up in bed in the middle of the night, how he needs to see his daughter, right this instant. He'll remind himself not to talk about how much money he won or how she hasn't grown or any memories really. *Maybe*, he'll think, *I'm better now*. And the giant oranges. *Don't forget the oranges.*

* * *

LET'S NOT FORGET: THIS is the story of lost enterprises. Of boarded-up pizza joints, lonely stuffed animals sans tipsy game operators, echoing parking lots with floating trash, and neon lights toppled over like sandcastles. A ghost city. In 2012, the Revel, a $2.4 billion casino, opened. The Revel was the most anticipated undertaking in Atlantic City at that time; the entire exterior was built with glass, as if it could disappear at night. A casino that disappears into thin air—which it did, just two years later.

It's fair to say that the Revel did not have luck on its side. During construction, lightning struck a worker's bucket lift and killed him. Three construction executives died in a freak plane crash. This was another world my father could have dreamt in, abandoned in rotting, unlucky luxury. Hotel rooms with punched-out windows. Echoing concert halls with families of soprano rats. Seagulls building velvet nests, declaring their own American dream in feathery, squawking, bird-shit glory. Jim Whelan, the former mayor of Atlantic City, said "Atlantic City is like Dracula—you can't kill it, no matter how hard we try."

These days, if I close my eyes, I can hear Bruce Springsteen's "Atlantic City" playing in Tony's Baltimore Grill, a surviving Atlantic City pizzeria, or maybe in our old Chinese American takeout amid the hiss of the wok firing. Sometimes I imagine my father in the future: in his late nineties, strolling along an empty boardwalk with me. He walks with his arms cradled behind his back, as elderly Chinese folks often do. We walk, and he points out how the howling waves sound just like they do in the South China Sea. What kind of luck do I need for this to come true?

WONGMOM.COM

MY FRIEND BRANDON AND I ARE WALKING IN WHATCOM Falls Park in Bellingham, Washington, where I teach. The forest is full of ancient ferns and massive banana slugs and white people slathered in Patagonia. They stare at us while also trying not to stare at us, and in the trying, they trip over rocks and sticks. It's been many years since I've seen Brandon, and he tells me about reading his late father's journals and finding surprising stories, poems, and other threads that connected to his own life. Then he shifts the conversation. "Your mom said something to me on a bus, like what, seven years ago? I really needed that." We are walking up the interwoven roots of a massive oak tree. I do remember: on the 12 bus in Seattle from Capitol Hill to downtown, my mother moves over to take a seat next to Brandon, a total stranger to her, and tells him something (this is for Brandon only to know). And the next thing I know, she's inviting him to stay with her on the Jersey shore. "I wish there was something like Wongmom .com. Like you could just type in what's been on your mind and press enter. It's your mom's voice, saying exactly what you need to hear." I laugh and tell him that's funny, but Brandon is absolutely serious and stops walking. "No, really," he says. "I need Wongmom.com."

And then I remember there's this video of her I took once, at a thrift store in Seattle, where she wags her finger at my phone and says out of nowhere: "Jane, I'm psychic." When I feel hopeless or angry or grief-stricken, I watch this video on loop. I watch and eat my Cheetos and laugh-cry, tears shellacked in cheese dust. There she is: my mother beaming her ferocity forward again and again, toward some future-past-present only she knows. Everyone who watches the video leans in together like trees in a windstorm—baby hairs touching—to listen to her powers. *Tell us, tell us!* From Theresa Hak Kyung Cha's *Dictee*: "Beginning wherever you wish, tell even us."

You do want to know, don't you?

2

ROOT CANAL STREET

The doctor places his hands on the patient's face
and exerts pressure on the upper maxillary nerves.
This creates a temporary numbness similar to
what happens when one's foot goes to sleep.
—DIANE LI, *The Barefoot Doctors of Rural China*

All this shimmery ache in one place . . .
—DAWN LUNDY MARTIN, *Life in a Box Is a Pretty Life*

1-9 AND 3-O (FIRST LOWER MOLARS):
Rich people have good teeth. Even the back molars, which are deep
caves where bioluminescent animals live. If I open my mouth, you can
practically see the glowing lure of a lantern fish—with teeth so big,
it can't even close its mouth. A fellow classmate I'll call Kristin was
a popular, rich girl in my middle school and probably had polished
molars like spotless K-Swiss sneakers. For my eighth-grade graduation, my mother and I picked out a floral A-line sundress from Lord
and Taylor. It was important to look rich, even if you weren't. For this
dress and all our dresses, my mother worked until her palms were
bruised and cut from lugging MSG bins and hacking spareribs at the
restaurant. Or in later years, peppered with paper cuts and bouts of
vertigo from sorting mail at the post office.

"This is the dress," my mother nodded, spinning me around, despite the fact that it was most definitely not $19.99, the absolute max for clothes. The year was 1998. There was no red sticker, no coupon clipped from junk mail.

"It's too much," I protested.

"You're so pretty in it. Now straighten your back when you walk," she said, and so I stretched myself upward, as if pulled by a string. But when I showed up in the same outfit as Kristin, I felt the peonies rise from my dress and smack themselves onto my cheeks. Sneers from Kristin and her mean-girl clique seethed through fence-straight teeth, glowing like little white ghost babies: "What a wannabe, what a loser. Copycat!" And then, worse: "Ew, what's her name, anyway?" There it was: the familiar giggling of erasure, of buying fancy dresses without blinking. I wanted to tell them that I saw the dress first, to brag about the geological thickness of my mother's palms and how they better not mess with us. I wanted to shout: "My name is Jane Wong, motherfuckers!" Instead, I wore my oversized Gap hoodie over my dress and imagined cowering in a locker or being absorbed by the peeling plaster of the hallway. Ultimately, Kristin and her friends' parents chose private high schools because our public school was "not great." Read: our school had too many immigrant and Black and Brown teenagers for their liking.

Rich people have teeth so white and smooth and straight, sometimes you want to knock those teeth right out and stuff them into your own mouth.

8 (CENTRAL INCISOR):

I don't know how many years go by, but it's many. I think I must be a senior in high school by now. I'm on my way to Bard College in the fall, which is important because I am the first in my family to go to college. I leave two strips of Crest whitening on for 10 minutes, a bit over what they suggest. For extra sparkle. I foam at the mouth like a rabid bat or a broken washing machine. In college, I can become whatever I want: poet protégé, artsy pixie dream girl. Even hipsters are supposed to have white teeth, right? No one needs to know that I'm from Jersey. Let's say: California, New York, whatever "New England" means. These are good, convenient answers.

Whitening strips can't fill cavities, though. I touch my aching tooth in the dentist's waiting room and it wobbles with hot pain. I imagine infrared maps flaring rainbows out of my mouth.

"We send reminders. By phone and by postcard," the annoyed dental hygienist tells my mother. She glances down at her records and raises an eyebrow. She doesn't even say how many years have passed since my last visit. Instead, she mouths the number into the air, silently, like a catfish gulping water.

"I know, I know. We're just so busy." My mother laughs nicely, but really I can tell she is rolling her eyes at the lecture. She has her hands curled around her credit card like a squirrel around a nut. "Single mom," she adds.

My molar feels like rotting roadkill—soft all around, but held by strong bones.

The hygienist doesn't care about the busy life of a single mother who works overtime. "It's called an annual visit for a reason."

As we leave the office, post-fillings, my mouth is swollen and half-numb. I'm drooling from the right side. I wipe it away with the back of my hand. I look down at my spittle and notice a shimmering pink smear. Why in the world did I wear lipstick?

Repeat: it's important to look rich. Repeat: you must be put together at all times.

My mother and I link arms as we walk out. "Ta th ink we thon't know wha 'ann ual' eans. We're not upid," I mumble out of one working mouth corner.

"That's right. No one tells me how to live my life!" my mother declares in the parking lot. The skinny strip-mall trees nod and sway back in agreement. *Yeah, what she said!*

7-1 (DECIDUOUS BABY, LOWER INCISOR):

When her first tooth came in, my mother must have thought it was a shark's fin, peeking out of the water. Or maybe a slowly disappearing piling along the Puget Sound, with little spiders in each wooden stake, trying to live their lives against the wind. Of course, she thought none of these things. Partly because she didn't know about sharks or old Pacific Northwest pilings, and partly because she was just a baby. My mother came into this world at the start of the Cultural Revolution, in a tiny rural village in Southern China, outside of Toisan. You have to take a dirt road for hours to get there. The farm fields stretch so far, they blur together like soup.

To say food was scarce would be an understatement. Pau Pau, my maternal grandmother, made my mother's favorite dish daily: boiled rice soup with little bits of sweet potatoes. Sometimes there was a peanut pancake. An egg or bit of meat, on your birthday. Tucked deep in the countryside, my family didn't think of Mao Zedong as a man, but as a faraway idea. Politics just happened and no one really knew who, what, when, where, how, or—most importantly—why. My mother's first tooth sprouted like a rare white yam. Her tooth shone in the twilight, and Gung Gung, my maternal grandfather, held her as she protested its arrival. Her first tooth came in before Gung Gung was taken away by city officials and jailed. And thus, he reveled in his firstborn's panicked cries, in her mouth's declaration: *I am ready to tear through the world!*

In the countryside, dental problems were the least of your worries. Basic health care needs were barely met. Idealistic, Mao's Directive on Public Health from June 26, 1965, sought to extend medical services to rural areas; doctors began to make occasional village visits. Usually, villagers had to walk or bike hours to reach a larger town with medical care. There were few, if any, dentists. When there was a rotten tooth, doctors would be called on for an extraction. Without hypodermic needles and Novocain, doctors would use acupressure. Acupressure for dummies: for exactly one minute, apply pressure with the thumb and forefinger to a spot on the cheek and on the jaw. Then, draw the tooth.

Tooth extraction was commonplace. Prevention, including toothbrushes and toothpaste, was not readily implemented or emphasized. "I loved sugarcane," my mother told me. "It was a special treat. I loved it more than anything."

Sweet baby teeth, falling out for sweeter adult teeth. Falling out. What I'm trying to say: my mother doesn't have any real teeth.

9 (CENTRAL INCISOR):

On the morning of my high school graduation, my mother comes into my room with a set of four ivory teeth in her open palm. They look like a row of seats in a theater. "I'm sorry," she sighs, holding her aching jaw like a fish caught by a hook. "I can't smile in any pictures today." I look up at her, her beauty radiating with the rising sun behind her. The mole above her left eye: a glowing planet not yet discovered. My mother is, quite simply, beautiful. At this point, she is in her late thirties. I tell her not to worry about it. I won't smile in solidarity.

The weekend following my graduation, we drive into New York City together. Through the cool hull of the Holland Tunnel and straight to the crowded, neon-lit streets of Chinatown. We need to see the dentist to fix my mother's fake teeth. Her current row of implants has lasted six years. I can't tell if that's a good or bad deal. Along Canal Street, the air is thick with the smell of fish breath and long fried doughnuts being dipped into steaming jook. Decked out in a pink silk wrap dress, giant tortoise shell sunglasses, and perfectly curled hair and eyelashes, my mother is the last person you'd expect to find following a sketchy 80-year-old grandma in a labyrinthine search for an unlicensed Chinatown dentist.

Repeat: you must be put together at all times. Especially when you have no insurance and no teeth to put together.

This was one of the many trips I took with my mother to Chinatown. We'd go to fix her teeth and buy some roast duck to bring home. Sometimes I'd grab a slice of pizza in Little Italy before we'd meet up with the grandma at the prearranged location. It was always just the two of us—never my brother, or my father when he was still in our lives. A freakish mother-daughter ritual. Other mothers and daughters had manicures, spa dates, hikes, and river-rafting retreats. Us: getting fake teeth fixed in Chinatown. Bonding over crowns.

An open secret of sorts, unlicensed dentistry in Chinatown is a widespread practice that often takes place in the dentists' homes. Most of them used to practice in China, but haven't received their license in the U.S. yet because of diploma issues or language barriers. Back when I used to go with my mother in the late '80s and early '90s, unlicensed dentists could charge $100 for a root canal and $130 for a broken tooth. In cash, of course. The same services in a licensed clinic are worth at least five times this amount. Such practices go beyond Chinatown too; under-the-table health care exists in low-income neighborhoods across the country. "Everyone knew the neighborhood dentist," my friend Catina told me when speaking about the housing projects in New Haven, Connecticut. According to the Dental Implant Cost Guide online, a single tooth replacement option in the U.S. costs between $1,000 and $3,000, not factoring in the appointment costs, X-rays, and the crown itself. With all these expenses included, it can cost $4,500 for one tooth. And if you've lost most of your real teeth, multiply that number by x amount of rot. My mother brought $600 in cash for an entire row of teeth.

Speaking in Cantonese was free, no added charge. My parents arrived in the States in their early 20s, not knowing a single word of English. How are you supposed to navigate the supermarket, let alone the American health system? The paperwork? It's enough to make you want to stack phone book after phone book behind the front door. Keep what you don't know out. Insurance and American medical care was (and is) expensive and hard to decipher, especially with language and cultural barriers. *Why is there so much white?* my mother must have wondered when she ended up in the hospital to give birth to me. White, a funeral color. White, the color of rich-people teeth. Flushed and exhausted in an itchy white gown, she must have been scared in so many ways, but unable to vocalize her fears.

Each time we went, we saw a different dentist. Probably on account of the shoddy treatment my mother received each time, and was trying to avoid. At least, I imagine so, if I factor in the sound of my mother moaning in pain and raising her hand to mean: *Nope, not acupressure.* At first I thought I was there to keep her company during these "bonding" trips. But then I saw my presence as something else entirely. I was there to witness, to document, to make sure she was okay—not hurt—at the end of it all. To protest if something wasn't quite right. But it always felt that way to me: not quite right. The dusty floors. The disorganized workstations where the dentist molded teeth, bits of pink putty and cement everywhere. The dentist slurping up noodles in a T-shirt before the procedure, a chili oil stain by the neckline like a ruby brooch. But at the same time, I understood why. Why I was there, waiting for her with a strange grandma happily chomping away at the baked goods we'd bought her. There: teetering nervously on a folding chair, listening to my mother's rising and lowering whimpers. There: deciding when to run to her aid. There: filling the needs of a community that can't afford basic health care.

When my mother smiles for my high school graduation photos, her mouth is closed. I aim for the same closed-mouth smile, curling up at the edges like an unfurled map. But her eyes. They gleam and gloat like glowworms.

TONGUE (FLAILING):
Here's how you find a dentist in Chinatown. Look for an "herbalist" ad in the free Chinese-language newspaper. Or better yet, ask a friend of a friend of a friend.

We typically used this latter approach, which always included a grandma, a stranger. Related or not, we always referred to elderly Chinese people as grandma or grandpa. These grandparents were often sent by friends of friends to help us find dentists. But we had to prove we weren't snitches first; they ultimately decided whether you were trustworthy enough to even have your teeth fixed.

During our post-graduation visit, which would be the last of the Chinatown dentist visits thanks to insurance, this particular grandma loved Chinese pastries. She had an insatiable sweet (fake) tooth. Trust rolled itself into buttery dough.

We met her at a bakery, which was bustling with fresh egg custard trays and grandchildren tapping their greasy fingers against the glass. *This one! And this one!* In my movie brain, I imagined there was some sort of secret signal, some spider sense or whatever that clued us in. A tip of the hat, a wink, a cuffing of the left sleeve. But that's not true. I can't remember how we knew she was the Grandma, but we knew.

She looked like most Chinese grandmas: hipster chic. Red beret, floral polyester blouse, jade bracelet, ankle-length checkered pants, polka-dot socks, clear jelly sandals. Her pattern mixing was accidentally on point. I was obsessed.

We bought the Grandma whatever she wanted. We held her paper-thin hands and told her so. A cornucopia for crowns: crispy almond biscuits; pineapple buns with golden cracks like some fantastical goose egg; hint-of-sweet red bean buns; hot dog buns with sweet bread and scallions; salted egg buns; airy sponge cakes shaped like boats; egg tarts with their pools of custard glory; and chewy winter melon cakes with sesame seeds. When she offered one to my mother, my mother shook her head and gestured to her throbbing mouth: *I wish, I can't.*

"Oh. Of course, how silly of me," the Grandma laughed with a full belly, her beret bobbing with her.

Soon, she'd take us through a winding maze, through a million alleyways bisecting Mott, Canal, Bowery, and Pell, to arrive at an electronics store selling long-distance phone cards and minuscule watch parts. Three or four stories above, the dentist and his wife/dental assistant would be eating their lunch in T-shirts and sweatpants: noodle soup with a side of pork and pickled vegetables. The Grandma would buzz the apartment. We would be early.

But, before that, back in the bakery: "You, pretty daughter," the Grandma waved a melon cake at me and pinched my arm hard. "You need some fat. Won't you have some with me?"

2-0, 2-1, 2-2, 2-3, 2-4 (LOWER LEFT), HEAVILY WORN, POSSIBLY BRUXING:

Mao's Directive on Public Health argues for basic know-how and against the educational rigor of medical specialties. He calls for just adequate doctors in the countryside: "If this kind of doctor is sent down to the countryside, even if they haven't much talent, they would be better than quacks and witch doctors and the villages would be better able to afford to keep them." Right after, he adds: "The more books one reads the more stupid one gets." The Goldilocks of medical knowledge: not too little, not too much. "Just right" means just enough. Despite this plan for doctors to reach the countryside, my mother doesn't remember them coming to her village. She tells me: "We'd have to go to the closest town, which was tiny. It wasn't a city. It would take hours. Sometimes a doctor could treat your teeth there." In later years, after my mother left China in the early '80s, the Chinese government under Deng Xiaoping's leadership established more dental schools and programs, increasing public access to oral health care.

In 1996, 10 medical practitioners in New York City's Chinatown were arrested. Nine of them were immigrants. When we went to my mother's dentists, they spoke openly about practicing illegally, pointing out how hard it was to pass state exams because of the language barrier. I think about these dentists, crouched over a confusing textbook with an electronic dictionary in hand. Of dental diction being worse than everyday speech. Of new procedures and laws and technologies. Of wanting so badly to just sit in a park and watch birds peck at bread. Of closing the book—its thick pages like a mushroom's lamella—minutes in or failing the test months later, in a mixture of embarrassment and resolve. And of needing to still pay the bills and put food on the table.

There is very little news coverage about this practice of unlicensed dentistry. When an article does appear, it's often about how patients are duped by medical impostors who prey upon them. Or about the community's reluctance to report illegal dental services. In Chinatown, in a community that still feels the impact of Maoist China, generation after generation, who would report anything to an official? Especially to a police officer who doesn't speak their language? Who wouldn't be worried about getting in trouble? With limited resources and an aching tooth, what can you do?

DISTAL COMPOSITE (UPPER SECOND PREMOLAR, AMALGAM FILLING):

How to make things (secretly) last: draw out honey by adding warm water; wash and dry plastic ziplock bags to reuse; after frying, pour oil into a container to salvage; make stock out of bones and vegetable ends; save Dutch cookie tins to use as a sewing-kit receptacle or seed library; add a few drops of dish soap to a bin filled with water to wash dirty plates; rip paper towels into fourths; unwrap presents slowly during Christmas to save fancy paper for next year; scissor a tube of toothpaste in half to scoop out what's left; scrape out remaining lipstick with a bobby pin, etc. Repeat: it's important to look rich.

5, 4, 1-3, 1-2 (PREMOLARS):

What is care?

I've always loved the interior of Chinese medicine shops. The mounds of dried mushrooms, chrysanthemum leaves, nuts, and tinctures and powders of all kinds. Conpoy, dried scallops, look like yellowed teeth. The herbalist knows literally everything within each jar, some jars as large as me. This is the kind of place my grandparents feel comfortable in. This is where my mother went when she first moved to the U.S., before she grew used to the white coldness of the CVS or Walgreens counter, with tiny pill bottles the size of perfume vials. Headache or indigestion or toothache, it was off to the herbalist. For the herbs, of course, but mostly for the care.

In fact, when Gung Gung's cancer first showed up, he announced he was going back to China for his medical care. During his hospital visit in 2008, I was abroad as a U.S. Fulbright Fellow in Hong Kong. I remember seeing him in the mainland, chatting casually with a doctor in Cantonese. The room itself wasn't obsessively clean or sanitized. There weren't any screens on the windows. Crickets jumped through, every so often. Someone was smoking cigarettes nearby. Bedpans clattered about, percussive. A decade later, when he fell ill after bouts of chemotherapy, he was in a hospital in Seattle. When I visited him, he was deflated—in spirit, especially. There were so many tubes and a laminated chart above his bed that read: *Doesn't speak English.* His nurses only spoke English. I felt helpless. I thought about their silence causing him more discomfort, the distance between them hovering about the white walls. Would you call someone who can't talk to you over to hold your hand?

Care, in a language you don't want to lose.

When Gung Gung passed away from cancer in late 2017, he was tucked in a makeshift bed, in my grandparents' warm Seattle apartment. He was wrapped in a soft velour blanket with cherry blossoms.

A little while before, he had made strips of salted pork, and the strips lay deliciously preserved on paper towels on the side table. Salt and meat perfumed the air, a kind of potpourri. My mother held his hand and told him he'd always be with her. She held and talked to him, keeping him there until she couldn't. She still talks to his portrait every day, back in Jersey: *Lo Dau, look at this squash I grew! Huge! I'll make some for you.*

1 (THIRD MOLAR, WISDOM):

Nowadays, my mother and I go to Chinatown for the roast duck only. We wander the streets aimlessly, looking for trinkets and snacks. Everywhere we turn, I keep imagining the Grandma popping out and cuffing her left sleeve, maybe winking a little. My mother, thanks to her government job, has medical and dental benefits now. She has dentures too, and let her illegal implants fall out. I have miraculously decent teeth, despite my paralyzing fear of doctors and dentists. This fear, considering how I grew up, seems rational. I still don't go often enough, even though I've had health insurance since I was a graduate student and continue to now, as a professor. *Ew, what's her name, anyway?*

Dr. Jane Wong, motherfuckers!

After six years of avoiding the dentist, I went in 2017. Nervously, I walked into the office off Denny Way in Seattle. Of course, I picked the cheapest plan, and only one office is available to me. As I waited, I noticed the April issue of *O Magazine* on the side table. I freaked out a little, waving my arms around like a sugar-high hummingbird. A friend had sent me an email with a photo of my first book in *O Magazine* that morning. "I'm in this," I told the receptionist, as if that would make the possibility of cavities go away. "It's poetry month! Morgan Parker recommended my book and I'm in here."

"Let me see!"

"That's me! Oprah!" I cried out. My shame from avoiding the dentist loosened from my sides, a grateful mudslide.

"Wow, damn!" The receptionist gave me a high five. We high-fived like we were making a really good sandwich with our two hands.

Despite the high five, I cried throughout the cleaning process and examination. My mascara ran under my protective eyewear. I must have looked like a panda in a paintball fight. I cried and squirmed and, truthfully, wished my mother was there with me. Waiting in the other room, teetering on her chair, listening to make sure everything was okay.

By the end of it all, replete with red marks from the dorky eyewear, the dentist told me: "No cavities. You have a good set of chompers. Take care of them." Honestly, it was a miracle.

5-5 (DECIDUOUS BABY, UPPER MOLAR):

I'm not a baby, but I've still got some baby teeth. I think I must be four years old. This is the first of the Chinatown dentist visits. This first visit is less private. The dentist has converted a basement into a waiting area, where another family sits with me. Another little girl pouts, going on and on about her lonely cat back at home, maybe somewhere in North Jersey. There are touches that let me know this dentist is aware of us Chinese American kids: old *Highlights* magazines, wood puzzles with one piece missing, and a porcelain bowl with White Rabbit candy. Candy, here. Of all places.

My adult teeth are here and more are coming. I knew it was inevitable. The Tooth Fairy wasn't Chinese, and so I never looked under my pillow. Instead, I just waited and cried for new molar sprouts, dental insurance, and more White Rabbit candy.

As I wait for my mother, I try to meditate. I don't know what that word means quite yet since I'm four, but I know that if I stare at a fat beetle climbing the ceiling, I can slow everything down. Everything disappears. It's so quiet, you can hear the lights humming any song you want. I meditate and dream of toothless things: an aquarium full of jellyfish floating by, their tentacles wrapped around each other. Baleen whales, mussels, earthworms, spiders, lobsters, feather stars. I drift off into my imagination until I remember I'm supposed to listen for one thing and one thing only: my mother's voice. Pain or no pain or something on the verge of too much pain. I come back, at the ready. I am here. I train my toddler ear. I love loyally, richly. *Tell me when.*

GHOST ARCHIVE

afraid?" I start to type what I'm afraid of, but the list is so long, I delete it. I click enter and wait for Wongmom.com's response. The cursor blinks, eyelashes of anxiety.

```
||||||
||
|
```

There's only one surviving photograph of the restaurant I grew up in. After the restaurant failed and my father disappeared, my mother threw away all the photographs that reminded her of that place. One day they were in our family photo albums, and the next day they weren't. There's a photograph of my father cooking that I remember— he is holding a wok, sweltering with wok hei, the heat crisping the edges of the photograph golden brown. He is wearing his paper chef's hat, marbled with grease and sweat. Most of all, I remember that he is smiling, a rarity. His teeth are strung up in a celebratory banner— each one rotting and on full display. There is a cigarette tucked in his shirt pocket. Behind him: a pink plastic tub of shredded cabbage, brimming at the ready for egg rolls.

But it's hard to say, truly, if I'm remembering this correctly. The photograph, like many others, is long gone. I don't know if my mother dumped them in a giant clump or if she took her time, tearing them apart one after the other. Maybe I'm trying to remember something more beautiful than it was. I think about how writers talk about doing research for their books. How they sift through archive after archive of family documents and historical records, their piles growing like skyscrapers. I think about how they can point to official resources, photographs, tape recordings, letters, newspaper clippings.

What happens when your archive is a ghost? Cha again: "Beginning wherever you wish." On one hand, my family's stories have not been documented because of dismissive erasure. Were the stories of low-income countryside immigrants worth recording? Who counted? Who mattered? On the other hand, secrecy was a matter of safety. What you don't know keeps you alive. What's gone means a new life. My mother's birthday keeps changing because of the lunar calendar, but also because her father changed her age so she could marry my father. How old is she, really? Does she even know? "Don't I look good for my age?" she laughs, caressing her smooth face.

I grew up with mythology over the archive. With the stories that my mother tells me, each one roaring from the belly up, like a strange many-headed beast. Maybe that's why I'm a poet. Maybe that's why I want to unfurl her stories—our stories—like an anteater's endless tongue. Maybe that's why I keep asking questions.

What do you do when you're afraid?

Wongmom.com finally answers my question: "Look at you and me! Look!"

3

A CHEAT SHEET FOR
RESTAURANT BABIES

HOW TO LOB AN EGG INTO A PARKING LOT: Wait until it's dark, settled-in dark, not sunset dark, say, 9:00 PM. The sound of breaking is better when you can't see it happening. When your father isn't looking, go to the fridge and steal two eggs from the bottom of the carton stack and wrap them up in a small towel, folding the towel like you would an origami cup. Sneak out through the back of the restaurant, mind the potholes, and circle around front to the parking lot. Unfold the towel and give your little brother one egg. When he says the egg is too cold and it smells rotten like unbrushed teeth, tell him to shut up. Ground your heels into the gravel, as you imagine baseball pitchers do to gain traction. Give all your anger over to the egg. Breathe your hot breath on it. Hold it up to the sky like an offering, a sacrifice, this careful thing that could have grown into something else. Tell your brother there is nothing to be afraid of. Tell him to stop shaking; he is no incubator. With your arm bent back at 45 degrees, hurl the egg high into the air, into an arch any city would welcome as a bridge. Hurl the egg and do not think about anything—not about how your father sloshes an aquarium of whiskey, not about the growing piles of bills you will translate later. You must give the egg all of it. You can open your eyes or close them; it won't matter since you won't see it land. But you will hear it. You will hear your brother squeal like a pig at mealtime. You will hear the splat—the crepuscular glob of the yolk spreading across the hood of a car. *Poor car*, you'll think. *Poor, stupid car.*

HOW TO LOCK YOUR BROTHER IN THE MEAT FREEZER: Say the following with love and intention:

"You won't even last five minutes."

"It's 100 degrees outside."

"Mommy said you have to get the spareribs."

"Look, I can see my breath in here. Huuuuh-huhhh."

"I'll give you $5."

"Let's go to Alaska."

"You aren't afraid, are you?"

HOW TO BE IN ALASKA: You live on the other coast, the Jersey side, and the wildest thing you've ever seen was a goose eating potato chips at the beach. But in the leeching cold of winter, in super sad February, you can escape anywhere. You can be transported to the opposite side of the country. To travel, you must wait until closing time, around 11:00 PM when the parking lot empties and your mother begins shaking the ants out of the MSG bin. They scatter from their salt haven slowly, begrudgingly, like teenagers when the mall shuts down its lights. Pull on your boots and grab two brooms from the supply closet and run outside. Ask your brother where he'd like to go. *Alaska*, he'll say, arms high in the air as if a puffin would adopt him any second. Earlier, at extra lonely 5:00 AM, before you woke up, a snowplow's jaw pushed all the snow from the parking lot up against the streetlamps. Take your brother's arm and give him a broom, bristle-side up. *Don't ruin the expedition*, you'll say, *or I'll send you back to Jersey*. As if Jersey was punishment enough. With the alien light of an Alaskan sun, dig the end of the broom into the hard snow—a mix of ice, gravel, and car oil. Climb up the mound, declaring coordinates along the way. 64.2008° N, 149.4937° W!

At the top, sit with your little brother, your back against the streetlamp, the bare warmth of electricity running through this conduit, this lifeline. Close your eyes, frost thickening along your lashes. Imagine what it feels like to be so far away from home. To leave this parking lot, this strip mall, this state, this way of life. Imagine traveling to places beyond Alaska—Hong Kong, Seoul, Cairo, St. Petersburg. Vow to leave Jersey the instant you graduate high school; link your two pinky fingers together and promise yourself you'll leave. As you fall asleep, surrounded by glaciers and your mother's sharp voice slicing through the ice, your brother declares everything he wants to see right now: sand, yak, mud, ice, caribou, polar bear, volcano, fox, rainbow fish, ants, ants, ants.

HOW TO PRETEND TO FALL ASLEEP SO YOUR MOTHER PICKS YOU UP: You've seen it on TV before—how children fall asleep in unlikely places and how parents look at them with pure wonder and affection. You've seen parents pick them up gently, kiss them, and tuck them in someplace safer. Don't worry; you have an upper hand in falling asleep in unlikely places. You have your choices: dining booth, supply closet, under the sink (if it's not leaking). To pretend to fall asleep, become a floppy, waterlogged noodle. Leave a book or a can of orange soda on your chest so that, when it inevitably falls in fake sleep, your mother will hear it and be compelled to come over. Slow down your breathing. Ever. So. Slow. Become a hibernating bear, a sleeping alligator. Dream of the ways she will find you—not hours later when she finally closes the restaurant and you actually fall into real sleep, but when she is finished cutting strips of wonton, refilling the water pitcher, and carrying dirty plates stacked tightly like the layers of an onion. Dream of the kiss on the cheek. Dream of the real feeling of her real arms wrapped around your back. Dream of her picking you up like a sack of sugar, a wet bleach rag, a suitcase she packed diligently many years ago, in a country 7,186 miles away. Open up that suitcase and see what you can find.

HOW TO READ IN THE HALF DARK: Contrary to the advice of any decent optometrist, you won't need that much light. Your eyes are good at adjusting. You can think of yourself as a cat preparing for a nightly hunt, if that helps. Head next door to the dry cleaners with your copy of *Matilda*. Look in to see if anyone is there. The owner will be in the very back of the store, steaming a shirt—the smoke trailing like a campfire someone forgot to put out. Head straight for the changing room. Pull back the velvet curtain and settle in. Clean the space as you would clean your apartment—the apartment you imagine having when you are 38 and, to the you-must-be-cursed elixir of disappointment and empathy of your entire family, still alone and still unmarried. Push the fallen pins to one corner. If there is lint, roll it up like a dung beetle—with purpose and slow precision. Your eyes should have adjusted by now. You should see light at the bottom of the curtain, intermittent waves of custard yellow. Start reading and practice your telekinesis, one dust ball at a time. And when the owner opens the curtain 10 minutes later, lower your eyes so that the light doesn't flood in too strongly and make you hiss. The owner will say hello to you in Korean because that is her language, and you'll say hello in Toisanese because you haven't forgotten your language yet. You'll look past her scoured, pink hands to see a customer behind her—an impatient white man who wants his suit measured *correctly* this time. You will meet people like this later in life. You will date these men for years. The ones who will mark you as laborer, as not worthy of their time, as easily disposable, and you will add them to your revenge list.

HOW TO PASS THE TIME (REMINDER: ONLY RICH KIDS ARE ALLOWED TO SAY THEY'RE BORED): Brush your hair 50 times; untangle hair from a wool blanket; shake up a can of orange soda;

defrost shrimp; defrost your hands; chase the curly-haired white dog who lives along the train tracks behind the restaurant; brew honey water; water the jade plant, covered in sticky dust; wash the bok choy until it runs clear; scrub the MEAT IS MURDER graffiti off the restaurant; scrub the spray-painted dicks that keep coming back; hiss at boys; whack at flies; draw snails on the backs of menus; stick gum under the table and see how long it takes to fall; sweep up piles of your father's cigarettes on the back stoop; breathe in deeply; breathe out deeply; ahhhhhhhhhhhhhhhhhhhhhhhhhh; scrape grease from the griddle; scape grease from your fingernails; drop wonton wrappers into the fryer; roll grapes under the fryer and imagine their apocalyptic melting, days from now; punch a bag of flour; cough from the punching; recite your revenge list; listen to the sound of gravel under tires; clean the muck out of the curly-haired white dog's eyes; roll your brother into the empty MSG bin, delicious crystals stinging his baby arms; wipe clean the new NO MSG sign; teach your Yeh Yeh to say "apple" in English (*No*, he says, *teach me how to say "gwaa zyu uk kei" in your language*).

HOW TO CARRY DISHES: Carry a pile of dirty dishes with both your hands to start. You don't learn to shoot a basketball with one hand first, do you? Then, after a few weeks, carry the dishes in the crook of one arm like you carry your textbooks. When you feel bold, stack crushed soda cans on top of the dishes. Put one foot in front of the other—this rule of thumb can also be applied to dancing with boys, which unfortunately won't be relevant to you during middle school (or high school, for that matter). Don't forget that you quit dance club after one day. When you naturally bump into the prep table and drop a dish, its porcelain center splintering in all directions like the sun's rays, do not listen when your mother laughs and says: "And who would marry you?" Instead, keep putting one foot in front of the other until you reach the kitchen sink: a wide, deep crater. Lay down the dishes, the refuse of others, the barely chewed pieces of beef fat and gnarled stems of broccoli. Raise your outrage—who is rich enough to leave food behind? Wash the oyster sauce trickling down your arm like thick squid ink. Add these customers to your revenge list for making your family cook Chinese American food—sticky, sweet food your family had to learn to make. This food is not your mother's, father's, grandfather's, or grandmother's. Don't pretend to know what duck sauce is. No one knows. Never eat this fake, plastic food, the photos of which are oversaturated and laminated above the ordering counter; wait for the real Toisanese food that your mother makes during 20-minute lunch and dinner breaks. During dinner, help your mother carry your favorite dish—whole tomatoes, egg, rice, ginger, soy sauce, and sesame oil. When your mother was pregnant with you, she grew tomatoes all around the small duplex in Matawan that your four uncles, Ngin Ngin, and Yeh Yeh lived in. Think of your mother at 21, sitting on a mattress in the duplex's attic, squirrels running across the beams. Imagine their feather duster tails tickling her feet. Imagine her eating a tomato like an apple, the juice trickling down to her knees. Think of the bright green vines wrapped around you as you eat your favorite dish, the tomatoes as sweet and tart as your burgeoning heart. Forgive your mother for being so tough on you; you don't know what she will have to carry over the years—the bills, the food on the table, the disappearance of your father, the work. Yes, the work. And the overwork. Don't you forget. You can't forget: just look at her hands, canvas-rough and trembling, wanting to be held.

HOW TO WRITE YOUR REVENGE LIST: Start with the cruel ones. The neighborhood boys who threw rocks at you, who picked up smooth, flat rocks from their landscaped yard and threw rocks at your backpack as you walked home. Add the ones who ignore you, the ones who look at clouds more than they look at you. The ones who have low expectations. The guidance counselor who placed you in lower-level

English, despite the stack of novels you read every week. Add the untrustworthy ones, the ones who smile too wide and compliment your hair while pointing out your too-large ears. Add the creepy white guys who always sit next to you on the bus, in the park, anywhere really, and ask if you are Chinese and if you can speak English. Imagine stabbing them like stabbing the foggy eye of a steamed fish. Add the popular girls, the rich kids, the customers who get frustrated and yell at your mother because they can't understand what she's saying, the kid who punched your little brother in the stomach, the politicians, the racists, the fetishists, the abusers. Add them, add them. Think about adding your father who will leave very soon and will always, somehow, be leaving. Think about how he gambled away everything and drank and smoked and lied and never spoke to you. How, when you were little, he didn't pick you up from band practice and you had to sit with the teacher for four hours until your mother came. How the reed of your clarinet grew moldy from your own mucilage. How he decided to go to Atlantic City that day and kept going there like a moth drawn toward light. Think about it, yes, give it a thorough evaluation, but please, do not add him. In decade-long increments, when your mother tells you he called and asked about you, do not flinch in anger or grief or longing or plain curiosity. Though you are a heathen, pray that he is still there, still alive, still able to blink and wonder from time to time, *Where is my daughter, where is the girl.*

AND WHAT TO DO NOW, NOW THAT YOU'RE OLDER AND FAR AWAY: There is not much to do now that the restaurant is long gone; you'll find this idleness disconcerting and will want to grab a broom to sweep or stomp or throw. You'll want to hiss for the sake of hissing. You'll want to chase raccoons just to find your likeness, your feral child self. The hours will grow shorter, the smells less pungent. Instead: move to New York, to Hong Kong, to Iowa, to Montana, to Washington, to a place so full of moss, it'll grow inside your apartment—the bearded green lining your windowsills. Call your brother, your mother, call them in apology, as in: *Sorry it's been so long, and what did you eat today?* Stop by your Pau Pau's apartment in the Central District for lunch; devour her salted fish and wipe your greasy mouth with pocketed Alaska Airlines napkins. Marvel over how your brother has grown exponentially taller than you, how he stands like an evergreen tree, rooted, no longer shaking. Listen to your mother laugh like a bursting tomato, seeds spilling everywhere. Over a bowl of tong yuan soup, forget and forgive your father; let the daikon and rice balls soften your aging face. When buying groceries, open an egg carton and check if anything's broken. Let the eggs feel heavy and round in your hands and do not calculate the physics of projectile motion; you were never good at science anyway. Read and write in good light, in hovering white light, in egg light, in a bed you share with someone and then no one. Do not be afraid of loneliness; remember your teenage self and what your mother told you right after your father left, the both of you struck by the sting of salty wind along the Jersey shore: "If I was allowed to choose, I would choose to be alone." Allow yourself to make your own decisions. Become your own book, your own hand holder, your own revenge in language struck with a good cleaver. Repeat the little Toisanese you know to your grandparents, in this world and in other worlds: ngoh mh sik gong, jousahn, joigin, jousahn, joigin. When you return to the strip mall 20 years later, the restaurant will still be a restaurant and there will be a small black-haired girl from another family, another restaurant-baby life. Do not look her in the eye. Do not tell her who you are. Do not ask her to draw you a picture on a menu or how long it takes for her to devein shrimp or if she falls asleep behind the fronds of potted plants. Does she stick gum along the ribs of bamboo? Is she a rat too? Don't ask her. It will be too close, too rotten, too down-to-the-bone honest to reach out and tell her everything you know.

GHOST ARCHIVE (LOOK)

AND SO I LOOK. THE PICTURE HAS A SEPIA UNDERTONE. A muted glow like someone dipped it into chrysanthemum tea. The restaurant is blurred in the background. You can barely make out the metal glint of pots and pans behind us. I'm sure one of those bowls was used to cut my hair. Clumps of hair falling like wood ear fungus. The photograph is scratched and smudged, little reminders that someone has held this, again and again.

I don't know who took this photo. An aunt or uncle? A customer? My mother is holding me, her head tilted in the left-hand corner, her chin resting on the polyester of my frilled clown-like dress. How old am I? Two? Three? Her black hair is utterly black, and so is mine. Our hair touches and melds together. I'm lifted above her face. My plump cheeks are unbearably rosy. It almost looks like the American dream actually came true: Look how well fed this child is! Look at her mischievous smile! Isn't she smart? She must be smart (my uncle said to me once: *Jane, you're the smart one. You're our only hope*). My mother holds up her blurry finger, caught in motion, like she's wagging it at me (*JANE, I'M PSYCHIC, JANE I'M PSYCHIC, JANE I'M PSYCHIC*), like she's playing a game with her beloved baby. But the truth is, I don't remember ever playing a game with my mother. She was too busy cooking, cleaning, packing for work, and putting out metaphorical and literal fires at the restaurant. Dousing flames with flimsy buckets. She admits that she wasn't ready to be a mother at 20. She tells me when I'm 37: "I never played with you. I feel bad about that now. When I'm a grandma, I'll play with your baby!" *My baby?* Something impossible churns deep within my chest and I want to cry, but I have to stop myself from turning into mud.

I follow my mother's advice. I look at her and me. I look so hard, I bore a rotting hole into the sepia. This is the only photograph she kept from the restaurant days. This is the earliest picture of me; I don't have any baby photos. I stare into my dark eyes like they're nests. I want to know: What does that child know? What does that Jane know that I don't?

4

GIVE US OUR CROWNS

WHAT I IMAGINED IF I WAS CROWNED MISS PRETEEN NEW Jersey 1997: all the piñatas in the Garden State bursting open simultaneously, each foil-wrapped strawberry gem shimmering forth, covering the ground completely. My mother's iridescent heels? Covered. Especially the left shoe, peeling at the big toe like a week-old banana. All the glitter falling from above. Like all the CDs in Fresh Kills, hitting the sun at the exact bliss-blind moment—to cover everything forever, ad infinitum.

And so I sat there, looking up at the spackled ceiling, my hands cupped together to collect.

When I closed my eyes, I saw 100 exploding donkey heads made of confetti streamers.

When I opened them: Miss Preteen New Jersey was being crowned in blonde, blue-eyed glory, surrounded by her family (who would never need her to translate medical bills or shove as many Taco Bell fire sauce packets into her pockets as possible because they're free). My new pageant friend, whom I will call Carol, was undoubtedly the most beautiful and brilliant person in the room. She turned to me: "It's okay. They always win."

Carol was an 11-year-old state champion in math. A big fan of unicorns and green apple Jolly Ranchers. She wore an A-line gold dress with stars all over it. The stars were kaleidoscopic and even the smallest babies in the audience were mesmerized. She wanted to be a pediatrician. A few hours previously, the pageant counselors had given each of us a pillowcase to sign like a yearbook (to remember, like our dreams when we slept) and I had only three entries on mine: one from Carol, whose cursive *o* looked like a bald man with a hat, one from a 10-year-old composer who wrote a sonata for her talent portion, and one from my own mother—if you count her accidentally using the pillowcase as a napkin. Creased in a wrinkled corner, her lipstick smudge resembled a bright red poppy.

I'm Chinese. Carol's Black. Cue: piñatas in reverse, donkey bellies sucking candy back up like greedy vacuum cleaners. The banana peel of my mother's shoe: tongue out. My palms now turned toward the ground as if I belonged with the potatoes and the beets. What I later regretted, leaving my short stint in regional pageant life: not keeping in touch with Carol, not asking her what she'd specialize in as a pediatrician, not clapping for ourselves and our futures, not saying back to her: "We'll get our crowns."

* * *

ON THE 5:30 AM 594 commuter bus from Seattle to Tacoma, on the way to being the Professor, I'm applying my mascara in three swoops like a swallow diving into a nest. I apply only when the bus stops at a red light. I am poised, ready at the yellow. A teenager watches me from across the seat, her headphones as large as earmuffs. I can't tell if she is feeling sorry for me or taking life-hack notes. Most likely the former, but I can't help but hope for the latter. Would this be her future self, half-ready, half-vain on a bus that would get her only halfway to her destination? Who would want a bleary-eyed future self applying makeup on a bus?

With the intensity of a drool-faced stalker, I used to watch my mother apply makeup. As a small child, I sat on the bathroom counter, my legs dangling. My ankles knocked harmonically against the fake wood grain, offering my mother a soundtrack. I held onto her pinky finger, which dipped into the softest lake-blue eye shadow—her favorite color. I curled into her eyelashes as full as a horse's. Between working at the restaurant, grocery shopping, and hanging up laundry to dry, my mother always slowed down for the rituals of beauty. Sometimes, at night, my mother would rise from the dark of the kitchen, the television glowing like a demon's mouth behind her. My mother in her avocado-and-honey face mask: a terrifying reptile. Eels of braids wrapped around her head like a slippery tiara. Eyeliner in precise black cursive, pink lipstick blotted on a tissue or the back of her hand. Blush circling her cheeks like an impossibly fluffy cloud. Growing up, I watched, memorized, practiced.

My mother is the reigning queen of the divine—if you swap out a scepter with a flyswatter. A sample photo shoot: my mother, in perfectly lacquered lips, chopping the head off a chicken, the rubbery head rolling right into my glitter-nail-polished hands. A close-up portrait: the bronzer of her cheeks deepening with the steam of boiling fish head broth. Far off in the background: me, a lipsticked replica, ravaging a bag of shrimp chips.

When the pamphlet for Miss Preteen New Jersey came in the mail—amid overdue bills and the weekly Super Savers Coupon Pack, which she clipped with meat scissors—she could read only half of it (she was just two weeks into her English night class). What she did know, in the language of pretty: that her daughter would never roughen her hands by pulling up root vegetables or burn them from fryer grease or too-hot pot handles. Her daughter would be on the cover of the pamphlet next year. And with this certainty, my mother taped the pamphlet on the fridge and circled the date of the pageant like circling both our fates. Did it matter that I broke plates by just looking at them (in my defense, I really had been working on my telekinesis)? Or that I had no friends who came over to play? Or that, in the U.S., what was deemed beautiful and worthy tended to look like Cindy Crawford or Kate Moss?

Grace? Popularity? Whiteness? You can make a face mask out of anything.

* * *

IN CHINA, DAILYMAIL.COM REPORTS, women are inserting small plugs into their noses to appear more "European." Or, you can clamp a product I found online called "Nose up Lifting Shaping & Bridge Straightening Beauty Clip" onto your nose for 15 minutes per day. Just 15 minutes. Reports and articles on beauty trends in China suggest the same thing: China values Western beauty standards. The eyelid surgery, the breast implants, the hair and skin bleaching. By Western, they must mean white. How is this different from U.S. beauty standards? *They always win.*

Something I do not want to admit: all throughout high school, I used a whitening product. It was labeled "brightening," and I was convinced whatever chemicals within burned the shit out of my stubborn teenage acne. But really, it was a whitening product with niacinamide. Niacinamide stops melanin pigment from reaching skin cells. The face wash was depleting my pigment. I was disappearing, a translucent jellyfish. Looking back at my senior class photo, I see my pale face float away from itself, like the thinnest sliver of Dove soap down the drain. I was as white as Carnation milk.

The whitening face wash was expensive and from Japan, and we'd buy it under the table from a friend of a friend in Chinatown or at the hole-in-the-wall discount Asian beauty store in Marlboro. At the beauty store, the women behind the counter peered at me like I was a seahorse in an aquarium—impossible. Questions floated outward in Cantonese, relentless waves, as my mother pulled me forward, closer to the translucent women.

They pried at my body like a pickle jar: *Where did you get your surgery? No surgery? How are your eyes so big? Are you sure they're natural? Have you modeled your eyes before? You'd be a star in China. What is that mole near your neck? Can we fix that? We can fix that.*

At 22, while living abroad in Hong Kong on the Fulbright Fellowship, I spent a long weekend in the Philippines gorging on Jollibee spaghetti, fresh mangoes, and fried fish, and getting tan along the Pacific. On the other shore, the Jersey shore, being tan was something people laid down in a microwave bed and paid lots of money for. Pauly D on *Jersey Shore* bemoans cloudy weather because you can't get a tan. I grew up in a culture slathered in orange-glow self-tanner (warning label: use only as directed, only if you are white, only if being tan is a choice).

When I saw my cousin back in Hong Kong, she was mortified by my tanned skin. "We need to go to the beauty store right now," she said, grabbing my arm.

For my family, tan meant laborer, meant farmer, meant everything my parents had tried to leave. Meant where I come from. My mother in fields of oxen, persimmon trees, and shattering sun. Her face framed in freckles like a robin's egg, like a constellation I would be so lucky to name.

In the beauty store with my cousin, I didn't look anyone in the eye, didn't touch any of the whitening products. The face washes, serums, and moisturizers glowed like radioactive material. There were so many. The store itself was so white, the overhead lights like lasers of ivory erasure. Yang Mingxuan, a Chinese woman, told CBS News in an article about Asian beauty trends ("Latest Trend Sweeping China: Lighter Skin") that her ideal skin color was "even, white, luminous and smooth [like] silk, like the egg white of a boiled egg."

To be egg white. Not: yellow yolk. Not: yellow skin, Yellow Peril, yellow fever.

The beauty consultants kept touching and pinching my skin as if I were a specimen under a compound microscope. I felt nauseous. It was all too much. Lingering by the door, I touched the mole along my left clavicle. My brown mole felt warm, like a mouse huddled in its burrow. My mother has a matching mole above her left eye. Watching my mother put on makeup as I sat on the counter. I'd touch her mole and then mine. I'd do this a few times: her mole, my mole, her mole, my mole. A telephone line, an activation. "Leave Mommy alone," my mother would cry, annoyed. These moles were ours. These moles linked us. I think back to how the beauty shop aunties wanted to erase my mole: *Can we fix that? We can fix that.*

As my cousin filled her wire basket with "brightening" beauty samples, I clutched my mole protectively. I imagined my mother in Jersey, halfway across the world, stopping whatever she was doing and touching her mole: activated. This touch was the beginning of love and its labor.

* * *

IN 2000, 16 YEARS after she left her home village in Southern China, my mother returned. This was my first time in China and her first time back since leaving. I was 16, my brother 13, and my mother 36. My father had just left our family like a storm going through another town. If my mother was going to return with a failed marriage and credit card debt piling like firewood in an ever-hungry hearth, she would be well dressed.

The dirt road was her runway—all her old classmates and extended family members stood in hushed awe as she walked. She strutted with her head held to the sweltering sky, her hair gleaming like a black diamond among the flowering persimmon trees. She walked in a red-and-black-checkered Calvin Klein shift dress, with her signature patent leather heels, a raw silk shawl, and a bold red swipe of lipstick. Her heels dug into the dirt, loosening yams and worms. She walked with confidence, resilience, and power—as if saying: *Look, I made it.*

Akin to throwing roses at her feet, everyone complimented my mother in the deepest tones of Toisanese: "The village beauty is back and more beautiful than ever," and "Have you been modeling in America?" And the most powerful compliment of all: utter silence and the glimmer of jealousy from long-lost cousins—and myself, awkward limbed and pocked with acne. Even the persimmon trees and worms lowered their heads as she walked past. Twirling in spitting dirt, thickening in the throat: *I made it. Look. I made it.*

As we walked through the labyrinthine alleyways of the village— past scrawny chickens, thin bags of rice, and broken plastic stools—my mother pulled me inside one particular doorway. The room was dark, dusty, and sparsely furnished. A rickety chair stood in one corner and there was a glowing altar with a few incense sticks and two rotting oranges. The oranges were cratering into themselves, little palms of citrus. My mother took in a deep breath and let it out slowly, as if giving the room its embers back.

"I want you to see this," she said. She walked over to the far-right corner and pointed to a wide, bare plank of wood. It was cool to the touch. "I slept here with my three brothers and my sister." She ran her pink nail-polished fingers across the splintering grain. "Jane, I could have been a doctor. I could have been . . . what do they call it on TV? With those sparkle dresses and they look like queens . . ."

"Miss Universe," I told her.

"Miss Universe," she repeated. "Leng neoi," she called me. Or maybe she was referring to herself. "I could've been anything."

We drove back to Toisan that day and stayed at my second uncle's apartment in the city. Sharing a bed with my mother and brother, swaddled in a purple velour comforter, I imagined the hushed words swirling within my mother's dreaming head. *Where is her husband. Look at her spoiled children who can't even speak Chinese. She forgot her home. She forgot where she comes from. She's a foreigner now. Her red lips. Where is her husband. Her red lips. You know what they say. What they say.*

Were these words in her head or mumbled when she walked along that dirt runway? Did I hear my mother whimper before bed? Did I see her sitting at lunch with village elders when they asked about her husband and told her what she should do to bring him back (the gambler, the drunk, the absent father)? Did I see her curl and uncurl her fists under the table? Did I see her marry my father the year before I was born? Did I hold her tan, teenaged arms as she carried bundles of water spinach, the flecks of water cool against her skin? Did I?

What my mother would have said in her dream: *Tell me what they say. Get out of this dream and say it to my face.*

My mother never entered a pageant, never went to college, never felt like she could refuse assimilation—the stakes were too high. Assimilation promised safety (it didn't) and ensured acceptance (it didn't). What she didn't do, I did. My mother saw me walk during the Miss Preteen New Jersey pageant. Leng neoi, in a puffy dress not quite white—more like a used napkin. She braided my hair in a long French braid and tied it neatly with a thick red ribbon. I walked onstage like an octopus, lumbering slowly across the floor. Regardless, I imagined her in the audience saying to a random stranger: "That's my daughter. She wants to be a writer. Look at her. Just look."

* * *

AT 37, MY DIVORCED mother is told by her date, over dinner: "I think your culture is so great." And then a couple of weeks later, he says to her, in front of my brother and me: "If I turned you over, would there be 'China' stamped on your ass?" This man was the first person my mother dated after the divorce. He was white, rich, tall, and formerly married to a Filipina woman. My brother and I would watch him squeeze my mother's thigh in public. We'd curl and uncurl our fists, imagine hitting him with sticks. He would do things like compliment her straight black hair, wear ugly baby-blue ties, and take us out to lobster dinners and say: "I know this is different from Chinese food, but this is like royalty . . ." They were together for a month before my mother dumped him. "It's like I woke up one day and thought: *he's a bad man,*" my mother told me. "I don't know how they are supposed to be, how I'm supposed to be. Maybe we come from two different cultures." What she didn't mention: that he had an Asian fetish and that she laughed in his face when he told her to quit her job at the post office.

At 33, over a bowl of lukewarm soup, my date told me: "I bet all the boys in high school had crushes on you and you didn't even know it." How sweet of him to say, I thought. Sweet like frosting on top of frosting I didn't want. I grinned too hard, pageant-worthy in the glow of a fake candle. "I bet," I said. The soup was made of locally grown tomatoes, fennel, or whatever. My lipstick did not smudge onto the spoon. My date was handsome, bearded. They all are, aren't they?

At 15, my diary read: *If I don't get kissed this year, I'll explode.* Piñatas of the Ugly One, the Nerdy One, the Weird One: exploding. I think of all the middle school and high school boys I knew. The ones that threw rocks at me at the bus stop, the ones that kicked my ankles as I walked, the ones that pushed by me like I was simply the air: there, but not. And worse, the ones that whistled at my mother, shouting, "Love me long time!" from classroom windows when she came in as my guest for an AP English presentation. She had decided to wear her cheongsam since I asked her to talk about immigrating to the U.S. She wore it proudly, the only cheongsam she had, the black silk flowing from her body like she had carved a canyon. She'd had it tailored in Chinatown years before and wore it with silver kitten-heel sandals, which I coveted and wore around the house, pretending like I had somewhere fancy to go. "What are they yelling?" my mother asked me in the parking lot, bending to fix her sandal strap. More whistling, more laughing. "Nothing, Mommy, let's just go," I growled, flushed with fury.

My first kiss was when I turned 19. It was my birthday and I had thrown clumps of grass in some guy's face and apparently, he was into that. It was earthy—not in the food-review-of-chanterelle-soup kind of way, but in the dirt-on-our-lips-and-body-odor kind of way that confirmed that I had chosen to go to Bard, a hippie liberal arts college, on a scholarship. I'd end up dating Grass Boy for five years. He would become a botanist.

All my boyfriends have liked the fact that I was unpopular in school. My mother's failed dream of me being popular somehow benefited my dating life. I seemed quirky, like someone straight out of *Ghost World*, or, even more precise in its Asianness, Lane Kim from *Gilmore Girls*. Kazu Makino of Blonde Redhead, flanked by twins. The Asian pixie dream girl. Loves Belle and Sebastian and secretly dyes her hair blonde or blue. Is this a way to be white too? Ex–pageant failure, ex–whitening gel slatherer. Whose dream girl?

Something I do not want to admit: seven of my exes have been white, and only two have been people of color. This makes me as uncomfortable as the image of eels swarming on my mother's head. As uncomfortable as a record playing: *If I turned you over, would you have "China" stamped on your ass?*

Though my white boyfriends are liberal, sensitive, and anti-racist, right? Right? What I've come to learn about dating white men: they adore that I'm petite. They are obsessed with my big eyes. They say they want to marry me and then they disappear. The first girl they date after me is Asian. They tell me I'm a badass, a rebel, a brilliant one, and when they realize I actually am, they get mad and leave. They laugh when I tell them not to fucking "boop" my nose. They ride bikes and climb and are really into documentaries on war. They love telling stories about living abroad and yes, local markets are the best way to get to know a place. They are really into learning about my cultural traditions but make sure to ask me if that's right, authentic, okay, or something I do, and if not, that's cool, they're just curious. Tea: "Am I pouring this right?" Joss paper: "I think I saw something about this on YouTube." Taking your shoes off: "Oh, shit. But whatever, it's not like I was running around in dirt." Longan: "Am I supposed to eat the whole thing all at once?" Upon meeting my family: "Should I bow? I don't know." Everything they don't know: point, ask, point, ask, point, ask. They show me off. When a beautiful Asian woman walks into a room, they look at her. They tell me they don't have a fetish, a preference. They've dated "all kinds of women" and yes, well, one or more of their exes happens to be Asian, but that's a pure coincidence. They are trying, really hard, to understand white supremacy and ask me what they can do. And can I say it without being so angry? When I'm angry, I don't look so pretty. And when I'm angry/ugly: Why does everything have to be about race? Didn't they just change their Facebook profile picture and donate to [insert link]? They would donate more, but they are saving up for a [insert gadget, fancy car, vacation] to brush up on their [insert foreign language] skills and have a well-deserved adventure!

And even if they are "really" trying and "really" listening, I still wait for the moment when they will say something not-quite-right or something absolutely, completely wrong. I prep myself for that raised eyebrow, that whip of the head, that side-eye that my body falls into a bit too easily. My ex-fiancé, on our second date, used the term "round eye" casually and I called him out loudly—in front of the entire bakery. He seemed both surprised and bemused by my sharp callout, by my lecture on Orientalism and Yellow Peril. Didn't he do his research on me? Didn't he know that I teach Asian American literature? (Oh right, straight cis men don't have to do the is-my-date--a-serial-killer research.) He claimed ignorance. He claimed that he didn't know anything about the history of this term, said he heard an Asian American person say it, said he would never use it again now that he knew. I tried to remind myself of his job. But isn't that the thing? Like, look at me, I *can't* be racist if I've devoted my life to [insert white-liberal-feel-good job]? Dating white men, I've learned that I have to explain and explain again, until my breath is thinned by their defensiveness, thinned by my whirling exhaustion.

There's this card game called Red Flags: The Game of Terrible Dates that I played at a party once, in which I learned I was pretty good at getting people to overlook red flags I'd made up, i.e.: *Okay, they might have 10 secret Instagram handles like makeluv2u69, but they will make you freshly baked cookies every day!* Which just confirms that I'm terrible at seeing red flags in real life. Or rather, I see them, and paste over them with what I want to see. If you combine red and green on the color wheel, what do you get? A palimpsest of DO NOT PASS GO. And yet.

When I met my previous ex—a man I'll call the Bad One, someone I dated before my ex-fiancé at the end of my 20s—he would call me ugly. He was one of the white boyfriends. My ears: ugly, too big. My hair: ugly, thinning, he was sure of it. My nose: ugly, too flat. And so I slept in my makeup for two years. And then for two years after that. Ritual, habit. Foundation seeped into my pores, mascara pooled around my tear ducts, eye shadow gathered like old relish. The Bad One cheated on me exclusively with Asian women. He bought me tight white pants from J. Crew in a double zero. I held my breath. I kept sleeping in my makeup. I wore my hair down to hide my ears. No ponytail, no hair bun for two years. And then for two years after that. Ritual, habit. I kept all of this a secret; I was so ashamed. I was afraid to tell my mother. Years later when I finally told her, I could hear her humid seething over the phone, her breath like a hot knife sizzling through lipstick.

In Hong Kong, I remember walking to meet my friend who lived in Wan Chai. I was late and I walked fast, holding flowers for her new apartment. Three white men snickered at me and one of them reached out and grabbed my ass. It happened so quickly, so blatantly, I stood there for a few seconds, speechless—my ass stinging from the force of his putrid touch. I could hear them laughing, could hear them talking about getting Asian pussy that night in their thick British accents. And I flipped. Neon anger spewed from my ass up and I turned around and ran toward them. They saw me running and I remember being shocked by how shocked they were. They ran and I chased them screaming for a block, shaking my bouquet like a weapon: DON'T EVER FUCKING TOUCH ME, YOU FUCKING DICKFACES!

Pageant interview question: "If there is something that viscerally scares you about white men, why do you date them? And what does this say about your understanding of self-worth, of beauty, of internalized racism, of not being white? Don't you know better (and don't forget to smile!)?"

What I've come to learn from dating the two men of color in my life: it's complicated, but I get it. You don't ever need to explain. Is it a coincidence that they are the only exes that I'm still friends with?

Note to self, note to you who needs this. Right now, get a Sharpie marker and circle: I'm fucking done explaining. Circle again and again. Orbit this.

* * *

FIRST TURN:

Nyla Edwards, who fundraised the majority of her pageant fees through a GoFundMe site, was crowned Miss Preteen New Jersey in 2016. Local Jersey newspapers reported that she loves volleyball and acting, and that she was looking forward to organizing a coat drive for her community. To see a Black girl with a crown, many years later, means young women of color see themselves reflected and celebrated.

Not enough, but something. The equation of whiteness equals beauty is learned so young that I'm not sure if this idea ever goes away, but it is imperative to celebrate our excellence and futures now.

SECOND TURN:

When I turned 33, my friend Hannah sent me a gift of eye makeup remover, a beautiful Korean beauty bottle that you have to shake to mix up. When I shook the bottle, milky liquid swirled like a new galaxy. "Clean your face, begin anew," she wrote in her birthday card. When a new galaxy forms, clouds of gas and dust collapse under their own gravitational pull, balloons of the heart. Stars swirl on dresses, on the freckles along my mother's nose.

THIRD TURN:

As a teenager, in her home village, my mother cut open a boy's foot in school. He sat behind her in class and kicked her chair every day. She turned around and told him, "If you kick me one more time, I'll cut your foot." And so she brought a knife to school and wedged it between the chair rungs. When he kicked, his blood spilled like schools of red snapper. My mother ran so fast through the fields back then, her hair left a comet streak—black glitter in mountain air. The reigning queen of everything beautiful. He probably had a crush on her and she didn't know it. In 2000, when she walked into her home village with dirt rustling around her, this kid was the last person to greet her. "Remember me?" he said, kicking off his plastic sandal and pointing to the scar on his foot. They both laughed in the mosquito heat. His toe was like a tree burl. "You haven't changed," he said.

FOURTH TURN:

I'm not the Asian pixie dream girl. I'm the type who rearranges the flowers on my grandparents' graves and waters them with the sloppy but dedicated precision of the clouds above.

FIFTH TURN:

Give me the mascara globules from my eyes, blooming black anemones. Give me the tangy lipstick I eat off my mouth. Give me thick salve for my aches, for the slump in my back. Give me wild eyebrow hairs like unruly sprouts after a forest fire. Give me the trees, the broccoli stuck in my teeth. Give me glitter heels so bright I become an anglerfish. Give me my bare baby face. My white hairs like daikon, my wrinkles like dog-eared books. Give me farmer, laborer, ardor.

* * *

TOWARD THE END OF my fellowship in Hong Kong, flipping through the channels, I saw it on TV: the Miss China International competition. The screen exploded with rainbow confetti and metallic ribbons like sunbathing snakes. I came in at the beginning of the interview round. Tall, thin, and pale Chinese women went up to the announcer's mic, one by one. The next contestant smiled wide, her white teeth: marvels of engineering. Her nose: straight as a pine tree. The announcer introduced her as the winner of Miss China Europe, a pageant for women of Chinese diasporic heritage. Her home: Denmark.

The interview unfolds in Cantonese. They ask her a question about the charities she supports. There's an uncomfortable silence. She doesn't understand the question, doesn't speak Cantonese. She stands there onstage, smiling, waving, and nodding for a whole two minutes—the length of time it takes to put on eyeliner or wash a nonstick pan you fried an egg in. The flutist in the orchestra awkwardly starts playing. You can hear the small click of another contestant's heels.

I leaned in closer to see if she was crying. Not a tear, not even a welling-up or trembling lip. She was a professional. I wanted her to feel something, to have her mascara run down her face like shadows along a riverbank. Feel! Something!

With the pageant still on TV, I impulsively called my mother in Jersey. "There's this woman in a beauty pageant. She's not even from China," I told her. "I'm going to enter. I'll write an essay about this. You know, like go undercover about all these whitening products and messed-up expectations about Western and Chinese beauty. Really dig in. Expose it all from within the pageant. What do you think, Mommy?"

There was a brief pause on the other end. This, as they say, is the moment we've all been waiting for.

"Chi sin! Are you crazy? What if you win?"

WHITE HAIR

WHEN I ENDED MY ENGAGEMENT, MY MOTHER FLEW OUT TO
see me. We went over to my aunt's house in Renton, near Seattle. My
family fed me avocados like a baby, scooping the ripe green middles
like soft-serve ice cream. Pau Pau gets free groceries from a local nonprofit supporting Asian elders. That week, there were 15 avocados to
eat, little dinosaur eggs piled high in a brown paper bag. Pau Pau had
never seen this fruit before and gave them to us. They also gave her
10 bags of pasta she doesn't know how to cook, so I signed up to eat
miniature elbow macaroni exclusively for the next year.

To say I was a mess would be putting it lightly. I gummed at the
fruit, overripe, and smeared it on the roof of my mouth. Half crying,
half eating, I was convinced I was fully cursed. I hadn't washed my
hair in over a week. The strands hung around me like tangled cords.
My mother, aunt, and cousin Angela surrounded me at the kitchen
counter, taking turns touching my shoulder with electric care. My
mother and aunt in their 50s, Angela in her teens, and me at 37. Their
words swirled around me: *I'm worried about you* and *We are here for
you* and *What do you want.*

"I want to dye my hair."

There's a cat meme I recently saw on softcore_trauma's Instagram:
"the traumatized urge to change your aesthetic instead of feeling your
feelings." The cat wore round yellow sunglasses and had a sheet mask
on. That. I wanted that.

In the bathroom, my mother sat me down and clipped my hair into four equal parts. "I don't know what you're talking about. You don't have any white hair," she shrugged. But then she lifted a chunk and declared with an archaeologist's glee: "Oh, I found them!" She started to paint my hair with the dark brown dye, rubbing it in until my nose stung with a chemical reminder that I was indeed awake.

"I'm gonna get you," she laughed, massaging the dye into my whites. My mother dyed my hair with such slow tenderness, section by section, that it calmed my entire nervous system down. I felt my wires flop over, flattening soda. Somehow (I didn't know how), it was going to be okay.

When I was a child, my mother would wash my hair on Friday nights around 11:30 PM, after closing up the restaurant. She'd lather roughly, her red nails digging into my scalp with a rage I wouldn't understand until I'd also experienced toxic men and their chemical needs. Pure Pantene fury, the suds thrashed around my bony shoulders. As she dipped my head back under the faucet, I couldn't see a thing. Just the hot sting of shampoo, my father with his smoker's cough hacking something up nearby, and her hands softening, slowly, along my scalp. After she rinsed me clean, she whirled a soft towel around my head. It was then that she hugged me on the bathroom floor. She cooed to me: *my Bao Bao, my Red Rabbit, my Rat Baby*. She squeezed me so close to her breast, I felt her organs link with mine.

At my aunt's house, after I'd let the dye sit for an hour and washed it out, they all came over. The women moved into the light, inspecting my new hair.

"Huh, weird," Angela said, her head tilted. "It didn't work." She was right. Nothing had happened at all. The whites remained, peeking through the black like silkworms. My white hair had refused the dye.

"It's a sign," my mother said, holding a single white strand out like a tightrope. "Don't pull them out. Something in you is stronger than you are." And with that, she let the strand go.

5

A JANE BY ANY
OTHER NAME

NOT JENNY. NOT MICHELLE. NOT KATIE. NOT CINDY. THESE were the names of the girls in my grade school class, oftentimes in triplicate so they had to be called Jenny L., Jennifer H., Jen T., and so on. Jenny was the most popular name of all. A name that shines like a penny you make a wish with.

When I tell my friends about how I got my name, they think it's hilarious. It says a lot about my mother. My mother, very pregnant with me (I envision my fetus self not as a watermelon, but as a hot air balloon filled with fire and a basket of perishable snacks), was working the cash register at the restaurant when it dawned on her that she had to give her daughter an English name.

To fit in. She says this phrase at least three times. *To fit in. To fit in. To fit in.* As if casting a spell upon America—the incantation traveling from shore to shore. And so, when the cash register slams shut like an alligator's jaw and the door jingles open, she asks the stranger who walks through.

"Can you name my daughter?"

The customer is truly from Jersey and does not skip a beat. "Yeah, sure. How about Maria?" The customer is Mexican American and is picking up an order of chicken and broccoli with some spareribs on the side. We are known for our spareribs—slow cooked for hours and lacquered in sweet and salty hoisin gold. The burnt ends are chewy, luscious like fermented lava. I used a spare rib as a pacifier growing up. My teeth strengthened, deliciously. My mother folds over the brown bag twice and staples it shut, the receipt dangling like a flag without a country.

Her mouth opens. She struggles. Her tongue doesn't know where to reach. She hasn't gone to night school for English yet and won't go for a few more years. She gets as far as "Ma," which is actually what she's about to become. She falters with the rest, which falls away from her like cookie crumbs. But, despite living in the U.S. for less than a year, my mother is already a Jersey girl. She also does not skip a beat. If there's something that has never changed about my mother, it's that she never wavers. "No, sorry. Try again."

The customer cradles the food in the crook of her arm and says my name while walking away. The food can't get cold, and she's got places to go. My name travels with her, a drowsy bee, almost buzzing out the door.

"Jane," my mother repeats after her.

The phone rings and my mother picks it up. But before she takes another order, she covers the phone with her hand and shouts so that the Customer Who Named Me can hear her over the car's engine: "Thank you! See you next time!" They both smile and wave at each other like queens sharing a parade float.

The best part? My mother does this again with my brother, Steven.

* * *

EVEN THOUGH MY NAME is common, it wasn't ordinary then or now. I have trouble finding my name on magnets at gas station rest stops. Which is actually fine, because why would you want a magnet with your name on it anyway?

When I was born in 1984, Jane was not a cool name. Jane lacked some serious '80s flair; my name didn't have shoulder pads or any sort of turquoise fluorescence. Growing up, I never knew another Jane. It would take me until graduate school, in 2008, to meet one. In fact, I met two Janes at the Iowa Writers' Workshop, both poets I admire. Underneath one of my Facebook photos, one Jane commented, "Hi Jane," and then the other Jane commented, "Hi Jane," and all three of us "liked" everything. This is how rare we are these days.

My name is short and blunt like the bowl haircut I had for years as a child. The *a* is sharp and nasally—meant to be sung by someone with a deviated septum. Meant for someone with the peak of a white person's nose, not flat and small like mine (it will take me over 30 years to love my nose). Sometimes my name sounds like a rusty tool you use to fix a broken sink—inadequate for such daily annoyances. Sometimes it bellows forth like a goat sticking its head out of a barn after a sudden downpour: "Jaaaaaaaaane."

My name startles me, especially when I'm not expecting it—when someone calls out for a Jane at the grocery store or the gynecologist's waiting room. Whenever I hear a stranger call my name, my spine always stands a bit straighter, as if I'm being hit with a ruler. My name is not allowed to hunch over, not allowed to overflow like a pool of foamy sludge along the shore, not allowed to shove handfuls of chips into its salt-stunned mouth.

Stand up straight, my name demands. *Or else you'll stay like that.*

* * *

MY FIRST NAME AND last name are common in two very different continents, empires. My name: a reluctant, rickety plank or a deep crevasse no one can forge. Let's start with my last name, which is how Chinese people do it. For I'm also trying to prove to you that I am a little bit Chinese and not a total failure—not a gweilo, a white ghost.

Wong, one of the most popular Chinese surnames, could mean "king" or "yellow" depending on what kind of family you are from. Considering I come from a poor farming family, a peasant family, it's definitely the latter (how I've always hated the word "peasant," how it's often confused with "pleasant," as if poor people are so nice, so happily stupid). But let's say yellow like gold. Like sumptuous, buttery 24-karat gold. I want to be gold-leaf yellow, the kind of edible gold a baker uses tweezers with to crown an impossibly moist cupcake. An egg-yolk drooling Wong, Meyer-lemon Wong, canary-singing Wong.

In the hellscape of middle school, I heard all the insufferable jokes. *Wrong Wong. Jane Slong. Jane Bong. Wonky Wong. What's Wong?* Amid all this inanity, which continues into adulthood believe it or not, I have to remind myself there are some great Wongs. There's Anna May Wong from the Roaring Twenties, the Chinese American Hollywood starlet born in Los Angeles, near Chinatown. She was in *The Toll of the Sea* (1922), one of the first Technicolor movies. The colors were as sharp as the stereotypes that cut through her, in all shades of sickly seaweed. Early in the film, we see Anna May's character, Lotus Flower, giggling with infantilized glee, demure in her ignorance: "Christian lady at Mission tell me America fine place. Women free—can spend all husband's money." This perceived threat of the cunning "Dragon Lady" was set up from the start, intermingling with her submissive Madame Butterfly trope to create the perfect storm of accented Otherness. Kenneth Harlan's character, Allen Carver, clutches her body tightly over and over in this scene, pulling her in with his greedy hands. This is what I notice when I watch and teach the scene: his hands all over her—her shoulders, her arms, her face— grasping with wild desire. Cementing her worthlessness under the tyranny of the white imagination, *The Toll of the Sea* ends with Lotus Flower drowning herself in the sea. At least according to Wikipedia, Anna May said it herself in a 1933 interview with *Film Weekly*: "I was so tired of the parts I had to play." In 1935, when it came time to cast *The Good Earth*—a film that tells the story of a family from rural China, adapted from a novel written by a white woman raised in China, Pearl S. Buck—MGM did not consider Anna May for the part she wanted: main character O-lan. They gave that part to Luise Rainer, a white actress, whose yellowface performance as O-lan was later awarded an Oscar.

I shake my head with my Wong sister, in solidarity. What someone so talented can withstand. It makes me furious with love. After being denied the role of O-lan, Anna May decided to spend a year traveling throughout China—starting with her ancestral village. She tells the *San Francisco Chronicle* in 1936: "Perhaps upon my arrival, I shall feel like an outsider. Perhaps instead, I shall find my past life assuming a dreamlike quality of unreality." I think about that dreamlike quality, about desiring that throbbing link of ghostly lineage. I recognize that desire to find something that will reassure you: you belong. Anna May, as I will discover, is Toisanese just like me. I wonder how far our ancestral villages are from each other—if I could walk the distance in my mother's heels. I pull our last name closer to me, a tether in a Technicolor I reimagine. In the future, Anna May gets to be whatever kind of Wong she wants—in real life and in the movies. She gets to star alongside Michelle Yeoh and Stephanie Hsu in 2022's *Everything Everywhere All at Once* in a googly-eye dripping flapper dress. She gets to douse all that racist Hollywood mess with golden gasoline and light it on fire. Imagine the glow of that yolky warmth held to your face.

There's also Gwen Wong, Faye Wong, Ali Wong, and Lee Anne Wong—a growing list of famous Wong sisters to start. Gwen was the second Asian American to be a centerfold in *Playboy* (China Lee being the first). In her iconic photo from April 1967, her black hair is impressively bouffanted, and she's outfitted in green. One hand pulls at her argyle knee sock and the other rests on a towering stack of colorful pillows. In this mod art scene, she's utterly balanced, her polished loafers kicked to the side, her breasts bare in their blunt confidence.

Gwen's family ran the first Chinese restaurant in Cincinnati, Ohio. She, too, was a restaurant baby. In a 2020 story for *Playboy*, she shares how David Bowie asked her out while she was shopping, but she was too busy to care. When she quit her job as a Playboy Bunny to spend more time with her children, she went to college—with *Playboy* contributing to her tuition. And later, returning to her restaurant-baby roots, she became a food tester for *Bon Appetit*. As of 2020, she proudly owns more than 3,000 cookbooks.

And then there's Faye Wong, whom I idolized from her roles in Wong Kar-wai films like *Chungking Express* (1994) and *2046* (2004). The OG cool girl, she moved to Hong Kong in the late '80s and sang in both Cantonese and Mandarin. I remember watching *Chungking Express* by myself in college, late at night when everyone else was out partying. I sipped Fireball from my solo cup alone and pressed play. There was Faye, whose character has the same name, singing her Cantonese cover of the Cranberries' "Dreams." With this soundtrack, Faye sneaks into the apartment of Cop 663—played by Tony Leung (aka my forever crush)—in long pink rubber gloves. She pours goldfish into a cloudy tank, throws flip-flop sandals behind a couch, dances with a soda can in hand, and changes the labels to his canned food (all sardines!). It's hard to explain what it was like to hear Cantonese, a language I associated only with my family, spoken in this way—oddly, rebelliously, creatively. In that dark dorm room, with my gross cinnamon booze breath, I fell in love with Faye and her overgrown pixie cut and yellow sunglasses. When she was on her 1994 music tour, she wore exaggerated long sleeves because she said she didn't know what to do with her hands. I can relate; at poetry readings, I usually linger by the cheese table so I have something to do with my hands. Also in 1994, the Hong Kong paparazzi caught her carrying a chamber pot, bleary eyed, to dump pee into a community toilet. That refusal of glamour skyrocketed her toward exponential coolness.

And what about my first name, the name gifted to me by a stranger? Jane was widely used in the 16th century for English daughters of noblemen, a new option to replace the popular name Joan (a name that sounds sweet and melancholy. A name that holds a kind of ennui "Jane" can't have). There are two queens from this time period in England: Lady Jane Grey and Jane Seymour. Lady Jane Grey, also known as Jane of England, was a queen for only nine days. She was eventually executed because she posed a threat to Queen Mary. In a painting of her, Jane looks like a ghost puppet in overflowing burgundy robes. Her arms are spread apart in an impossible hug, like a bear trap that can't close. She looks terribly severe and unhappy. Looking at her, I feel my whole body react—involuntarily shaking itself loose, limb by limb. And of course there's Calamity Jane, notorious in the public's imagination for wearing men's clothes and drinking herself under the table. She's idolized. The American West loves a badass. An ox-team driver, a sex worker, a cook, a nurse, a waitress. What often gets left out of Calamity Jane's narrative: a supporter of the murder of Indigenous peoples. Some people might use the term "frontierswoman," but this is what this term means. None of these Janes look like me, and I am pretty sure that, even though we share a first name, they would take one glance at me and shove me firmly under their heeled boots.

Instead, I imagine Anna May, Gwen, Faye, and me sharing pork and crab soup dumplings at Dough Zone in Seattle's Chinatown-International District, resting them gently on our spoon cradles and then puncturing the tops with our teeth, fatty steam rising victoriously. I think about this slurping scene a lot, about generations of Asian American women nourishing each other across time, space, and so much unnecessary loneliness. This is us: the Wongs, linked by name but also by ferocity, resolve, and vinegary tenderness.

* * *

IF I'M GOING TO be honest, I keep forgetting how to say my Chinese name. There's no guarantee at all that I'm even writing or saying my name correctly at this very moment. I have to call my mother every few years and ask her to say it out loud. My mother speaks to me only in English these days. My Chinese name opens like an old jar of fermented garlic. "Can you say it again?" I ask her over and over, until I'm dizzy with its unrecognizable pungency. I say my name out loud, lifting it to the air like my favorite amusement park ride, the swing carousel. My name: flung out to the farthest corners, the guttural tones blurring together. Was I saying it right? I wobble in my shame, like I'm about to shit my pants. *Can you say it again?*

The only time I hear my name naturally is when I'm around my grandparents. When Gung Gung was alive, he would announce my presence like it was the time of day. It was Hang Neoi o'clock! He affectionately added "neoi." I loved how resolutely he said my name, as if it opened doors. Yeh Yeh and Ngin Ngin nicknamed me Bao Bao, my cheeks as large as baked pork buns. *Bao Bao*, they'd say, holding my face up to theirs, my big eyes shining on them like a seaside lighthouse.

When Yeh Yeh fell seriously ill, my brother and I visited him at the hospice. On the ground floor, the receptionist asked us: "Who are you here to see?" My brother and I looked at each other, completely flustered.

"Yeh Yeh," we said in unison. How could we tell her that we don't know our grandfather's actual name? How could we explain that our grandparents earned this title, the grandest of all titles, and let go of their actual names? The three of us looked at each other, not sure of what to do.

"Let me just go through some Chinese-sounding names, how about that?" she finally said, trying her best to help. My brother and I went, floor by cold floor, hoping to find him. Amid the vases of plastic daisies and halls of empty gurneys, our shoes squeaked against the linoleum. Finally, on the second floor, we saw our uncle, who led us to our Yeh Yeh. When we saw his actual name for the first time, on the whiteboard outside his door, we stared at it with wonder. And then we looked away with guilt, which bloated through us like quick oats.

In Seattle's Central District, my one surviving grandparent, Pau Pau, laughs, tipping her head back like a pitcher of water, when she says my name. Once, when my aunt and I visited her, we let ourselves into her studio apartment. She always leaves her door unlocked. Pau Pau was cutting the ends off string beans when we entered, the little green tails gathering in a pink plastic colander. She looked up and laughed in soft surprise, *Hang Neoi*, the scissors scraping her fingers. *Pau Pau*, I greeted her, weighing her warm, papery hands. A spot of her blood rivered along my palm lines. I held on tightly until it stopped bleeding.

To write this, I ask my mother again. I call and ask her to remind me what my name means. "It's like something naturally fragrant. Something you like. Like lavender or chamomile. But not actually," she tells me. "Your Yeh Yeh named you. He knew I missed home. Your name sounds like missing home, but it's not."

Not actually? But it's not? Confused, I ask her to write it down for me in Chinese. She pauses for a bit. "Oh shoot. I forgot how." I can hear her in the post office break room, waving down a Chinese co-worker of hers. "Jane, I'll text it to you later, okay?" After all this talk about my name, she tells me that her co-workers are having a party during break today. On the other side of the country, I imagine my mother with a party hat, the elastic strap along her chin. I imagine her lunch whirling inside the microwave behind her. She tells me there's a wheel you can spin to win a prize. "Let's see if I'm lucky today!"

The text comes through later that night. My Chinese name is written on a white napkin. One of the characters looks like it has dimples. When a Chinese American friend of mine looks up the characters (I'm completely illiterate in Chinese), she finds the words "vegetable" and "fragrant." Homesick with top notes of various vegetables and a hint of chamomile, eau de parfum.

Shu Hang. Is that my name? In the bewildering cosmos of my name, I have to let go of precision, clarity, and correctness. I say my Chinese name like speaking into wet sand, muffled in sloppy grit.

* * *

AT ANY GIVEN TIME, it's bound to happen. I try to extra-enunciate in my best learned voice. And yet. And still.

"It's nice to meet you, Jade!"

The places you'll find Jade: dinner parties, conference networking groups, dressing room chalkboards. Sometimes I correct them. Sometimes I just let it go. It's not worth listening to their embarrassment, their arms-waving-over-their-heart apologies. One time, when I corrected a white woman, she said, "Oh my god, I'm sorry. How do you spell that?" As if there's an exotic way to spell Jane. And my favorite of all, correcting another white woman: "It's actually Jane. Not Jade. My name is Jane." She had the nerve to respond: "Are you sure?"

Am I sure of my own name?

I was born in Long Branch, New Jersey. My mother loves telling me about how I looked like a doll, with my big eyes, bowl haircut, and perfectly frilly dress. "When we'd go to Chinatown, strangers would take pictures of you. They'd ask me if they could take a picture with the China Doll."

"That's creepy," I tell her.

"Yeah," she shakes her head. "Sometimes I thought they were going to kidnap you. And make you model for GapKids." My mother wanted me to be a GapKids model so badly, she'd risk me getting kidnapped by white couples. She used to rip out the GapKids ads from magazines to show her friends, tapping the pages with her finger: "Don't you think Jane and Steven should be Gap?"

Despite being a fluent English speaker and reading early for my age, I ended up in ESL for two years. This was back in the day when you were pulled out of your regular classroom and walked to the "trailers" like you were about to be quarantined. The trailers were outside and linked together with a shoddy boardwalk. The nurse's office was there too, full of nosebleeds and taffy-colored vomit. Being pulled into a trailer was like wearing a "kick me" sign on your back for years.

I hated everyone in school and didn't say a single word out loud until the fourth grade. And thus, because of this silence and the fact that I looked foreign, the teachers and administrators assumed I didn't know English. So what if she's clearly writing a novella in her Trapper Keeper? So what if she's read all the books in the classroom three times already?

And there I was, in a stuffy trailer, refusing to do yet another puzzle map of the U.S. The ESL teacher pointed to the trailer door with its rusty hinges and slapped a sign on it that read "DOOR." She smiled at me like a murderous clown. "DOOOOOOOOOOR, Jane. Say it with me. That's a DOOOOOOOR." I sat there, my eyes burning a flame so bright it could light a million torches held by rats in mutiny.

The teachers and administrators forced me to play the little Chinese girl, dressed in pigtails and a red silk jacket, to taunt a dragon on Culture Night. They forced my mother to bring in wontons from the restaurant on International Food Day. And those wontons, made painstakingly by all the women in our family, were delicious. When a white bully, who looked me straight in the eye with glittering cruelty (*Ching-chong, ding-dong*, he sneered at me during recess, pressing my nose as if ringing a doorbell), doubled over and said the wontons were poisoned, they did nothing when all the kids started to fake cry and push their bowls away. You can imagine what followed: *Ew, dog meat, MSG is poison, dirty this*, and *dirty that*. Remember: my mother never wavers. "The wontons are fine!" she shouted with her arms raised, shooing them away like flies. I thought about the time it took to pinch each wonton closed, how each matrilineal thumb pressed its indent of care. "Who taught you to be like this?"

School was the reason I refused to speak for so long, the reason I stayed silent. I became an empty vault of held breath, an abandoned vinegar cellar. When a teacher called on me, I said nothing. When I was paired to work in groups, I doodled in my notebook and said nothing. In ESL, I said nothing. At the counselor's office, I said nothing. My silence gurgled salt water and spit it out. Instead of playing at recess, I sat alone and read and reread books, living in an imagined place of symphonic sound and color. I liked how Claudia Kishi talked about her outfits, how, in *Claudia Kishi: Middle School Dropout* from the Baby-Sitters Club series, she was really into moss-colored accessories and wore a Pebbles Flintstone ponytail on the top of her head. I wrote down what I wanted to say to Claudia, if I could say something that mattered. And then I'd cover that up with my arm, afraid someone would see it. I'd smudge my pencil lead with silver embarrassment, filling my notebook with stars I drew in metallic gel ink in one continuous motion. And just like that, I became another trope in their eyes: the Inscrutable Asian. Stoic, mysterious, unreadable. My teachers gave me low marks on participation. I wasn't a "team player." I wasn't "like the other kids." What I really was: angry. I was angry that I couldn't be who I really was. I was angry that they wouldn't let me figure out who I really was. Who was I? Jane? Shu Hang? Little Chinese Girl? I had no idea. I tunneled into the interior corners of my seething loneliness, one college-ruled line at a time. I hugged my Trapper Keeper like a flotation device, like it was the only thing that kept me above water. Even from a young age, I was plainly aware that I couldn't escape the vast ways I was seen and unseen, made and unmade.

These days, I can't seem to shut up. Words spill out of me like the ribboned guts of a sea cucumber: unstoppable, self-protective. I write, I teach, I insist. But, at the molten core of my voice, I always wonder: Am I a traitor for writing in the language of the colonizer?

* * *

I COULD CALL MYSELF a dove, a winter melon. I could fall in love with my name in ripe, unabashed sunlight. June Jordan writes in "Poem about My Rights": "My name is my own my own my own." Repeating "my own" makes the phrase echo and ring in perpetuity. I think about how protective I am of my own name, how I hold it close to my body like a Band-Aid I can't seem to pull off. To be seen, to be human, to be singular.

* * *

HOW MY EX-BOYFRIENDS WERE named: after a Rick Springfield song, after a great-great-grandfather no one remembers, after a person in the Bible before his parents stopped bathing and decided to become hippies, after months of deliberation and divination via a book of baby names his parents paid real money for, to use just once. They often tell me their middle names—which they prefer and wish were their actual names. But I want to ask: What is the difference between a Frank and a David? What good is a name you never use?

"What's your middle name?" they ask me.

"It's just Jane Wong."

"That's it? You really don't have a middle name?"

I've always wondered why they thought this was strange. What were they thinking? How simple, how pedestrian, how plain? Jane Wong? Just two syllables? Just two skips of a rock in a pond? You only need rain and a pothole to skip a name that short. Two syllables like two taps of the gavel in *Law and Order*.

It's funny how someone can make you feel like you need a middle name. I actually considered getting one, as if one could "get one" like picking up a kitten from the shelter. I could be one of those cool Asian Americans who had an identity awakening in college and use my

Chinese name. Jane Shu Hang Wong. Or, because we are often mistaken for each other, I could use my mother's name. Jane Jin Wong. As I filed this in the back of my head as something to think about, I opened up Facebook and saw my little brother had changed his name for a brief moment: Steven Jay Wong.

I texted him immediately: Jay?!

He texted back: So what? My friends say it sounds cooler.

I didn't know this could be a thing. My brother completely made up "Jay." Was it after the bird, handsome with its mohawk? Or was it to be closer to my mother and me, sealing our family triumvirate through our first initials: Jin, Jane, Jay? My brother is earnest enough to do something like that, and I love him with the fierceness of a wolf pack for it.

Here I was, a grown woman, trying to come up with something I never desired in the first place. Honestly, I didn't want any embellishment. I didn't want this extra flair to be someone I'm not. Not the supplemental, downy softness my ex-boyfriends desired of me: no Rose, no Sophia, no Isabelle in the middle. I don't care how plain "Jane" sounds, how old fashioned, how no-frills. I don't care that there are a million Jane Wongs in the world. For once, I want to put away my glitter, my bright red lips, my patent leather boots. I want to hold my name up like a simple blade of grass and ask my baby cousin: *What color is this?* Not emerald, not chartreuse, not forest. *Green*, he'll say. My name, just like that.

* * *

THROUGHOUT MIDDLE SCHOOL, I had an alter ego named Wayne. My best friend at the time, who I'll call Lara, was the tallest girl in our class at six feet and growing. She collected terrifying Victorian dolls with collars like frilled lizards and loved sipping steak blood, which her family poured into tiny Dixie cups clearly made for tequila shots.

I took steak blood shots with them, cackling like a vampire. My lips were filmed with salty jus. Lara loved Wayne the most. And when I was over at her house, Wayne would cause all kinds of trouble.

Some things to know about my alter ego: she's a cheesemonger and lives in a cheese cave. She plays R&B tunes on the clarinet and is known for her airy renditions of Boyz II Men. When boys throw rocks at her (which happens to Jane, coincidentally), she kicks them right in the balls. Wayne is a thief, a total flirt, and wears her boyfriends' T-shirts as minidresses. She has bright blue hair, the color of a sour blue raspberry Fruit Roll-Up.

Once, at Lara's house, Wayne made a concoction from all the booze in her parents' liquor closet, the curaçao swirling together with the rest of the clear and honey liquids like an extravagant bath bomb. Moving from cabinet to cabinet like a jewel thief, Wayne fortified the cocktail with hot sauce, Welch's grape juice, horseradish, red liquid from cocktail cherries, and clam juice. Lara and Wayne (both wearing yellow kitchen gloves because who would want to touch that cocktail) poured the mixture into an empty Coke bottle and spent the whole night convincing Lara's little brothers to drink it. One of her brothers took a sip and curled up in a ball and cried like a broken sink. Lara and Wayne poured the entirety of the concoction into a bowl of cereal just to see what it would do. Wayne wanted to hear the sound. The sizzling incineration of each Cheerio, glugging its way down to the bottom of the bowl. She took a picture of it with a disposable camera and told Lara she was going to send this to her boyfriend in lieu of a love poem.

For the record, all middle schoolers are weird people who tiptoe around the edges of indelicacy. And it's obvious that my alter ego was more akin to building an altar for who I wanted to be—or who I truly was, at least partly. I needed Wayne, my familiar stranger. I needed her to refuse what people expected of me. Jane: polite, quiet, shy, deferential, forgiving. The media taught me these roles, returning to lovelorn, docile Lotus Flower in *The Toll of the Sea.*

Later in life, men will expect me to be their "babe," their "baby." They'll play me Velvet Underground's "Sweet Jane" in the morning, as if this has never been done before. They'll kiss me hard—my lips splintered with blood. They'll whisper, "You're bad, you're rotten," as if I was supposed to be good. I will get messages on dating apps like "will you be the Jane to my Tarzan?" and "you remind me of Lucy Liu." In 2017, many years after the Bad One, I will fall for a man who shows up at one of my poetry readings in Seattle, a man who says my name like scaling a waterfall. He will love me in all my contradictions and never call me "babe" or "baby," just Jane. After a year, I will let my guard down and tumble into each cherry-blossomed tree, each muddy mass of moss. And he will leave for work in the wilderness and tell me days later that he never loved me, that none of it was real. I will become some other entity, some ghost self. Insert for a name: any girl. I will fall silent again. I will walk through the world like an aphid-thinned leaf. I will beg to have my name returned to me, boomeranged back. My mother will call and carry me through heartache once again. *Get up, Jane, get up.* I will hold my name fiercely until it grows new selves. Pups, sprouts, offsets, green suckers of the self. I will listen to the sounds of garbage trucks outside and their prehistoric arms, crushing everything we throw away, and demand that every single person see me—fully and completely—as I see myself. Somehow uncrushed, growing still.

*   *   *

MY MOTHER LIKES TO tell me about a blanket I named "Nose" as a toddler. The blanket was completely falling apart, threadbare and pilled. I used to stuff my nose with the soft cotton, twisting it up so I could only breathe through my mouth. According to her, I spent a lot of time twisting up the cotton, like I was trying to get the perfect ratio of cotton to nose. It was important that the cotton was still connected to the blanket. "You couldn't sleep without Nose. You'd cry: Nose! Nose! It was weird. I was worried there was something wrong with you." In her telling, I love how my mother says this last part, as if this couldn't possibly be her daughter, this weirdo, this future poet.

Nowadays, I sleep in fists. I can't help it. When I wake in the morning, my hands hurt from being curled up all night. I shake them loose in the early fog, wings flapping. At night, I surround my bed with books, pillows, and plates of leftover pizza just to know something is there. Too many bad or disappearing men, too many real stories that terrify. How could anyone sleep peacefully?

When my mother visits me in Seattle, she always sleeps in my bed with me. Apparently, most people put their parents up in a hotel. I would never. My mother would be offended. She takes up the entire bed, her legs and arms outstretched. She makes little animal noises when she sleeps. Little squirrel chirps and toad moans. I always sleep stick-straight, at the edge of the bed like I'm about to fall off a cliff. "Are you a mummy?" she jokes. She tells me that, when I was a little baby, she'd have to stick her index finger under my nose to make sure I was still breathing. "You never move. Why?"

Once, sleeping with me in my Seattle studio, my mother jolted up in bed and shouted at the top of her lungs: "THE BONES!"

"What the hell mommy!" I screamed, startled awake. Then I started to laugh uncontrollably, the dry heat making me cough. Then she started laughing and coughing so hard, she kept smacking the wall. Then I kept going, my face aching with laughter, like I'd run miles escaping a bear that wasn't there. It was like this for some time—this rollicking train of laughter and tears and drool and gulping. My neighbor slapped the walls back, transmitting an important message: *Stop it!* Rolling around in bed, legs kicking in the air like synchronized swimmers, we chanted in our early morning delirium: "THE BONES! THE BONES THE BONES THE BONES THE BONES THE BONES THE BONES THE BONES THE BONES THE BONES THE

BONES!" (The butcher had given us free beef bones and she'd forgotten to put them in the fridge.) When I sleep with my mother, I never sleep in fists.

My mother and I get our names mixed up all the time. Jin Ai translates to something like "simple" and "love." Her maiden name: Huang. We look alike; it's more than obvious that I'm her daughter. We have the same lips, the same smile, the same mole, the same proclivity toward eating things that take patience to consume: we bite each single corn kernel, carefully crack open every peanut, dig our claws into each absurdly tiny crab leg. When I lived in Montana, I received her W-2 in the mail. When I get mail at my childhood home in Jersey, she forges my signature, pretends to be Jane. Our names sound similar, ringing together like bells: Jin, Jane. Because America is America, some of her co-workers call her Jean instead. And some people spell her name Gin, which welcomes a plethora of dad jokes about getting my mother drunk.

"We are the same," she tells me often. "We have the same light inside. It's so crazy bright, some bugs come to us and some just go blind. Do you know what I mean?" *I think I do? Can you repeat it again?*

I love these stories of hers. The Insect Light, the Nose Blanket, the Customer Who Named You. There are so many, I can't recount them all in my lifetime: the time she cut open that boy's foot, the time she stole her purse back from a thief, the time we sang "Who Let the Dogs Out" at full volume after my father left, the time her sister-in-law broke all her plates and dropped me on my head—in all these stories, we meld into each other. These stories become mine, passed down through so much blinding light.

My mother didn't name me. Not my English name, not my Chinese name. She calls me by my true name: her daughter. Hers. Her reflection, her double. "That's my daughter," she says all the time, as if we are twin moons. She announces this to her co-workers who we run into on the street, to strangers by the sweet cantaloupe heaps at A&P, to me especially, when I am red-eyed and hunched in exhaustion. *You're my daughter.* In other words: *You will survive this because I have.* Jin's Daughter with the Crazy Bright Light. I earned this title and I move into it, a waltz of kin I know so well. Moths carousel around it, testing their trust.

GUTS

HALF A YEAR WENT BY WHILE I WAS LIVING WITH THE MAN who would become my ex-fiancé before I noticed the ants. The ants were larger than I expected—not the size you think of when you think of the word "ant." Ants large enough that I felt their bodies fall apart—armor clanging off piece by piece—when I tried to kill them with a napkin. It felt medieval to press down on their miraculous bodies like that; I hated doing it. The ants seemed to be coming up from our sink and bathtub, squeezing their bodies past the silver stopper. They poured out of each intestinal water system of the house, their antennae testing the humid air like a radio tuning to find my heart. At first, I tried to spray them away with multipurpose cleaner, but they kept coming back. Maybe they even liked the spray (I had sprung for something nice, Mrs. Meyer's Clean Day in lemon verbena). They came back thicker, stronger.

I didn't even type anything into Wongmom.com, but she pinged me, unsolicited. "You've got ants," she said, matter-of-factly. "Ants are workers. They don't stop. Something is running in your heart, tireless. Something bothering you?"

"What? No, I'm fine." I waved her away, flicking an ant, which somersaulted across the room. The ant landed on the bedroom window ledge, unshaken, and started to crawl back to where it came from: me. I typed this quietly, my fingers attempting ballet, so that my future ex-fiancé couldn't hear in the other room. He frequently made sarcastic jokes about how loudly I typed. And of course, I *had* to be a writer who typed like a charging rhino a lot.

"You have ants? Yes, or no?"

I stared at them circling the sink drain's perimeter, chewing on hair, toothpaste, my foamy face cleanser. They sipped at his mouthwash, a glassy streak of blue. Every small morsel we left behind, they interrogated with the curiosity of a scientist. I had even seen them carrying other insects before, a wing here, a fly segment there. I admired their strength as they sourced these treasures back to the drain. Meanwhile, I could barely lug the lawnmower out from the garage, my forehead necklaced with grassy sweat.

When I finally admitted to the ants, Wongmom.com told me I had to face what had been bothering me, what kept coming back. She told me that I had the power to send the ants elsewhere. She told me only I knew what needed facing. Then she added a wink emoji, and then an ant emoji.

"How did you find that one?" I asked her, shocked since she'd only just started using the red heart.

"Mommy figured it out," Wongmom.com said, proudly. "You type in what you want and boom! Ant. So smart."

My ex-fiancé's annoyed sigh drifted in from the other room. Before I could say anything, he came over and wordlessly slammed my door shut. With my loud typing, I was being selfish and inconsiderate again. I thought about flushing the ants out, guzzling some awful Drano down into the guts. But I knew what I really had to do. My ultimate fears, my gut feelings—they had been marching outward with so many spindly legs for months.

But it wouldn't be easy. Wongmom.com didn't have to tell me that. Sometimes the ants even nestled in my hair, blending in with each black strand not yet white. I'd find one crawling and pinch it off, dropping it to the ground. I'd stare at the crawling thing, perfumed with my meaty follicles. Was it now a part of me?

I remember an acquaintance's reply when I shared about leaving the Bad One, many years before my ex-fiancé: "You're so brave. I wouldn't be able to go through that." Since I'd barely told her any details about my relationship, only that I needed to escape, I didn't understand her comment. I didn't feel brave. Was it brave to run out of a burning building? When she said the second comment, she looked at me with a particular type of pity. Her head was lowered like a horse pawing at a carrot, her eyes wide and glossy. She tried to reach for my hands, but I held them behind my back. "I've only been with [her husband's name] and yeah, he gets on my nerves sometimes, but I guess I should really count my blessings. I mean, look what you went through!" She looked expectant, eager for details. A juicy carrot. What did she want from me? I regretted saying anything. I wanted nothing more than to curl into a ball like an armadillo and roll down a hill, wayward straw in my shell, far away from her perfectly ironed blouse with a satin bow.

Look what I went through! I was so brave, so gutsy.

My guts churned with fire ants as I made up some excuse to leave the conversation.

A few weeks after leaving the Bad One, I felt a pain in my side. I lay in bed, trying to get up every so often, but it flared so sharply, I couldn't move. It was as if someone had lanced me with a long sword—like a katana, one of those Japanese swords creepy white dudes love to collect above their fireplace mantels. I clutched my weeping wound. I looked up "appendicitis" on my phone, terrified of my body imploding.

What was more terrifying? My appendix bursting a deadly abscess or going to the doctor? I held out for three hours, but the pain wouldn't subside. Like a wailing kitten, I pawed at the phone and finally decided to go to the ER. It was my first time being a patient in the ER, and I felt so small. I spoke in such a low whisper that the woman at the intake counter had to lean her whole head out of the counter's frame. Across two ratty waiting room chairs, I curled over like a mouse stuck in a peanut butter trap. I waited for another hour to be seen. When I finally got into a room to get checked out, there were numerous young white male residents who buzzed around me, mumbling and knocking into things. They had fresh haircuts with well-done fades but couldn't find my appendix. *Huh, that's funny,* they said to each other. They ran some blood tests. *Hmmm, I wonder what's going on. What level did you say the pain was? A 7? Are you sure?* They kept coming in and out of the room, in and out, telling me nothing. *One second, Miss . . . Wong.* I wondered if I'd ever get someone to actually look at me. *Excuse me, I'll be right back.* I laid there in my starchy paper dress, feverish and vulnerable, not moving for fear of the pain spiking up and through me. I cried, tears leaking into my ears, and stared at posters of women's bodies on the wall, illustrations of fleshy vulvas.

An hour passed and, finally, a doctor came in swiftly. She began by apologizing for the residents who kept flubbing about me. She kept that apology sharp and to one sentence only. Then she told me I had colitis. My colon was swollen to four times its usual size. I imagined my colon like an inflatable tube at a kid's birthday party. "What has your diet been?" she asked. She was pretty, and when she saw that I'd noticed she was pretty, she spoke even more sharply. "Have you experienced chronic stress?"

I thought about the Bad One's hands tightening around my purpling body, the nearly rotten slices of frozen pizza I'd eaten for the past week. I lifted my head and opened my mouth to answer her, but nothing came out. She nodded for me in a brief camera flash of knowing, which my guts appreciated. She handed me a pamphlet on colitis care. The trifold flapped in my sweaty hands, its care routine being the first of many steps to clear my system.

Maybe this is the one constant in my life: the need to clear. The ants, my guts, concentric piles of shame. And it is more about clearing regularly—and doing so thoroughly. After our ant exchange,

Wongmom.com prescribed me more dragon fruit and sent a couple lovingly wrapped in scarves in the mail. She sent golden versions, sweeter and softer in the middle. They were so ripe; they were impossible to eat with a knife. I squeezed each center and fruit leapt right into my open mouth.

6

BAD BILDUNGSROMAN
WITH TABLE TENNIS

I PAINTED MY NAILS ON MY FATHER'S BRAND-NEW PING-Pong table. The table was set up in our garage. I remember it unfolding like the limbs of a praying mantis, charming but eerie. The table was so large it pushed everything to the side like a bright green bully. Deflated basketballs: sad little melons, piled up against a wall. Our box of Christmas ornaments: crushed in a corner, helpless in their slow, red shattering. There was barely any room to stand on either side of the table, and so my father had to practice close to the edge—a stance he knew well from playing round after round of blackjack, teetering dangerously past 21.

The nail color was not a color. It was glitter and I know this because I was 13 and all I wanted then was glitter. I wanted to be a chandelier of blinding beauty. I had this antibacterial hand gel from Bath & Body Works that had glitter suspended inside, flecks of iridescent silver and pink that I swear—when held to direct sunlight—could burn a laser straight into your eye. I'd rub this gel all over my shoulders, neck, armpits, even behind my knees, and sashay like a spinning disco ball. This glitter killed germs. This glitter drew all my crushes in, crushed by shards of lustrous desire. I even imagined my organs gurgling with glitter—my stomach and pancreas shining like a midsummer lake so sun-startling, you could fall right in. All that sparkling circulation within me. Didn't I deserve something this extraordinary? As an adult, my friend Ally would text me a site that sold glitter poop pills, so you can excrete glitter (it does say "do not consume"): *Should I buy it?*

I especially loved the feeling of glitter nail polish once it dried, rough and jagged to the touch. I'd brush my nails against my cheek, exfoliating better than St. Ives apricot scrub. How I loved this topography of beauty, this simple self-celebration. At an age when everything and everyone tells you to pick yourself apart, to feel terrible about something as small as your eyebrows and cuticles, I glittered carelessly. I spackled on coat after goopy coat, thick with dazzling protection.

* * *

MY FATHER LOVED PLAYING Ping-Pong. He grew up playing it as a young adult in Southern China. I imagined him playing on watermarked tables in parks full of songbirds and on dusty kitchen tables late at night—a cigarette dangling in his mouth like a fishing pole coming up empty. In Jersey, in his 20s and early 30s, he often went to his friends' houses, practicing his topspin and lightning-fast serves. They played barefoot or in too-big foam sandals that resembled marshmallows. I've always loved how Chinese families have these sandals, often candy colored, perched by the door—so irresistible to dogs and babies to put in their mouths. Playing Ping-Pong seemed like a very dad thing to do, fitting neatly into the stereotypes of what dads do on TV. They play sports poorly, make bad jokes, nap on the couch, grill burnt burgers, give terrible but earnest advice about growing up to their children. Instead of deadbeats and gamblers and gangsters and liars, for once I saw these skinny men—the original members of the Toothpick Gang—playing Ping-Pong as if they were TV dads. They marinated and grilled chicken wings with tongs. They trash-talked in gesticular Toisanese, hurling bad puns about each other's sloppy serves or Balding Uncle's low-tide hairline. *At least I don't look like a winter melon!* Sweat dribbled down their foreheads, rivulets of volleying concentration. Sometimes their toothpicks would fall out of their mouths. Sometimes their moves appeared elegant—the cursive swish of a conductor's arm, the swift and precise en pointe footwork. They always played with worn paddles, the rubber flopping off like a cold pancake. These Ping-Pong matches were a refreshing break from the whiskey-laden gambling circles in the basement.

This hopeful vision of well-adjusted familial life seemed preferable to everything else: my father's stinging anger encircling my mother like a lasso and his nonchalant disregard for us, bills, chores, daylight. More often than not, he would refuse to use words. He'd just grunt like a rock falling off a truck bed. Who knows, maybe I learned my silence in school from him. But as someone who fell in love with words at a young age, devouring book after book at the public library, I was always unnerved by his silence. Around him, I felt like a thin sliver of self—barely there. As a young child, I pretended that my father saved his words like pennies in a jar, keeping them for someone special. That, one day, he would spew out a tangled monologue of everything he kept inside, the script unfurling gloriously like a Fruit by the Foot, copper coins pouring all over the spit-covered floor. 173 volleys, back and forth across a net, in 60 seconds. That's the 1993 World Record for ping pong, set by Jackie Bellinger and Lisa Lomas. Imagine all the things my father could say to me in one single minute.

But then his friends started to play for money, betting on winners and losers. Bills, watches, even shoes were offered up. You could gamblify anything, as it turns out. My father wanted to start hosting games at our house, and so, the summer before I started eighth grade, he bought his very own table, expensive and superfluous. When he unveiled it, my mother rolled her eyes: *Does your table turn into food we can eat?* My brother and I were curious, though, and we tiptoed closer, the table like a magnet pulling us in. I remember touching the table's fresh coat of paint, which smelled like a lime dipped in all-purpose cleaner. The white lines were as crisp as a collared shirt my father would never wear. The table was painted AstroTurf green. I thought of ants running across its vast dimensions, searching for tendrils of real grass.

* * *

THERE WERE LIMA BEAN sprouts in yogurt containers all along my sixth-grade language arts teacher's windowsill. Their little green heads bowed heavily—almost kissing the dirt below. I stared at them often, watching for the slightest change. Did they grow a millimeter? Did they move closer to the light? After our unit on Lois Lowry's *The Giver*, my teacher asked the class, "What's the lesson learned here? What's the moral of the story?" I had trouble with this question, scribbling jumbled thoughts about Elsewhere and the freezing snow in my notebook. I wrote *I have no idea* in bubble letters and thought about all the red marks my teacher would bestow upon me. I turned to watch the lima beans instead. A fly was washing its face under a stubby stem.

Here is a story. On weekdays, while my father slept soundly after a late night of gambling and drinking, snores rising and falling like a rusty seesaw, I'd steal a couple of bucks for lunch money from the back pocket of his jeans on the floor. I've always wondered why he never gave me lunch money directly, why I had to sneak around this way like a raccoon stealing cat food. *Take it from his wallet*, my mother would direct me. *Take as much as you want. He pays for nothing.* Except his wallet only ever had a few dollar bills, if anything. Unemployed after the restaurant failed, he'd splurged on this beautiful Ping-Pong table while my mother paid the bills, cooked, cleaned, and worked the night shift.

As I dug around his empty wallet, shaking out coins like Tic Tacs, my father snored and dreamt about the precise cut of his topspin, about his orchestrated footing, about the hidden ways one could win. And on those no-bills days, when there was nothing at all in his wallet, I'd steal my friends' gnawed pizza crusts during lunch. I'd sit in the cafeteria and eat their nacho chip crumbs, funneled to my mouth.

* * *

IN MY MID-20S, I was at a party in Seattle talking with writers about books we enjoyed when a new acquaintance scoffed at someone's recommendation, written by a woman. "Please. That book reeks of daddy issues," he said, gulping cheap white wine. "I'm so tired of daddy issues. It's the same thing every time. I mean, my dad sucks too, but I don't need to write about it." I looked away nervously, staring at the towers of liquor on the table. My flinch made him zero in on me. He looked at me in a way that I was unfortunately used to: up and down, with a smug smile, the vulture-beaked curiosity in his twisted eyebrow. "Let me guess," he said. "You've got daddy issues."

"So what if I do," I blurted out, lunging forward. "Don't we all?" The rest of the circle took a step backward.

He looked at me, calculating what I'd learned about masculinity and power from my father, and long divisioned the likelihood of my failed past relationships. I watched him do the math and saw that he liked how the numbers crunched in his head. He could use me. He could be awful to me and chalk it up to daddy issues. He could show the work, the math. Yes, he decided he liked me. "Hey, what's your name again?"

What's the lesson learned here? What's the moral of this story? And where was my glittered self then?

* * *

NAIL POLISH REMOVER IS incredibly resourceful. You can use it in a variety of ways, including to get rid of leeches. A little nail polish remover will destroy a leech's ability to cling to your skin. Whether or not the leech makes a terrible sizzling noise, its soft body shrinking like a dying star, is unknown to me. Nail polish remover also removes grime from computer keyboards, breaks down superglue, and helps you scrub sticker remnants off glass jars. All these uses offer me a strange sense of relief. I've spent so many hours trying to get sticker gunk off spaghetti sauce jars, stupidly determined to reuse that which we throw away. Thrift store stickers are also notoriously sticky, clinging with supernatural strength. And, perhaps most importantly, nail polish remover can strip paint really well.

* * *

IN THE 1950S, MAO Zedong heralded table tennis as China's national sport, in part because it was an economical game. With Rong Guotuan's World Table Tennis Championships victory in 1959, he became China's first world champion. In a photograph taken upon his return to China, Rong cradles his shiny trophy and a bouquet of flowers, smiling in a suit slightly too large for him. He's standing in front of an airplane, handsome in his youth, with his hair cut so cleanly, you can see little loose barber hairs if you look closely. His soft eyes peer off into the distance, not quite focused. Mao celebrated Rong's victory, eerily calling table tennis China's spiritual nuclear weapon. In 1972, the year of the rat, President Richard Nixon visited Beijing, his decision shaped in part by table tennis. Ping-Pong diplomacy was real, opening up China to the U.S. via the sharing of table tennis players, starting with the World Table Tennis Championships.

What I discovered too: Rong was denounced as a possible spy during the Cultural Revolution and held under house arrest by the Red Guards. He took his own life in 1968, four years before Nixon's

visit. He was a librarian and spent his days surrounded by the fluttering pages of books. In his suicide note, he wrote: "I am not a spy;
please do not suspect me. I have let you down."

I take all of this in: Ping-Pong's intense history of competition,
empire, power, and violence. How it all occurred in a world of men
making decisions. How there was always more at stake than just a
game. "Playing games," meaning toying with someone's earnest inten-
tions, meaning getting what you want no matter what.

* * *

I LOOK UP "DADDY issues" on the Internet. The first thing that pops
up is from Talkspace.com, which describes "daddy issues" as a negative term for those "who have complex, confusing, or dysfunctional
relationships with men." The article continues: "It can describe people
(most often women) who project subconscious impulses toward the
male partners in their life." On another search hit from Healthline
.com, Amy Rollo, a psychotherapist from Houston, addresses the gen-
dered stigma of "daddy issues." Rollo states that "'Daddy issues' could
also mean that a woman desires a strong attachment with a man . . .
using the term is minimizing a woman's basic needs in a relationship."

I think back to that dismissive comment at that party and how I
didn't hook up with that guy. And how it bothers me that I need to
announce that here, like some trophy of proof. Like, see? I have an
ounce of self-respect. But why? Why do I need to say that? What do I
have to prove? What does toxic masculinity have to do with me, with
so-called daddy issues? At the rotten core of these questions: Who
placed all of this within me in the first place? This shame, this constant buzzing-horsefly play of power and powerlessness?

At a bus stop, I hack away at my chipped nail polish like an ice
mountaineer. The color flakes off in jagged chunks. "Oh no, did
you break a nail?" A middle-aged man walks by, giggling in falsetto

girlish shock. When I stare at him, he rolls his eyes. "Come on, I was just kidding."

* * *

WHEN I TELL PEOPLE that I love playing Ping-Pong, they say: *Of course you do. You probably started playing as a baby.* Meaning: you're Chinese and your parents made you train for seven hours a day at the age of four and you must be really, really good. They think I'm a shark. The truth is: I'm terrible at being Chinese, I don't have strict parents, and I'm just okay at Ping-Pong. I can serve pretty well and I love lunging for impossible volleys along the edge or barely over the net. I'm quick on the return, but not quite mantis-shrimp quick. I'm from Jersey and I talk a bigger game than I play. I double-over laughing when I accidentally hit a ball with my hand instead of the paddle. I love playing doubles and diving out of the way like a defective firecracker for my partner. I am loyal like that. I barely have spin, but it's there. I have a serve that I like to call "the soft serve," where I chop the ball so that it falls *just* over the net. I never played as a child and I never played with my father. He never let us play. Both his tables—his Ping-Pong table and his mahjong table— were forbidden territory.

I still hold a certain affection for the game. My brother and I play it sometimes as 30-somethings, well matched in our passable skill set. We're earnest in our decent serves and terrible backhand. Sometimes we play at this hole-in-the-wall bar in Jersey called Players Billiards, where the bartenders are required to pull a netted curtain around us so we avoid hitting pool players. The Ping-Pong "table" is just a wooden slab placed over a pool table. You can still see the deep pockets of the pool table underneath. It's definitely lopsided, with little teeth-mark dents that we avoid like potholes. This is what I actually love about Ping-Pong. In this cozy shell of a game, we laugh, drink cheap beer, and completely lose track of the score—generous in our recalibration. We play just to play.

In my late 20s and early 30s, I used to bring my dates to the Zoo, a cash-only dive bar in Seattle. This was usually a first or second date. I used Ping-Pong to test them out, to see how they'd play with me. Were they sore losers? Mansplainers? Were they going to let me win, without trying? It was a terrible dad joke. To play a match to see if we'd be a good match. At the time, I thought the game could maybe reveal some red flags I couldn't see otherwise. One of my exes was a great Ping-Pong date, cajoling strangers to play doubles with us. He knocked the ball into the Skee-Ball chute instead, and we played with the new rule of unexpected baskets: winner takes all. I remember him lifting me up on the table at the end of the night and making out with him, hungry for playfulness. The bartender shouted, "Last call!" and we ended up dating for two years.

But on an early date years later, the man I was with slammed the ball hard on me. The slam actually cracked the white ball like an egg, which was sent flying toward the back of the bar. He dropped—no, threw—his paddle to the beer-sticky ground and raised his arms above his head like massive antlers, yelling: "I fucking got you! Did you see that? I fucked you up!" I could see spit frothing from the corners of his too-white smile. An older woman nearby turned. She looked me up and down with such pity and disdain, I nearly rotted into compost and crawled under the mandibles of the table. What was she thinking? What was he thinking? I'd be lying if I said I didn't cry in the piss-covered bathroom, shocked by the whole situation I found myself in. I heard an echo that night of the terrible guy from the party years before: *Let me guess. You have daddy issues.* How did this toxicity become my fault? I remember looking up at a line of scrawled graffiti in the bathroom: *for a good time, call yourself.*

* * *

WHEN I WAS A senior in high school, a friend sent me a care package in the mail. I had just met this friend at the Governor's School of the Arts, a free summer program for high school artists in Jersey. Excited, I ripped it open on the front stoop of our house. It contained a mixtape cassette, metallic purple nail polish, pressed flowers, and incense sticks that had broken apart in the postal journey. Incense ash flew everywhere, perfuming the yard with earthy patchouli. My mother, who had been watering her pansies, started screaming. "Oh my god! Oh my god! It's him!"

"It's just incense, Mommy! Who are you talking about?" I held up the crumpled hippie bits to her face so she could smell them. "See?"

She sighed heavily, relieved. She thought they were ashes. "I thought it was the Chicken Bone Man. He dropped dead in China on a massage table. I always knew something was going on with your daddy's friends," she said, shaking her head. She didn't know the word "sketchy" at the time, but she implied some serious sketch. And it's true: growing up, I noticed there was always something worth a side-eyed glance in my father's inner circle. Something less innocent than it seemed, something lurking underneath the table. I could never figure it out. Why did the trunk have 50 boxes of cigarettes? Why did a pregnant teenaged girl stay at our house for a month? What was happening in that basement when City Uncle stormed out of our house, his hand covering his misshapen jaw?

* * *

PART OF BEING A teenager is the desire to destroy something. To break something apart so fully, you can see its pulled seams, its tangled organs. At 13, I felt this feeling churn within me, this rage, this pimple-popping lusciousness of rudeness, this gleaming desire for sudden destruction. The thing is: I had no interest in diplomacy, no interest in sportsmanship. There must be a special kind of joy you get from no longer taking shit, from teaching someone else a lesson, from rightful revenge and teenaged feminism that can see far into the glittering future. Is there a word for this? I wanted to propel my 13-year-old self into the Zoo and have her tell that awful date to fuck off, her bedazzled middle fingers up.

At 13, I leaned against the AstroTurf green of my father's table, glitter nail polish inches from the net. My father hadn't even hosted his first match yet. It was still so shiny, so new. I thought of my mother, passed out in the early morning on the couch. How I pulled off her slippers and draped a blanket around her. How I lifted her work tote off the floor and placed it back on the kitchen counter. I thought of my brother, cowering in the closet when my father would start yelling. How soft his hair was when I held him. Or maybe I thought of my future self. How I'd play Ping-Pong for endless hours at the Union with my roommates in Missoula, laughing with raucous joy. We'd do this every week, for what we called Forced Family Fun Friday. How I'd gotten Nick, my boyfriend at that fast-forward time, a Ping-Pong paddle with Hello Kitty in a Green Bay Packers outfit. Because sometimes it was also about joy and love.

I picked up my nail polish remover and held it upside down, pressing a cotton ball against the bottle's opening ever so loosely. Cool dollops of acetone fell on my father's table like dog drool. Did I relish in the slow bloom of the remover as it ate away the fresh green paint, my mountain peony of joy? Leaving little splotches of white, like curdled milk, like clouds I saw so many wild animals in? Later in the day, when my father discovered his table ruined and came running with his boots on for me in the house, he should have known I was in school. That his daughter goes to school. I imagined him wordlessly seething, mumbling his bottled-up anger, searching the perimeter of our house—an anger that reached so far back, he too was teenaged and frothing destruction.

Maybe none of this was on my mind at the time. In the early-morning quiet of the garage, maybe I simply didn't care. Can you imagine? Not caring? I cleaned my nails carefully. I took my time. I wiped the crescent moons with the devotion of a mother cat. The crickets were still chirping outside, pearlescent dew on their muscular legs. I shook the bottle of glitter polish so that it radiated something I could only know at 13. It swirled with glossy guts. Isn't this how it really is? Returning to the wisdom of a younger self? How strange it is to learn in reverse. Against the ruined green backdrop of the table, I held my glitter fingers out, tiara tangents of my full self—victorious, bad. For once, just once, I grew dizzy with my own power.

THE WATCHER

I ALWAYS LEAVE DOORS AJAR. I DIDN'T REALIZE THIS UNTIL I moved in with a man who'd walk past as I pooped with the bathroom door open, half grossed out, half in love: *Really, Jane?* Really what? I couldn't really answer that question. Was it serious that I had to leave doors open? I grew up in a house where a closed door meant something terrible might be happening. The basement door was always closed when my father gambled with his friends, cigarette smoke leaking through the bottom. A closed door meant my parents screaming at each other, something falling to the ground like a thick vase. Meant me as an adult, pressed up against a locked door, begging a man for a way out or in. Since childhood, I've slept with my bedroom door ajar, my eyes hawk-trained on the slivered opening. Just in case. I am waiting for the creak of a serial killer's step, waiting for the shadow of a man who will clamp a hand over my mouth. That's when I'll bludgeon them with my books, which I always sleep with.

Via telehealth, a therapist told me that I have hypervigilance. Hypervigilance being an intensified state of assessing danger in your environment. When she said this, I turned away from my laptop and looked at the wood grain on my desk. "Uh huh," I said, tracing a swirl. It had taken me a full two years to find a woman of color provider. I was so anxious, I shook the entire time as if there were a constant wind chill. Would this be a good fit? Did the therapist like me? Was I incapable of healing? Was I too closed? I knew I wasn't supposed to think these questions, but that doesn't mean they didn't pop up like stubborn stigma weeds.

I think about Wongmom.com telling me to look. By look, does she also mean watch?

When I was forced to stay on a tuk-tuk for six hours in Bangkok in 2007, I wasn't a champion Watcher yet. This was when I was a Fulbrighter trying to write a novel (I didn't; I wrote prose poems) and was in Thailand for the weekend. It took me two hours to finally realize the driver wasn't going to let me go, despite the fact that I had emptied my wallet. His searing eyes were on me while he filled the gas tank. I kept pulling up my bra strap, which kept falling down. I was 22. Even then, in the suffocating gasoline heat, I kept thinking, naively: *Maybe he'll take me to my hostel eventually.* And when I finally ran away into a busy market after pleading to use the bathroom, I didn't even think to turn around to see if he was following me. I kept going and going, lost and going, and took another tuk-tuk back to find my very sweet college boyfriend, Grass Boy, beaming after playing at an Ultimate Frisbee tournament with other expats, dripping sweat and sod. "It was so awesome!" he said, his cleats clicking against the floor. "How was your day?" I wanted to rip apart his stupid Frisbee and his stupid safety with my bare teeth. I wanted to see his slackened puppy face when his beloved Frisbee got ripped to plastic shreds like iceberg lettuce, but I knew he'd bounce right back and smile: *No worries, Jane, REI will refund me!* He was such a nice, nice first boyfriend.

What do you do when you're afraid?

I keep typing into Wongmom.com.

* * *

I WROTE AN ENTIRE book of poems on fear, *How to Not Be Afraid of Everything*, which is also a book about anger, love, hunger, and nourishment. In the title poem, there's this passage where I talk about being the Watcher:

> Can I say I always look behind me? I *always* look behind me. I always take a step forward like I'm about to save myself from toppling over.

I think about how I phrased that as a question: "Can I say I always look behind me?" Whose permission do I need to say that? Who am I demanding to hear me? Am I cursed to be the Watcher forever (that repetition of "always")? Hypervigilance is exhausting. Swiveling my head around like an owl, trained against creepy men, makes for a terrible neck. When I finally got my first massage in my mid-30s, the massage therapist recoiled from me. I was a brick with hot flesh. "That's not good," she whispered. She thought I couldn't hear her. But I did. I didn't even know how to be massaged; she kept telling me to relax, but I thought I was relaxing. On that plush table, I felt like a failure. *Be a noodle in a giant vat of soup!* I kept repeating to myself, drooling into the headrest doughnut. *FLOP, NOODLE, FLOP, DAMN IT.* I hope my mantras helped her.

* * *

IN RESPONSE TO MY query, Wongmom.com instead sends me some encouraging thoughts on my writing progress and reclaiming loneliness: "Good for you! There are beautiful things out there! <3" and "It's ok by yourself. Sooner or later everybody spends time with themselves." I "heart" the first message.

What do you do when you're afraid? I think she's telling me to write. Sometimes I think poetry is the only space where I can watch myself, a space where I can stand in the center of a kaleidoscopic house of mirrors, reflected back in so many strange (sometimes too true) ways. When I walked into one of artist Yayoi Kusama's Infinity Mirror Rooms, an eternity of fireflies buzzing around me, I felt so *relieved*. That's what writing poetry is like sometimes—that infinite awe, that seeing, that relief. My mother tends to answer my questions elliptically, and I try my best to sit with her words and really look. I need to see these "beautiful things." I want to slurp them up; I've always been hungry for gorgeousness.

When I was little, I fed stray cats in our backyard. There was one black stray who was pregnant and I'd give her some extra canned food. I'd scoop the tuna pâté like ice cream, dolloped onto a plate. She never let me pet her, but she'd come up to the plate eagerly, chomping the tuna with her sharp teeth. She had such pretty emerald eyes. Our family cat, Noodles, would grow jealous—mewing with his own emerald eyes in the living room. This stray would bring me awful gifts. Dead mice, mostly. She'd drop those tiny beasts out of her mouth like they were Gucci bags. But one day, she came by the back door and nudged a tropical fish toward me. It was oddly beautiful. She had gifted me a regal angelfish, striped in brilliant swathes of blue and yellow. The wet fish was perfectly intact, laid out like it was a museum specimen, but obviously very dead. "Where did you get this?" I asked her. She touched a white-socked paw to the fish's neon fin, as if to say: *Pretty, right? I got it for you.* Even in these macabre gifts I didn't ask for, bundled in the stray's murderous love, my younger self was moved. There it was: a gesture of genuine emotion offered to me, a poem. "So pretty," I thanked her.

A month or so after leaving my ex-fiancé, I was on my way to take my rescue dog to an off-leash dog park in Seattle. We had agreed to co-parent our dog, who was a little over a year old at that time. As I got closer to the park, my dog started to squeal with chattering exclamations of joy, pawing at my shoulder from the back seat. "Almost, cutie!" I told him. But then, when I got closer, I saw that the park was closed for maintenance. There were at least seven lawn mowers whirling through the tall grass, chopping a large salad of allergies. He kept squeaking from excitement, but I had to turn around and find another park. As I turned the car around, that's when it happened: I started to wail. Crying, I gulped at the air. I wiped my gushing snot on my arms. My dog instinctively moved into a flurry of puppy licks, nudging me with his sweet silver fur. It was embarrassing that a closed dog park would set me off like this: I was alone, again. *How did this toxicity become my fault?* I took big breaths in and out. Once I felt better and stopped crying, we arrived at another park. When I let him off leash inside, he waited for me, heeling as he does. His soft fox ears, peppered with red and silver, shimmered in the sun. I fed him a lamb lung treat, and his wet mouth smiled. He was so, so beautiful. And we loved each other so. I nearly cried again—this time with inexplicable joy. There really was so much gorgeousness in the world. "Good boy!" and off he went running, playing with new friends—doing what he does best.

* * *

WHAT IF I'M AFRAID *to write this memoir?*

Before Wongmom.com answers—or maybe it is her answer—she wants to know: "why didn't you heart 'it's ok by yourself'?"

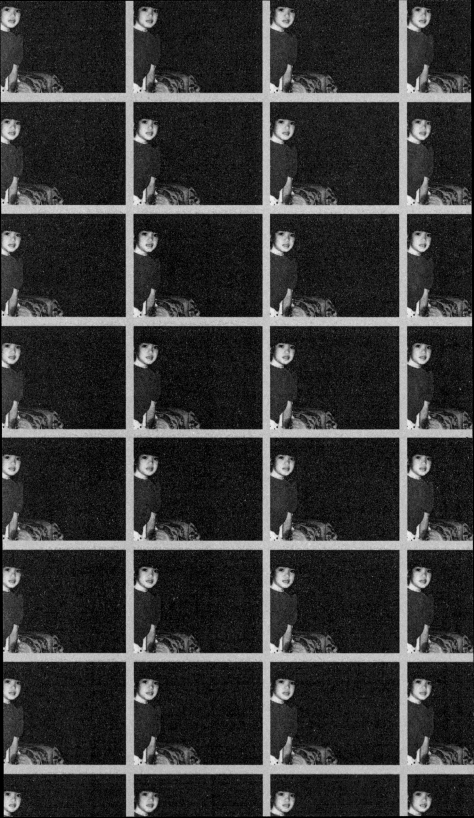

7

THE OBJECT OF LOVE

THE BAND

There's this joke I have with my close friends. There's this band called Jane and Her Ex-boyfriends. A rotating cast of overzealous drummers, cruel bassists, patronizing guitarists, and faux do-gooder celloists. All I do in the band is scream and play the egg shaker.

THE OBJECT OF LOVE

I think about what it means to write about heartache and the hope of love. I've written only a handful of love poems. All of which have turned into heartbreak poems months or years later. I think about what Toni Morrison said during an interview with the *Guardian* in 2012: "The times I didn't write, maybe I was in love. Or beloved. Somebody was [...] making me the object of love."

Am I in love now? Am I writing now? I have this habit of buying new journals—clean, crisp, and empty. Without the ensuing pasta-sauce stain or leaky-pen marks or jagged, ripped-out pages. Most of my journals are half-finished, some even less. A bridge that simply never made it to the other side. I keep buying more notebooks, opening them up in the middle to see if they have enough weight to lie flat. I creep around Kinokuniya, touching Japanese stationery, dreaming of the perfect ruling, the perfect matte, semigloss finish.

What could make me fill those pages? Why can't joy be the thing? I think about what I'm "allowed" to write. I was told by several people in the book industry to focus only on the Chinese American immigrant experience, on growing up poor in a strip mall take-out restaurant. Immigrant gold, intergenerational trauma dessert. I remember an email I received once from a community member, a white woman, who asked me to read at a local poetry event the next day. She wrote: "we need you, women need you, white Bellingham needs to hear your powerful poems." Then she emailed me again after I politely declined, asking if she could read a poem on hunger on my behalf: "Can you send me a poem or two to read they may touch on diversity. Chinese restaurant or not having enough to eat . . . I will read for you???" And then yet another email when I didn't reply: "We gathered a variety of spicey poets." They're so hungry for immigrant trauma, they lap at blood before blood can even exist.

But isn't love mine to hold too? This shimmering dip in the heart, this rattling terror? Wasn't it some kind of love that led my mother to cross that shore? Isn't love what siphons nourishment to the organs? As a Chinese American woman, as the child of immigrants, how can I divorce my experiences from love and fetish, terror and hypersexualized violence? Can't I write about all the parts, all the tentacles, all the mycelia that make me who I am?

Morrison continues: "Look, five years I spent on some books. I suppose you could love somebody for five years. Maybe. I don't mean lust. You can do that forever. But I mean really love them, the way you say you love children. I don't know. But that means I would have to remember all the times I was in love." I keep coming back to these last two sentences, which haunt me. The not knowing. The wobble, the wreck. The reluctance to remember being in love. Why is writing about love so hard to do? It is so hard to do. Writing is my singular love, my truest love, because I can control it. Even in doubt, I touch its familiar face.

THE REMINDER

I have been told by almost every man I've ever been with that I'm difficult. That I make it impossible for them to love me. That I'm selfish, that I'm intimidating, that I always do what I want to do, that I don't listen, that I need to—*must*—change. And, with the Bad One, I was told I was a monster. That I shouldn't live because I made his life absolute fucking hell. Once, I saw a GChat thread on his computer where he joked with a friend about killing me. What do you do when you read something like that? And did I think, in the slinking sewer of my difficulty, that I deserved it? Did I nod back at that glowing screen, left open for me to see?

When I was four or so, I protested a family trip to Chinatown. Going to the city meant parking far away and walking dozens of blocks as my family grocery-shopped for hard-to-find Chinese vegetables and herbs. I stubbornly dragged my legs on the ground and refused to get up. Each time my mother would try to pick me up, I'd groan and flail on the floor, skittering away like a cockroach. *I won't go!* My mother screamed at me: "What is wrong with you? What kind of daughter is like this?" *I broke a leg!* I lied. I kept refusing, even when my mother threatened to take me to the hospital and drop me off there due to my "broken leg." It was only when I saw the ER sign that I finally admitted I lied. I felt terrible and sulked in my shame. "Now that's a good girl," my mother said, smugly, rocking my baby brother in her arms. My father slammed on the gas pedal, and we all lurched forward as if to vomit. My cheek smashed red against the window. He stared at my mother long and hard as she clutched Steven. "Let's go," he spat. We were late to meet his friends.

My mother was called difficult too, by my father.

But after my father left, my mother changed. She praised my strong voice and told me we were exactly the same. On the way to the beach, she belted out Destiny's Child's "Independent Women." She told me we were uncontrollable brilliance. Infinite moons, dragon's breath, a parade of fireflies. Later, in my late 20s and 30s, my mother would call me after each breakup with comforting resolve. "Get up," she'd say. "Go buy yourself flowers. You only need yourself! And Mommy!" I'd flop out of bed like a retired betta fish, swipe on eyeliner that always smudged because of my puffy eyes, and trudge to QFC in the previous night's clothes to buy discount marigolds, daisies, baby's breath, eucalyptus leaves—filler flowers marked with the red manager's discount. I'd rip open flower-food packets and dredge their semi-rotting stems in milky juice. I'd fill my tiny Capitol Hill studio with these B-side flowers in old pasta-sauce jars and write poems I wouldn't understand until years later. I'd write and write until I felt my blood moving again, hot pot of the self.

I am beginning to believe that difficult means independent. Let me say that more accurately. I am worried that being a difficult woman means I love myself. I love my convictions, my community, my writing, my intelligence, my gut and all its flora. And every single time I feel like I have to lessen myself because of men, I am difficult. Let me say that again. I am scared that being difficult means I want to survive. Let me say: I want to survive.

When I got into an argument with my ex-fiancé, who called me difficult, I left the room and sat in my closet repeating *I'm done I'm done I'm done.* My chest heaved with decades of exhaustion—thick lava, gray sludge cement. In panic, I was filling with hot slime from the inside out, burning. My breath—held, caught—was like a fox suspended in air before plunging into dark snow. I tunneled deeper, worm deep, *monster* deep. I gurgled snot. My breath was so out of reach, I pawed outward for it. During a panic attack, I have to force myself to open my eyes. I have to look around and call out a color I see. I have to hold onto a texture, a sound. I have to count. I have to remember something, anything. What socks was I wearing? Were they the ones with mustaches on them that my brother got me? I wiggle my toes, I count, I lug my anchored breath back. When I finally came out of this particular panic, I felt the icy silks of my dresses dangling above my head, undulating rivers of white, blue, and green. The heat had stopped working the night before in the house and I felt the cold surging through my hands. I tucked them into my armpits. We were in the middle of a snowstorm.

The heat came back on after my ex blasted the heater and pipes in the garage with a hair dryer, which I had suggested after a Google search for solutions. I heard the heat shuddering, hissing back. I heard him washing dishes. When I came into the kitchen, he offered me a ramekin with an egg he had boiled, peeled, and covered in salt and pepper. "You need to eat," he said gently. And: "I really do love you, Jane." Steam rose from the hot water in the sink. Later, he turned to stare at me, quizzically: "Do you think someone could fake a panic attack?"

That evening, my friend Michelle texted me to check in. And I told her I'd write down what she said to me verbatim, because I needed the reminder: "You are easy to love. It is a hard thing to remember when you've been through what you've been through. You are not hard to love. Loving you is not perilous or an arduous endeavor." Eight years prior, Michelle had sent me a similar text about how easy it was to love me. Current and future me still needs the reminder. Maybe you do too.

THE KNIFE

Each year, my stepfather Vinny asks my mother to marry him. I call him my stepfather, though technically he isn't. There's a cabinet in our house where my mother keeps the gifts Vinny has given her over the years: candles with "I love you" etched inside, a glowing heart that turns on a pedestal, dried roses suspended in bubbled resin. Wary of remarrying due to what happened with my father, she affectionately calls Vinny her "Forever Boyfriend." They met at work, at the postal service. As the story goes, Vinny—who fixes the mail sorting machines—went over to my mother's mail-sorting station and messed with her machine on purpose, right before she clocked in. He did this just to get a chance to talk to her, to make dad jokes and watch her smile and roll her eyes. He did this a few more times before he had the nerve to ask her out. They eventually ate chicken noodle soup and coleslaw at the Blue Swan diner after getting off work around 6:00 AM. As the world woke up, they yawned story after story to each other. Their teacups clinked harmoniously together, their diner mints softened. *Vinny and I never fight,* my mother tells me. *We are there for each other, but we also leave each other alone. I love him because he loves me for me. It's simple.* When he proposes, she gently says no every time.

Vinny is always somewhere under the sink, wrench in hand, fixing a leak. Nowadays, he's got a bad leg and limps, kicking the laundry basket down the hallway. After two brisk circles walking together around the neighborhood, my mother makes him loose-leaf tea and spoons honey in there, swirling a sweetness into this second life of theirs. If they're in a rush to go to work, he pours the tea into a plastic water bottle, which warps and crinkles. He goes to warm up the car for her. They shovel snow together, breath steaming in crystalline air. His favorite meal is the watercress soup she makes, and he makes an "ahhh" sound when he eats it. When my mother says, "Move your ass," he laughs because he taught her the word "ass," and she repeats it again and again, louder: "Move your ass!" They're out the door to go to work, in separate cars, even though they are going to the same place: the postal service. Their overtimes will be different; one of them will outwork the other. It's been 18 years and counting.

My mother doesn't use the word "hate" ever, except when it comes to my father. When they were still together, my mother used to write "I hate him I hate him I hate him" in her English notebook for night school. I waited two years after leaving the Bad One to tell my mother about him. Hadn't she done everything in her power to protect me?

I knew about my father's gambling, debts, drinking, and disappearances. What she protected me from: intimate violence. When I told my mother about the Bad One, she told me about my father wielding a knife in the kitchen at her. How the knife glinted in the air, a knife she used to cut off the heads of chickens. "Can you believe that," she said. "Your father did that to me. A *man* did that to me." My mother doesn't cry as a general policy. And so I cried for her, for the both of us, as grief poured out of every pore.

THE BAD ONE

When people ask me how I left, though no one really asks because no one really knows about my abuser, I tell them: I have no idea. I wish I could tell them. I wish I could tell you, if I knew. Could you say that it was one final thing, one last measured act of cruelty where I raised my arms up and screamed until the moss—which grows so well in the Pacific Northwest—catches fire? How does one measure exhaustion? These tiny splinters of self—caught in cuticles or floating off in air, in lungs good for breathing—are they mine? Even as I write this, I tell myself: Don't write about the etymology of abuse. Don't try to make sense of it, don't find its root. It has no roots. Just legs, dangling over the edge of something, chum or ancient fern.

THE BOXER

It felt good to punch the shit out of it. To punch between the eyes of fury I found, to knead my knuckles hard into bread that won't rise, to stun this sturdy cylinder of transgression. I kept punching the bag, tenderizing the hell out of a cutlet, even when the boxing coach told me I was doing it all wrong.

Earlier that day, I had called my friend Tessa, moping around my apartment in Seattle, placing mugs aimlessly in cupboards. Just to do something, anything.

"How did it end?" she asked.

Holding a mug, I thought of how my boyfriend after the Bad One used to buy terrible thrift store mugs. There was this one mug with a bear riding a train with the name "Dave" on it. Of how, when all the wineglasses were dirty and we were too exhausted from our bodies pressing against each other all day, we'd drink merlot out of mugs. In my fresh heartache, the mug I was holding was from when I lived in Iowa City, a robin's-egg blue mug with "Iowa Road Races" on it, accompanied by a random image of a tropical fish. I placed my mug into the cupboard, upside down, despite the fact that the mugs were stacked right side up. My roommate would hate that. I don't remember what I said to my friend, what it really was this time. Backing out of moving in together. My hypervigilance. The woman that wanted to be with him, maraschino-cherry sweet, asking him to open up her bottle of champagne—which I wish was a euphemism, it was so predictable. The timing of falling in love. What came before and what trickled down, sewage from the Bad One leaking into this new love afterward. My fear of not being enough, like a sad plate of lettuce with no dressing. Simply not being enough. Being difficult. So very difficult.

I don't know what I told her, but I somehow found myself in a boxing gym 30 minutes later, passing a medicine ball back and forth between Tessa and Michelle, the ball heavy as an avalanche.

"Why do they make us do this?" I cried, laughing at my flimsy arms, the ball touching the ground from time to time as I tried to ferry it forward.

"Come on," Tessa said, wild in her fitness, holding the ball with an ecstatic joy I couldn't comprehend or access. Michelle laughed so hard; she kept waving her arms like she was saying *Stop stop.* Our legs stuck out straight, our shoes touching, connecting. The ball lolled about, its leather face annoyed at me. I cried and drooled so much from laughing that the boxing coach came over and asked if I needed any help. In ancient Greece, Hippocrates apparently had his patients throw around stuffed animal skins to heal ailments. I imagined the ballooning skin of a cow thrown in the air, curing nausea. What exactly was this healing? What did I need help with?

The boyfriend who had just broken up with me was incredibly fit; he used to read books on the treadmill, used to run through the city at night, passing over bridges with a high heart rate, stopping only to take a picture for me of the Puget Sound, liquid silver. While he went running, I was most likely in bed, eating Swedish Fish, revising a chapter of my dissertation, wondering if I should lace up my nonexistent sneakers, wondering if that was what he hoped of me— what they all hoped of me. A future ex-boyfriend said to me, over the phone, after whispering *You're so sexy* over and over the night before, "I don't think this is going to work out. You're not active enough for my lifestyle. I'm sorry, but this is over." I wish I could go back in time and laugh at the audacity—howl a high-pitched cackle, spit a giggling fit, wallop a guffaw as large as all the medicine balls in the world combined. *What men are afraid of*, I'd say, between delicious chortles. *And the things*—chortle!—*they make up*. Instead, I started to weep, slumped in my never-enoughness. My ear hurt from being pressed so tightly into the phone. *Don't say it*, my interior self demanded. "I'll do anything," I begged that future ex, my voice like a slowly leaking faucet. *DON'T SAY IT*. "You want me to run? I'll run."

THE SPILL

At the Fred Meyer gas station in Bellingham, the pump surged and spilled all over me like a drunk whale spouting. In seconds, I was drenched in the stink of the highway, in the smell of men who turned their heads from within dimly lit bars to stare at me, toothless and salivating. In seconds, I was flammable. I was the slop of malfunction, sickened in the purest match light. My new dress: slick-soaked silk, a greasy reminder of what I supposedly wanted. People nearby heard me yell out. No one dared look at me. Weren't they respectable people? Wasn't I used to this? I: pretty, wretched thing, swimming in my shame?

Standing by my car, I tottered about in this heavily perfumed familiarity (wasn't I used to this?). I couldn't help but think of my pores, opening like sad clams, guzzling the stink. I wanted the gasoline off me. I wanted to strip down naked right there and use my own spit to wash myself clean.

The pump covered me in gasoline but missed spraying my eyes and mouth—the tenderest parts. What infuriated me: how, drenched, I thought immediately of the Bad One, of wanting the chemical rot of that memory off me, that liquored sweat. When I got home, I washed myself for an hour and it wasn't enough. The smell lingered along the back bend of my knee. How can one thing send us hurtling toward another with such fervent accuracy?

THE BAD ONE

Each day, I tapped a spoon against my chest to make sure I was there. Tap, tap.

The Bad One was good at making pork chops and mashed potatoes for dinner. When he was on food stamps, he stole pork chops from the grocery store and stole them well. He placed them into a reusable bag before checking out. The key is to look people straight in the eye. What a charmer. He made pork chops fried on high with Old Bay seasoning, sweet paprika, and crushed garlic. He liked to cut up garlic and smell it on his hands. In the summer, he gillnetted salmon; his hands had deep crevices, crevasses really, and the garlic flourished between them. He'd hold up his hands to my face and laugh, chasing me around the apartment as police cars spun their lights around us. We'd romp around so loudly, even the whiskey bottles hidden in suitcases and toilet bowls and high cabinets clinked and cheered. *Get her! Get her!*

One of his favorite games to play was to text me to bring over groceries so we could make dinner together, and then never buzz me in or answer his phone. I used to wait outside his apartment building with bags full of pork chops and asparagus, the meat leaking through the paper. My hands wet with raw pork juice, pressing the call button again. I waited until one of his neighbors let me into the building. They knew me by now. They looked at me and then looked away quickly. If they looked at me too long, they'd also be cursed.

I was the woman who cried into the walls, soft like tofu. The woman who couldn't take off her makeup at night because he couldn't stand to see her bare face. The woman who smiled in public like a pageant queen, pure varnish: the poet, the scholar, the best friend, the professor, the one who got away (who is this guy she's with anyway?). The woman who was too good at hiding, like a bag of rotting cilantro in the way back of the fridge. The woman who waited and hummed like a fridge on its last legs. *Let her in.*

I'd sit down on the paisley rug outside his apartment door and wait. I'd think about how easy it was to wait, how I can wait in line at the DMV and not push anyone, not even nudge. I'd think: patience is a virtuoso. I'd wait and start to cry and start to worry about my makeup running. In case he comes. In case he doesn't like my makeup running. I'd knock a few more times. I'd put my ear against the door like a good doctor. I'd become my smallest self and listen and hear the mice skittering in the walls. I'd hear the drunk inside roving about in his bed, turning the covers, pissing himself, laughing at me, calling me a stupid cunt, leaving me out. I'd hold the asparagus like lit sparklers, its spears packed tightly.

THE REAL

Four years after the Bad One, I spent one viciously hot summer reading and rereading *All about Love: New Visions* by bell hooks. In early June, an ex of mine had sent me an email saying I wasn't a real person to him. He said I was a fantasy. Nothing about me or about us was real. He wrote that our connection was based on something mythical and that he didn't actually love me. Just weeks before this email, he'd told me he was so excited to move to Bellingham with me. He had met all my new colleagues at Western Washington University, where I'd just gotten a tenure-track job. They remarked on how handsome he was, how kind his smile was. We took pictures along the South Bay Trail, the seaweed waving behind us on glittering rocks. We joked about how the kelp looked so delicious, we wanted to scoop it up in our arms and devour each crunchy cassette-tape strand. And even when he wrote such unkind words and deleted all photographs and references to me, I wrote back that I refused to believe him. I refused to believe he would say and do such a thing. He was better than that, right?

From hooks: "All too often women believe it is a sign of commitment, an expression of love, to endure unkindness or cruelty, to forgive and forget. In actuality, when we love rightly we know that the healthy, loving response to cruelty and abuse is putting ourselves out of harm's way." I underlined this so hard, I ripped the page open with the precision of an X-Acto knife. I was so tired of forgiving, of trying to believe the good in something rotten. I felt ashamed that I couldn't tell the difference between what was abuse and what was love. I had met this particular ex of mine many years after the Bad One. I thought I knew. I didn't. Not even a year later, a man I went on a few dates with would snarl *I could destroy you* into my face after we slept together. And even later, I would be left on a street in Denver, amid slammed car doors and thrown keys, all due to an argument over hotel reimbursement. When I told him I was afraid of his anger in that moment, my ex-fiancé said, "I'll take care of that for you," and walked away. And kept walking. He never came back to the car. You can decide which tone to read those last words in.

I worry I will tunnel into harm's way again and again, my mole nose flowering against its familiar walls.

THE BOOK

There was a time before the Bad One. There was a time when heartbreak wasn't cruel. A breakup could mean something just didn't work out. Nick and I went to the Iowa Writers' Workshop together. We spent each day dreaming up poems and making brothy soups and cuddling a sweet orange cat who loved bananas and anything that resembled a banana (her favorite spot was atop a yellow canoe, may she rest in banana peace). Along with a bunch of poets, we'd watch *Twin Peaks* and *Lost* and *Deadwood*. We'd dance at grungy hipster parties until we were drenched in sweat; play fiction vs. poetry softball; grade papers at Prairie Lights Bookstore; crawl home from George's and the Fox Head with too many beers and cheeseburgers; and debate sincerity, line breaks, and caesuras. We were both Asian American, so when Nick got me a Hello Kitty soap dispenser for my birthday, it wasn't problematic. It was perfect. Till this day, Nick is one of my most trusted readers.

When I told Nick years later about the Bad One, we were on tour for our first books. We were going to read at Prairie Lights together, a place where we'd spent countless grad school hours nursing single tea bags in the café, reading literary journals. After catching up, we started talking about forgiveness and about our capacities to forgive. Nick believed so deeply in forgiveness, in its radical shifts and surprising arteries. But I couldn't agree. I couldn't forgive some things. And so I told him about the Bad One. He grew really quiet, his hands clutched together. "You should have told me," Nick said. "I could have done something." But he couldn't have. He knew that. "I'm so sorry, Jane," he said, his voice wobbly and tender. I didn't go into detail. I didn't say much, and maybe that absence made it even more frightening.

"Wait, do you remember," he said, "that creepy guy in that bookstore?"

At first I didn't, but then I did. Back when I was at Iowa, I'd gone into a used bookstore to find a book of essays by Ralph Waldo

Emerson. I had just read "Circles": "The eye is the first circle; the horizon which it forms is the second; and throughout nature this primary picture is repeated without end." Earlier in a poetry seminar, we'd spent our time outside, looking for circles. My friend Hannah and I had sat on the edge of the Iowa River, watching ducks. The ducks were preening themselves, nuzzling their beaks into the crevices of their glossy feathers. We weren't talking about Emerson. We were encircling each other's hearts and minds, talking about crushes and longing and failure and expectations. We braided grass and daisies together. We beckoned the ducks to come closer, our hands extended. We dreamt about the possibility of publishing our first books, wondered if we could break the alphabet and have them paired together, always. Imagine how crisp, how glossy our spines would be! When our professor called on us to share, Hannah blurted out, "Duck circles!" and that's all we shared.

I went to the used bookstore to find a cheap copy. The bookstore was a complete labyrinth and I couldn't find nonfiction and essays, tripping over piles of paperbacks like crumbling cities. When I finally found the book, in the dark back corner of the store, someone tapped my shoulder. I turned around, and it was a middle-aged white man with a greasy smile. "Are you a student here?" he asked. I backed into the bookcase instinctively, the wood sharp against my shoulders. "Kind of," I said, trying to see if anyone else was nearby. No one was. Dust swirled around me like a horde of gnats. "It's good to study," he said smugly, and then reached into his breast pocket. He unfolded ten $100 bills and fanned them out in front of my face like a magician. "One night," he said.

It took me a minute to process what was happening, and when I did, he was still there, with his mouth slightly open. His hungry breath seeping out. The bills still in my face, metallic smelling and mold green. And when I screamed, I realized I didn't. No sound came out of my mouth. I pushed past him with my shoulder and ran out of the store, knocking more book piles over, the tiny bell on the door ringing. Not even a block away, I realized I had Emerson's *Collected Essays* in my hand and hadn't paid for it. And so I stupidly turned around. There he was, across the street with that same smug smile, oil slicked. He called out to me. "Did I scare you? Do you like that?" It was in broad daylight, noon. A stroller passed between us and the baby giggled and wiggled their toes. I dropped the book and ran.

"I remember. Fucking disgusting," I said to Nick. Later, we found out that the man was a registered sex offender and had accosted many young women in similar ways, including another workshop student.

"That creepy guy. And [the Bad One]. How can people like that exist? How can I be a father and know men like this exist?" Nick said. Such awful knowledge, crawling in the corridors of hope, safety. I couldn't answer him. We'd spend our second books writing about fear, violence, grief, empire, daughtering, kindness. Sometimes there are no answers.

THE OBJECT OF LOVE

Did I write? "The times I didn't write, maybe I was in love. Or beloved. Somebody was making me the object of love." Each time, I wanted to be beloved. In high school, I used to sit in front of a mirror and touch my face, imagining someone touching my face as if it were a blue flame. No one told me that being the object of love was mostly waiting. More than once, I've spent a writing residency waiting and not writing. In Washington, Tennessee, Wyoming, Kentucky. I've spent hours waiting for some stranger to write me back, like a mosquito coming back to bite the same spot, because who wouldn't lick a honeyed spoon? Waiting is the makeup-less face of the beloved. The pores of rereading texts over and over, scrutinizing each word, each punctuation mark. What did an emoji-less text mean? What did a kissy face, an upside-down face mean? I took selfie after selfie in good light, wondering if I was the only one sending selfies in good light. I worry I don't know how to be in love. I worry I only know how to be the object of love. Maybe this is what men have taught me, what I've internalized: to not be me. To not be real.

At my residency in Kentucky, I waited for my future ex-fiancé to call me, my chest spewing with a bubbling glee when he did. On the phone, he told me he wanted to start a new chapter with me, that he wanted to set down the luggage he carried and leave it behind. On my next residency in Wyoming, he sent me photos of his vacation in Costa Rica. He told me he met a couple on a boat and gushed about this beautiful, brilliant poet he was dating. I'd find out later in our relationship that he had been lying to me and had been sleeping with two other women at that time—including a woman in Costa Rica whom he had been sexting for a year. He broke down and begged me for another chance; I gave it to him.

THE ICE

I stripped off my clothes down to my bright blue bikini on New Year's Day. I ran into the frigid water at Golden Gardens beach in Seattle. Skin prickling among the driftwood. I was an icicle in the howling wind. To convince some random future ex that yes, I'd do this for you. If I gathered all the times I've said this to men—*I'm sorry, I'll change this, I'll do this for you, I'll be what you want, I'll sleep in my makeup*—how much driftwood would I have? I've always been bad at math.

Many years later, in the warmth of an orange August sun, I was at another writing residency. My days were spent reading and sun-bathing alongside a river that swirled around the residency estate like the very center of a snail's shell. But, one day, it started to hail. I was writing a very long poem about labor when little pellets of ice started knocking around all over my writing cabin, salting me like cod. Rabbits ran underneath trees to hide. In this freakish cold snap, I remembered doing that polar bear plunge to impress that mediocre man who never wanted me to begin with. I hated that I did that. I hated that I was pathetic in my wanting to be wanted. Here I was, writing a poem about the powerful women in my life—that "high heat lineage" of my matrilineal line, and I chose to go into glacial murk for someone not myself? I stared out the window at the river of hail, slumped in my shame. I wasn't powerful at all. I wasn't the daughter they had hoped for, sacrificed for. You know that saying? "We are our ancestors' wildest dreams"? Yeah, no. How could I be? How could I tell my students that self-love was of utmost importance when I couldn't even do it for myself?

But then there it was, in the window of my studio. A bobcat, looking right through me. With a mouse dangling in its cold, wet mouth, blood draining fast. The amber of its eyes flicked like a tongue. *What are you looking at*, it seemed to say. *Fuck*, I thought, backing away from my desk slowly, slowly. Paw by paw. *Myself.*

THE BAD ONE

I wanted to run, but where were my legs? Where was my breath?

He was not as good at lying as he was at stealing pork chops. He wanted me to know what he was doing. He liked it when I saw the lie. He held my neck with the hands he killed salmon with and squeezed. *I want you to know what I am saying.* He said he was grieving and that's why he got drunk and talked to girls online after I fell asleep. He said the condoms in the dresser were actually his friend's. He said he had low self-esteem, said the girls online cheered him up. That his skin felt like it was falling off. That he had to throw rocks at my window because I wouldn't answer him. That there were mice in the walls and how it was goddamn sick that they were alive and squirming in his rat traps. He held my neck and spat and held harder, a bouquet. My breath disappeared and I squeaked like the mice in the walls. *Your ears are goddamn ugly*, he'd say, drunk singing. *You're so goddamn ugly and useless and your pussy is rotten.*

THE WHAT-MAKES-YOU-HAPPY

I was home for the holidays after finally leaving the Bad One. I couldn't tell my mother about him. We sat on the couch together in Jersey, eating nuts. My mom draped a chenille blanket across our tangled legs and pointed to her bowl. Nuts are expensive and always a gift in my family. "All different kinds," she said. "Pistachio, peanut, walnut, macadamia, sunflower . . . it's hard to find them in the shell." She ran her hands through the potpourri of nuts like running her hands through her hair. Then she lifted up her nutcracker and knife, surgical tools. "I like the sound, crack crack. It makes me happy." I squeezed a fistful of blanket and watched as she cracked open a single walnut, which opened like a locket, the tan grooves falling apart, one by one. "See?" she said. The sound felt familiar, the icy fissures of myself splintering apart in fear. Crack, crack.

I loosened my grip on the blanket and started howling, sobbing, gasping, my mouth open like an undiscovered cave. I pawed at my mother, who held me in shock, who kept saying *What's wrong what's wrong my baby, what*, and I couldn't tell her. I couldn't tell her. My eyes burned red, my bones whittled down to a toothpick, cracking open. She held me, heaving, no words, blood-sick, until she slipped a small piece of walnut into my mouth, which softened in my ache. I might have choked. I might have swallowed the earthy meat. *Everything is going to be okay*, she said, wrapping me tighter into her lap, my head against the bowl. My hair was dusted with salty shells. *I want my baby to be happy. I'm not happy unless you're happy.*

THE BAD ONE

There were so many girls, I can't remember them all. They were all Asian and younger than me, and this fact settled into me like sewage in the belly. I thought I had vetted him out, thought that his ex being platinum blonde was a relief. Elaine Hsieh Chou's novel *Disorientation* has a scene where the protagonist goes through her white boyfriend's past dating history and discovers his Asian exes. But then Chou writes about the other possibility: "She could be someone's Asian starter kit." I was that starter kit, which is a particular type of horror. It was relentless: the shame of being a fetish, the shame of letting a white man do this to me, and why couldn't I stop it? I sunk into the mold of my own self-disgust. The first one he said was someone he used to tutor, a student. The second one, a friend of a friend he reconnected with. The third one, an escort found through Craigslist. They were on his phone, his computer, in the streets of this city I diminished in. Tinder, Bumble, OkCupid, Plenty of Fish, Match. What was left? Some I knew, some I didn't know. When I saw their pictures, I couldn't help but think: *Are we sisters?* Once, we went to a bar together and he kissed a half-Asian girl while I was in the bathroom. When I came back, she laughed with bright white teeth—the true sign of wealth. His eyes roved backward, nautilus of the sea. He told me that he had made out with her and that I needed to get the fuck out.

When he would fuck me, he liked to do so in front of the mirror by the door. The door I always wanted to open. He liked pulling my hair back and covering my face with his hands, pressing my head down so he couldn't see me. I couldn't see anything. I could smell garlic. I floated above myself, watching this scene, this woman and this man. Was she supposed to like it? Turn around and kick him, I wanted to say. Fucking kick him! Outside, the cardboard boxes by the recycling bin were fat with rain.

In the beginning, he asked mutual friends if I would be interested in him. In the beginning, he bought me clothes from the stores he liked, from the shopgirls he later cheated on me with. To start off with. Was it coffee? No. At a bar with beer and peanuts on the floor? He was wearing a jean jacket over a fisherman's sweater. He said he liked Bruce Springsteen. Aren't you from Jersey, he smiled. He sang "Nebraska" for me. Was it "Nebraska"? Or "Atlantic City"? In the beginning, he took his shirt off. In the beginning, I kept my shirt on. It was his shirt that I wore, flannel and as warm as a summer peach. I wrapped my bare legs around him. And my hair? Straight as pine needles, prepped for a forest fire. In the beginning, I laughed and laughed and didn't bother to consider why I was laughing. Did I write a poem that day? Did I write?

THE NONEXHAUSTIVE LIST

On one dating-app date, I meet this graduate student at an art museum. He looks nothing like his picture. I guess none of them do, really. Upon meeting me, he gives me a crooked grin and says: "You know, you look like my favorite anime character." And, before I can stop him, this stranger boops my nose.

On another date, this chef guy stops eating for a second and looks up at me, adoringly. "Do you know you don't have the epicanthal fold?" I churn in my disgust and keep eating my brisket poutine. The poutine is undeniably delicious and I feast before leaving.

On another, this time on Valentine's Day, a guy shows up in gym clothes at an ice cream shop. I ask him about electrical engineering, which he supposedly studies. He says "What? Oh. Yeah, uh, actually I don't do that, sorry." Even though I tell him I'm not interested, he texts me to invite me over for wine and cheese at his place.

Another: this divorce attorney asks me why writers like Sherman Alexie are cancelled and why we can't separate a writer's work from their personal lives. He tells me these male writers don't deserve this treatment. He asks me: "Do you think I'm an asshole?"

After this one guy goes down on me, he lies next to me in bed and turns to face me: "You're one of those bad Asians, aren't you?"

Once, a guy I'd dated came up to me on the bus and sat behind me. "Hey," he said. "Why did you end things? I need to know." I got off at the next stop, and it definitely wasn't my stop. Another guy, after I told him I wasn't interested: five block texts about why he was so great and that it was my loss. When I didn't reply, he followed up with yet another series of texts about being in my neighborhood and wondering if I wanted to get dinner.

On my first date with my ex-fiancé: "I wasn't expecting to turn on my brain," he said, bemused. "I had such a good time." Before the date, he had asked me if we'd be eating. I remember thinking: I don't know what to text back. I'd had dinner, but I always wanted to eat. I texted back "always ☺" and wondered if that was accidentally salacious. When he proposed to me three years later, during a global pandemic, he did so with a massive cheese wheel, the ring box hidden in Comté. I loved it. We pranced around the pungent wheel, giggling like newborn mice.

THE MESSAGE

My friend Darren tried to tell me first. There was a missed call from him and a text where he wrote: "call me, it's important." But it was too late: the Bad One's friend messaged me on Facebook. Every part of me ignited with fear, trickling gasoline and porcupine quills. In her message, she told me that the Bad One had passed away, that I'd meant a lot to him, that there was going to be a virtual funeral service if I wanted to come. I felt sick and tried to vomit in the bathroom, but all that came out was a sludge of clear spit. I sat outside in my yard in Bellingham for a while. I watched this northern alligator lizard I'd named Dragon sun himself by the lavender bushes. The air was fragrant with soft lavender. I refused to cut the lavender back and so it hung over the pathway, overgrown purple wands. Was it so bad to want to be brushed by beauty? I hung out with Dragon all throughout the early days of the pandemic. He scooted closer to me and lifted his brown reptilian head up sweetly, as if accepting a strawberry. When I finally called Darren, neither of us knew what to say. He asked me how I felt. *Don't read the obituary*, I begged myself. The last time I'd encountered the Bad One had been in email. I'd written that I would file a restraining order if he contacted me again. "I feel awful for his parents," I said first. "And I have this strange feeling . . . like I'm less afraid." Did I read? Did I write? Sometimes you write because you finally can.

THE OBJECT OF LOVE

When bell hooks passed in December 2021, I looked for my copy of *All about Love: New Visions*, but I couldn't find it. I panicked and started pulling my bookshelves apart, books lying all over the floor like a messy pile of matches. I started to cry in the middle of my book puddle, lost. But then I remembered: I had lent it out to a friend who was trying to leave an abusive partner. Maybe this was what I knew: that the loving response to toxicity and abuse is to help someone else out of harm's way. That maybe, to be beloved was not romantic. I love and am beloved by my community: my friends, my family, my mother. This love is consistent, across so many years. When I called Darren and told him I was slumped outside the Bad One's apartment by the dumpster, he came to get me and carried me all the way into his car. He sat with me in my studio as I cried into his lap, feeding me almonds and sticky fruit snacks. When I called my friend Diana, it took her only five minutes to get to me on that Denver street. I had been panicking and she slowed my breath. She walked with me, sat with me at the only place to sit (a bus stop), tried to feed me baked goods (I couldn't eat, but the buttery smell revived me), and took me to a tea shop until I could stop shaking and drive back to the hotel. My friend Brenda let me stay at her house for months after I left my ex-fiancé; she made nourishing soups for me, with a secret cinnamon stick swirled in the middle. When I called my mother, when I called Michelle, when I called Brenda, when I called Diana, when I called Darren, when I called Tessa, when I called. It's a long, beautiful web.

Reminder: I am bundled in such vast, buzzing fields of care. I am tangled in their love, rushing forward in laughter (necessary puppy memes to send), in nourishment (*You have to eat, Jane. I made this lasagna, this jook*), in listening and holding and touching. They offer their homes, their sleeves, their laughter, their reminders: *You are easy to love.* And it is easy to love. How I love to love! To love is vibrational, a sound wave humming through your belly and theirs. To love is easy, a rice cooker always on warm. I paddle through love, through glutinous rice. I pour my love back and forth in that looping river of community. I listen, I extend, I stand up, I hold, I stay. We are not objects, not things that can be polished, admired, graded. We don't need to explain ourselves. We don't need to feel shame or fear or judgment. We could be *real*. We are real. I want a romantic love like my intimate platonic loves. The object, meaning the goal, of love is to be happy.

"What makes you happy?" my mother asks me every so often. This is the simplest and hardest question to answer. In her book, bell hooks continues: "Learning to love in friendships empowers us in ways that enable us to bring this love to other interactions with family or with romantic bonds." She emphasizes how we can learn the art of loving from being in community. I think about how the toxic men in my life have been jealous of my community, my endlessly fertile fields of friends and family. Now I realize they were envious of my joy, my love. When I was getting ready to move out, my ex-fiancé inquired about the plants in the garden boxes—beautiful garden boxes he had built for me, out of what I thought was love. He told me the vegetables were definitely mine. He wanted my stuff cleared out. It was awful to pull up my starts, their roots dangling like lost ghosts, like pulled teeth caught in my throat. How I loved those little starts—Chinese chives, red lettuce, pea shoots, lacinato kale. I tried to save them—tucking them into plastic nurse pots, begging them to survive the journey. And even if they didn't, even if I had to start all over again, it was fine. Michelle had promised to send me seeds, after all.

THE MOMMY BOYFRIEND

There's also this other running joke. My mother keeps telling me that she'll be my boyfriend. "I'll be your boyfriend forever and ever," she says over the phone. And she means it. "I will take care of you and tell you how special you are every single day." She pauses, then starts to laugh uncontrollably: "But no sexy stuff."

WONGMOM.COM
(DON'T MESS WITH ME)

I MESSAGE MY FRIEND KEITH AND BEMOAN THE FACT THAT I'm not psychic. That I'm not as powerful as my mother, that I can't make things happen. Why didn't her powers trickle down to me? No one wants Janewong.com (though someone did buy that domain so I couldn't. Reveal yourself!). But Keith tells me: "Your poems are incantatory. You did inherit it."

I sit with this generous message for a while. Maybe I wasn't psychic in my regular life, but maybe poetry was the portal through which my powers came alive. In my first book, *Overpour*, there's a poem toward the end called "Ceremony" where I envision the future: "This is what we were promised: another life. / Today, I run with a flare in my hand like a bouquet of exploding flowers. / Today, I will not be transparent." I wrote this poem before leaving the Bad One, forcing a future I wanted, needed in order to survive. And isn't this memoir a kind of flare? Didn't I need to write that poem in order to leave?

In my second book, I don't have a clear memory of writing the last poem, "After Preparing the Altar, the Ghosts Feast Feverishly," in which my ancestors speak directly to me and have a massive feast. I remember being at the Lettered Streets Coffeehouse in Bellingham with my colleagues and telling them I had to go into the other room and write a poem. I was compelled, pulled into an alternate dimension by all my limbs. The poem came out in two hours and I barely revised it. I moved through that day in a haunted haze. Have you ever co-written a poem with ghosts? What I can tell you: amid the chaos of the world around me, my ghosts have my back. I think about what they did and didn't survive during the Great Leap Forward (also known as the Great Famine), a Maoist agricultural campaign that led to the death of an estimated 36 million people. I think about the acidity of starvation, the fields of bodies returning to earth. Did they fall in love during a time like that? Did they see me, a little restaurant baby with a severe bowl haircut, slicing bright scallions behind the counter? How long did it take for the flies to descend, to sip at grief? Through poetry, they led me around the spinning table of their desires. Through poetry, they demanded a future cornucopia. They demanded durian, omelets, steak, bitter gourd, pizza, flip-flops, my soul. The last line of the poem reads: "Tell us, little girl, are you / hungry, awake, astonished enough?"

Wake up to your powers!

Each day, I rub my eyes with poetry, bleary in foggy morning light. I clear goopy line after goopy line out of their corners. It's true. Poetry does make me feel powerful. Poetry's magic does loosen the sinking weight of fear. Even when I'm not writing, I'm writing. Sitting still in the raging heat of the bathtub, I guzzle language like salt. Stirring a thickening pot of jook, I kiss my ghosts' sticky foreheads. Then I get mad at poetry. I get mad at myself. I feel disgusted by poetry and its lyricism. How dare I poetize death. These were the real corpses of my family. These were real bruises on my neck. A man really did choke me. Real death, real vertigo, real addiction, real debt, real labor, real hunger. My father was really never going to call me. What if there's nothing to say at all?

I return to Lucille Clifton often, one of my central literary loves. From her poem "why some people be mad at me sometimes":

> they ask me to remember
> but they want me to remember

their memories
and i keep on remembering
mine.

I can't deny the psychic power, ancestral power, poetry power that moves through these magnetic lines. Even in my shame, I feel Clifton's words stir my fluids awake, frothing. I think about her insistence: "i keep on remembering / mine." And how that determination to remember *her* memories angers people. I love how "mine" sits on its own line, cemented in self-knowledge. Even if poetry fails us, we need it to survive. From the end of her poem "won't you celebrate with me": "come celebrate / with me that everyday / something has tried to kill me / and has failed."

There's another video of my mother that I caught on my phone, a perfect pairing to JANE I'M PSYCHIC. She's sitting in my aunt's car and she says to the camera: "Don't mess with me. Or you will become a frog." I play this one on loop too, whenever I feel the pungent need for retribution. It makes me inextricably happy to watch it. I send it to my brother in Jersey who texts back: LOLOL *typical*. She delights in the word "frog," which sits in her throat like a paperweight. I love the combination of seriousness and humor in her voice, in her glimmering eyes. Like, really, don't mess with her. The universe will become a croaking pond. Are you ready to feel the amphibious slick of your leg?

I wonder what Wongmom.com is afraid of. It almost seems like she's not afraid of anything. But isn't that impossible? To be fearless? I know this can't be true. Everyone is afraid. I need to know, so that I don't feel so alone in my fear. I type that in: "what are you afraid of, Mommy?"

8

TO LOVE A MOSQUITO

"IT DOESN'T COUNT IF YOU DON'T SEE BLOOD," I SAY, holding my palm up to my little brother's face like a mirror. I show him the blood—a lipstick smear right in the middle. *Smack*. Half a wing dangles from my hand. If you squint hard enough, it looks like I'm shedding my own skin. Steven nods because he is still young enough to agree to everything I say. We are eight and five respectively. We agree to precision. We agree to be a team. Climbing the fat arms of the sofa—perpetually spilling its cloud stuffing—we begin tracking the fluttering legs of another mosquito.

In the humid horror of August, in the afternoon where boredom widens like a forbidden cave, when Ngin Ngin falls asleep and dreams of another shore and another life, when we're not at the restaurant where our mother chops endless heaps of yu choy, we like to play a game we call Mosquito Wars. "Mosquito": a word we know well enough because of the buzzing pieces of shit that suck our blood. "Wars": a word (plural) we are beginning to understand as it relates to our family, layer by fraught layer.

* * *

A MOSQUITO CAN ONLY cover, on average, one to one and a half miles in an hour—at this pace, it can't keep up with a butterfly, bee, or locust. The gluttonous ones are slower and easier to catch. They meander about, heavy with their blood-full luggage and sugary song. We know it's the hungry, crazy, skinny ones you have to watch out for. The crazy ones that fly all erratic like they're performing an experimental contemporary dance no one wants to watch.

"Twenty-two. More than yesterday," I announce with the observational matter-of-factness of a field researcher. I tally this up in our Mosquito Wars notebook, each pen mark like a thin mosquito leg.

"Suckers!" Steven says. He repeats it again, pleased by its double meaning. "Suckers! Suckers!" He screams this so loudly, the stray cat who usually delivers us dead-animal gifts at noon runs away, a starling dangling in her mouth.

It's summer on the Jersey shore and all day, every day, dozens of mosquitoes bite our arms, legs, feet, faces, and butts (in order of terribleness). A bite on the butt is terrible because it's painful to sit with a bump like a pebble or a cough drop stuck in your back pocket, and no one wants to be seen itching their butt. Though a bite on your face is pretty bad too, especially if you get bit near your eye. Someone might think you have pink eye and are the type to go to cheap water parks where babies swim in their diapers. (And what if you are?) Also, with a bite near your eye, you'll always think about how close the mosquito came to your actual eyeball, how it could have sucked the softest thing by accident. (And what if it did?) You could have woken up with all your eye juice drained. No, I take it back. The face is definitely worse than the butt.

I'm highly allergic, so my bites puff up like perfect profiteroles, the heat of the bite radiating like a dog panting in dry heat. Over weeks, the bites turn hard like tree stumps. Then they leave little scars. Little reminders that you are a target. Then and now: the target of mosquitoes, bullies, racists, terrifying men. Later, when our father leaves us, it will be October—the scars of our bites as faint as autumn-leaf etchings.

I hate it when mosquitoes bite you when you sleep. It's sneaky, smarmy. Like that guy my mother hired to fix our back-door steps, which had holes in them like bagels. He put in one hour of work, left a bucket of concrete to harden, and ran away with the money to Florida to probably spy on his ex-wife. *Why don't you bite me to my face!,* I'd say, shaking my fist in the dark, daring the buzzing I couldn't see. The stray cat left us an extra dead creature that week, a bright red bird, as if to say: *Sorry for your luck, sorry for trusting someone.* I've always admired such gestures of empathy, how they shake loose the wrongdoings of others. As we killed more and more mosquitoes—this disgusting pastime, a kind of love—I hoped someone or something offered the insects their own gestures of empathy. Maybe rain and a new, stagnant pool. Maybe more night, more sleeping children.

* * *

WHEN WE'D GO OVER to a friend's house, a nice house, we'd look around and ask: *Where are your mosquitoes?* At their houses, our limbs would be careless, free. At home or at the restaurant, we'd have to wave our arms around like a windmill or do some jumping jacks since we learned that mosquitoes bite when you're still. That's when we discovered that some people have screens on their windows. Some people have air-conditioning. Some people have fancy-ass citronella candles and monster-truck DEET. *Ah,* Steven and I'd say in unison, nodding. *This is why they get us.*

In the daylight, my brother and I would seek our revenge. We'd work as a team to corner the mosquitoes along the elbow of a wall like corralling a herd of cows. We'd squat or sit or stretch in slow motion, and then—as swift as a face slap on *Jerry Springer*—we'd smash them right there! Oftentimes, we'd stand along the wall and stick out our arms like zombies, inviting them. *Over here,* we'd coo. *Sweet, sweet blood.*

A mosquito would hover over my brother's arm, smelling his honey-eyed baby sweat. Each time, my brother would wince and look at me with equal parts trust and terror. Family is like this sometimes, mixed with trust and terror. And more often than not, family solidly teeters one way or the other. Trust or terror: curled together in a tornado, or the tornado itself.

Right before the mosquito would wrangle its wanton, many-pronged mouth to pierce his skin, I'd clap it between my hands like a cymbal. *Smack.* How easy it is to end such suspension. Then, as per the rules of the game and for the accuracy of the tally, I'd smear the goop on the wall. A kind of painting.

Blood, my brother would say. *It counts.*

* * *

AT A DINNER PARTY or on a first date that won't precede a second, someone always ends up asking me what superpower I'd like to have. *Flight or invisibility?* And when I tell them invisibility, they always shake their heads and say something like: *Ah, you're the type to steal shit.* But I want to tell them they're missing the point. I want to be invisible so I can be completely present. I want to know what I can't. I want to see. For example, these past scenes:

Our Ngin Ngin, napping in the afternoon, after folding dozens of wontons, the flour settling into the creases of her wrinkled hands. *Maybe*, she dreams, *the mosquito that bit me 10 years ago in China is somehow still flying over there, carrying my blood across a grove of persimmon trees.*

Our mother, home from work at midnight, her hair—which smells like oyster sauce—pulled up in a wayward bun. She looks at the walls, covered in mosquito carnage and blood, and collapses into the bread-soft sofa. "I've raised wild animals!" She actually says this out loud, in Toisanese, to no one at all.

Our father, driving to Atlantic City on the Parkway at midnight, staying in the right lane to be closer to the ocean. He chews through a packet of SkyFlakes, crumbs along his beard—slightly damp from the humid air. *What if,* he thinks, *I never come back?*

Is this normal, to want to be there in the past, present, and future? As an adult, I ask Steven: "What do you know about our parents? Like, do you ever wonder what they must have been thinking?"

Steven shrugs. "I mean, I know they were arranged." Then he pauses. "Wait, what do *you* know?"

* * *

I KNOW NOTHING AND everything, unfortunately. I know that mosquitoes never bit my father. We'd joke around about it sometimes. How he would just be sitting there in his cigarette-burn armchair, invincible, while all of us waved our arms and legs around, swirling in a swarm of *zzzzzzzzzz*s. My mother, in July: "Maybe his blood tastes like cigarettes." My brother, in August: "Maybe his skin is all leathery like his jacket." Or maybe, year-round, his blood wasn't meant to mingle with ours.

How does the saying go? One's own flesh and blood? It's in the blood? Blood is thicker than water? Blood siblings? In 1991, I remember being obsessed with the movie *My Girl* and that scene where Vada (played by Anna Chlumsky) asks Thomas J. (Macaulay Culkin) to be blood brothers. They're on this too-picturesque dock together and they catch a fish, which ends up dying. Vada takes the hook out of its mouth and nicks herself, blood running. She asks if they can become blood brothers. Vada convinces Thomas J. to pick the scab off his arm and they rub their blood together, finger painting. I remember being freaked out by this scene, by their blood mixing like that—but then, wasn't that the same thing happening inside a mosquito? Wasn't this flying nuisance just trying to bring us closer as a family, as we turned or drifted away from each other? For this valiant and free service, couldn't I love a mosquito?

Then there's bad blood. And getting blood from a turnip. I spend hours trying to find a blood-related idiom about someone refusing relation. What kind of idiom works for a father who says, *I no longer want to be your blood*? I look everywhere. But all I can find is a completely confusing metaphor. This super analog blog called "Chinese Idioms and Sayings" translates the saying as "the soft-shelled turtle eats the soft-shelled turtle." The idiom is used to describe "a person who turns his back upon family and friends"—blasphemy in a Chinese family. The saying just doesn't work here. I have a hard time thinking of our father like that, swimming around muddy riverbanks, eating other vulnerable turtles, claw by soft claw. No, I know that much. Our father may differ from our blood, but he is not the type to eat his own kind. I ask my mother if she knows the saying. "No, why?" she asks, incredulous. When I tell her I'm trying to figure something out about my father, she cuts me off abruptly—"There are no sayings for your daddy."

* * *

WAS OUR GAME CRUEL? Was it so bad to want to seek revenge? *This is our blood*, I kept saying to myself. *It belongs to us.* This was different from the scenes on TV with kids burning ants with magnifying glasses and cataclysmic sun. Or at least I wanted to believe we were kinder than that. Once, one of my creative writing students wrote about how she put her goldfish in a peanut butter jar as a kid—half peanut butter, half water—just to see what it would do. We were in week one of our nonfiction unit. During office hours, I asked her: *What is the emotional weight here? What did you glean from this, later in life? Is this connected to another scene you haven't written yet?* She shook her head and chewed at her long hair. *I don't know. And I'm scared that I don't know.* I told her to write that down. And then I asked her if it was creamy or chunky peanut butter.

To support the righteousness of our cruelty, we could tell ourselves whatever we wanted. Like, we needed to kill the mosquitoes in order to eradicate disease. Or, we needed to kill them to bond with each other. We needed to ruin the walls to be noticed by our parents. And what do we notice, if we don't turn away? *Look at you and me! Look!* What courses through a family—slithering underneath the carpet like some other kind of undesirable insect, something worse than a mosquito? The gambling debts, the cheating, the hands raised, the disappearing. Everything we didn't know that led to all of this. Half-lit knowledge. What scares a family into silence. My parents were at war with each other from the moment they were arranged to be married. My brother and I inherited this war and witnessed cannons, daily. My father accused my mother of cheating; my mother said he spent all her money at the strip club. They hurled names at each other in Toisanese—words we didn't know that nonetheless held a guttural ache. My father held my mother's shoulders to stop her from screaming. My mother packed her suitcase again and again, throwing silk, tulle, and polyester every-where. The little wars in our family, the little fires igniting around us like a garden of deadly nightshade. What terrified me the most was when my parents stopped screaming. Silence: a dark field I wouldn't dare to trespass, whether I was invisible or not. What we remember, what we don't want to remember. My mother kept a lot of danger hidden from us, and what I saw and knew, I in turn kept from my brother. We were a domino triptych, a protective triumvirate.

Days after our father left, my brother dug out his old dinosaur toys from a broken cardboard box and lined them up on his windowsill, a parade of vegetarians. A green brontosaurus and an orange stego-saurus, one after the other. "In case he forgets which house is ours." Because, once or twice, my father shook a stegosaurus at my brother and smiled.

How swiftly a life can change, how easily. We can kill a mosquito with the palms of our hands, just like that. And just like that, my father's gambling debts pile so high, they become a mountain no one can climb, and the restaurant fails and we must go. My mother almost gets laid off because the local postal facility closes. She adds two hours to her commute each day and works night shift for so many years, she develops vertigo. Just like that, her cochlea wobbles and she vomits, but she refuses to go to the hospital. She stays at home and we stay with her. Everything happens so quickly, time collapses. My brother and I forget to grow up.

* * *

HOW CAN I DESCRIBE to you what it feels like to protect my brother from our father's refusal to be in our bloodline? In this one moment in time, he's 26, and has been recording year after year of the NBA play-offs to watch with our father. He wants to visit him now, our father, but wants me to come. They live only 20 minutes apart. The plan is to deliver the tapes and to set up a time to go over the next week to have some "father-son time." "You can stay in the car," my brother says. He knows I'll be too angry to leave the passenger seat. He knows to keep me strapped in my safety belt or else I'll lunge.

I drive with my brother to our father's house. I am sitting in his car, watching them. It has been years, maybe five, since they've seen each other; it has been longer since I've seen him, but I've lost count. My brother opens the screen door and it squeaks like a dog toy. My father is there, the door only half-open. In my brother's hands: the old VHS tapes, the ribbons curled neatly inside like a bundle of fresh pasta. He knows our father only has a VHS player, and so he held onto our old, clunky machine all these years despite having a DVD player. My brother also knows our father loves basketball, and so he's been practicing his layups even though he's a seasoned hockey goalie.

How swiftly, how easily.

My brother holds the tapes out with his arms, smiling awkwardly. Our father shakes his head and puts his hands in his pockets, closing the door so slowly. He doesn't notice me at all in the car. I swear they both age another five years. The dead grass sways in the wind around them. My brother returns with the tapes, hugged tightly to his chest.

"What happened?"

"I don't want to talk about it."

I ask again, reminding him that we are a team.

My brother puts his hands on the steering wheel and stretches his fingers out as if to keep them from becoming fists. He turns to look at me and, for once, I wish I'd turned away. His face, marveling at his own fear, realized. His eyes flicker about like silverfish.

"He said he was too busy."

I can't describe to you my anger. I can't describe what I wanted to do to that screen door, what I wanted to say to my father. I can't describe the vicious ventricles of my heart or the depths of revenge and devotion. I can see myself giving my writing students advice: *Try! See where it goes, even if you fail.* And I can't even take my own advice. Sometimes I'm at a loss. Sometimes I have to quit, sword down.

* * *

THERE'S THIS OTHER SAYING I found while searching for blood in a Chinese family: "Tiger father begets tiger son." Like father, like son. I never liked the order of that. What if: "Tiger son begets tiger father"? I will spend my whole life wanting this. For my father to be more like my brother: the tenderhearted one, the team member, the dinosaur who quietly chomps on leaves, the trusty one who stays by your side, even when he's deeply uncertain and afraid.

Say it out loud with me: "A tiger, a son, a tiger, a father!"

* * *

AT OUR AFFECTIONATE BEST, my brother calls me "seester" and I call him "little bro."

Seester, when are you coming home? Seester, can you look at my résumé? Seester, remember when we'd lock each other in the freezer at the restaurant? Seester, maybe we should talk more. This nickname is one of my favorite things ever, and it makes me want to hug my brother so hard that I nearly crush his organs like beefsteak tomatoes.

The thing is, we rarely say "I love you" to each other. In fact, maybe we've said it out loud only once. I can't remember. Maybe we said it while tipsy and playing Ping-Pong, volleying affections: "I love you, little bro!" and "I love you, Seester!" But if we did say it then, we probably laughed to clear the air of sentimentality.

I worry we've toughened up in order to hide that we're both too tender. Ever since we were little, we've felt everything intensely. If we were our true selves, we'd walk around wearing matching sweatshirts with IN MY FEELINGS screen-printed on them.

I worry that it's my fault. I am the one who taught him to be tougher than he needed to be. When the neighbor kid who ate whole sticks of butter punched my brother in the stomach for no reason and he doubled over crying, I told him to stop, get up, and pay attention as I punched that kid back. Maybe our mother taught me this. She taught me to stand up for myself, to refuse the expectations of others. When a fellow postal worker told her that her pants were too tight, she wore even tighter pants the next day. She looked him directly in the eye and asked: "What exactly are you looking at?" She taught me to fight my fears away. That if someone was trying to make you afraid of them, they were afraid of something even darker. "No one can burn your light," she'd tell me. "I won't let them."

I could have been more gentle. I could have been the type of person who cups a spider and carries it outside, to a grassy field, and tells it to go wander the world. And sometimes I am. But other times, I am the type to flush a spider down the drain; I point the showerhead until the spider's legs curl up into a rosebud and then the water washes it out. Without warning, I crush ants with my thumb. My brother—then and now—is a kinder, gentler person. Maybe, if he'd been the older sibling, he could have taught me to care for the mosquitoes. Maybe he could have showed me how to gather them in a butterfly net, how to scoop them and carry them into the deep woods. Maybe he could have taught me how to wean them off blood with beet juice. To love even that which hurts us. To love at your fullest capacity, despite failure. My mother and I transmit a message to my brother while we dream: *We're trying, we promise.*

* * *

KOMARNO, MANITOBA, BOASTS THE world's largest mosquito statue. Erected in 1984, my birth year, the steel mosquito is perched not on an arm, but a rock. But the statue isn't still; its 15-foot wingspan turns one way, then another as a weather vane. I think about this giant fake mosquito, about how mosquitoes love stillness: an abandoned pool, a thigh at rest. Instead, this bloodsucking monolith shows us which direction the wind is blowing. Completely harmless and helpful, even, though I'm not sure how.

My brother, who is now married and in his 30s, bought a fixer-upper in North Jersey with the help of his wife's family.

"It's going to be a lot of work," he tells me when I call to congratulate him. I imagine my brother peeling back the old floral wallpaper, splotched with grime and cigarette ash. It covers the floor in strips like failed drafts of a novel. And on the bare walls, evidence of another life, another family: a smeared insect or two. He tells me he found tons of rusty razor blades in the bathroom cabinet, and how gross it was to throw them away.

"Did you wear gloves?" I ask him.

"Shit, was I supposed to?" He also tells me that he found old cassette tapes and wants to buy a tape player to listen to them. *Maybe I'll discover a new song or two.*

"Hey, remember when we used to play Mosquito Wars?" I ask him over the phone, helplessly nostalgic in Bellingham—2,967.3 miles away. We begin a lot of our conversations like this: Remember when we used the bucket where meat marinated as a kiddie pool? Remember when we fed each other spoonfuls of grape Fanta like hummingbirds to make one can last? Remember when we tried to buy a slice of pizza next door at Tony's and got so scared of talking to someone-not-in-our-family that we started shaking and crying? Remember when a drunk stranger knocked on the door and called for our aunt and we hid underneath piles of blankets? Remember playing in the sandpit by the railroad tracks behind the restaurant and the train's invincible roar? Remember the pill bugs crawling along Yeh Yeh's yellow electric blanket? Remember when, remember when?

(We do, we do, we do, we do.)

I tell him about a fact I learned from the guy I'm dating, who will of course become an ex, who will of course stay unemployed and live with his mother, who will of course make me pay for Airbnbs to hook up in. "Did you know that mosquitoes used to be three times bigger than they are now? Isn't that sick?"

"Sick," he echoes back because he is still younger than me and believes everything I say is true, no matter what. Over the years, he's learned to be patient with the things I say. *My sister is a poet,* he tells his friends at his wedding, proudly. I wrote a poem, an epithalamium, for him and his wife. When his friends ask me what that's like, to be a poet, he interrupts and tells them himself: *It means she says things differently.* I want to tell them he's kind of a poet too.

"Anyway." He pauses. "I have to go back to work." How could I forget so easily? He isn't five years old anymore. At best, the dinosaur toys are in the possession of some distant cousin. Our father wasn't invited to the wedding. I knew this was it. It took my brother 30 years to decide to give up on their relationship. Not because of anger or even disappointment. Sometimes empathy simply can't beat exhaustion. When he told me he wasn't inviting our father, my brother's beard was full, and he scratched at it like something was biting him. Empathy, out loud: "I didn't want Dad to feel awkward, since no one wants him there. I don't want him to feel bad." Exhaustion, not said: *Why bother? He doesn't.*

"Yeah, I should get back to work too," I say. "Congrats again on the house," and we hang up after saying a quick goodbye. The 2,967.3 miles stretch like saltwater taffy between us.

* * *

AT THE END OF *My Girl*, Thomas J. dies, swarmed by bees, trying to get Vada's mood ring back for her. Stung and stung again, her blood brother. My god, I think now, what a completely tragic movie to love as a child. That scene made me deeply sad all the time, and still I watched it. Even if it's Hollywood-drastic, that dedication moves me still. That commitment, that we're-in-this-together mentality, that refusal to strike out on one's own or be a rat abandoning ship, despite the wars that rage around and within us. I believe in loyalty. Maybe that's old school. Maybe that's the only Chinese thing about me. Jane and Steven. Our blood: thicker than water, thick as thieves, thick as mosquito vigilantes. There are some things I have to have faith in.

It's early September in the Pacific Northwest and cool enough for a sweater and a slow-burning firepit. On a whim, I call my brother. It's East Coast time, so I wake him up at 2:00 AM accidentally and begin by apologizing. It's over 80 degrees there, and the early fall mosquitoes are the hungry, crazy, skinny ones. He mumbles in his half sleep: "It's fine, I was playing video games anyway," and asks if everything is okay. We usually don't call each other unless something serious has happened.

I think about how Chinese families never say it, how we hold the word far away from our bodies like a shitting baby—with our noses turned up. How the word floats in a corner like a loner at a middle school dance, pores gleaming with awkward disco-ball light. How love is instead *have you eaten yet*, is carefully peeled Asian pear slices on a clean plate, is immediately offering the fattiest piece of pork belly, is *I paid the dinner bill when you were in the bathroom*, is sitting in the car while my brother begs our father to be a father.

"I'll let all the mosquitoes bite me so they won't bite you," I say.

"What?" He laughs loudly and I imagine him shaking his head, all these miles away. "Ugh, my seester, the poet."

For once, I won't be one of those poets who say: *What I'm trying to say is.* That line is a hiding trick each and every time. No, this time I just say it, ruthlessly sentimental. Without hesitation or simile or metaphor: "I love you."

And when he says it back to me, slowly, awkwardly, like "ugh, you know I love you," it's like dipping a toe in a needle-cold lake. When he says it back to me, I imagine all the mosquitoes in the world bowing their glassy wings.

AN ANCIENT
CHINESE SAYING

WONGMOM.COM IS AVOIDING MY QUESTION ABOUT HER own fears. She ducks under the wormholes of the Internet, hides under AdBlock and videos of unlikely animal friendships (I stay a while with the tortoise and baby hippo). AdBlock is like "talk to the hand," and I know she's trying to distract me with '90s nostalgia, waving around those clear glitter jelly sandals I coveted. But, just as she did in the '90s, she tells me to put them back on the shelf. We will be going to Payless instead. It's BOGO season.

Refusing to answer my inquiry, she decides to tell me an "ancient Chinese saying." She replies: "If you can't crawl, swim. If you can't swim, then take the bus."

"How can a bus be in an ancient Chinese saying?" I ask her.

"I'm telling you," Wongmom.com writes back, "it's ancient." She doesn't like it when I ask her about bus fare, about procuring exact change. I know she's trying to tell me to keep going, to keep writing this memoir, to push beyond my fear of failure and shame. *Mommy, can't we just crack nuts together instead?* My mother admits later, when I ask her about this ever-so-ancient proverb, that it's something more like: "If your horse is dead, then you have to walk. Now the horse is dead. Walk." I look this up and it really is a Cantonese saying: maa sei lok dei haang. She said she tweaked it for a more updated approach. I think she likes being a poet herself.

During the start of the pandemic in 2020, I barely wrote any poems. But I touched the shine, the goop, the wet, the cold, the heart of many things. I rolled out bao dough from scratch. I dug my hands into dirt to plant chard seeds. Once, the dough overproofed and its hardened top was like a seam on an old couch. Unnameable bugs chewed through my chard.

As I touched things, as I didn't write, my mother wore gloves and a mask at her postal facility in Trenton, sorting the mail and packages that kept you connected to your loved ones and to whatever you needed— medicine, ballots, flour, noise-canceling headphones, vibrators. I worried about her and her PPE. I wondered when the vaccine would be available for postal employees in Jersey. I kept refreshing the website, over and over. How could I be vaccinated when my mother wasn't?

I couldn't write. It was as if there were little stones stuck in my throat, grating me in graveled exhaustion. I kept scrolling through social media posts about daily word counts, about writing groups making progress on their projects. Who were these productive people? I kept scrolling, kept quiet, kept an exuberant spirit for my students. I kept myself in bed, touching the edge of my wrinkled sheet. I kept getting texts from white people who hadn't reached out to me in years, like *How are you, I just heard*, when the Atlanta spa shootings happened. When six Asian women were murdered, when the Atlanta police captain said the shooter was having a "really bad day," when the shooter said he had a sex addiction. Those texts made me numb. I called Michelle a lot and we touched our hot ears to the phones. Our ears like baked hand pies. I crushed the cabbage worms chewing through the purple heart of my cabbage. I cried so hard sometimes, my snot became a galaxy of its own.

Leading up to this book, anxiety and panic attacks poured out of me like glimmering wildflower honey. My anxiety was sticky in its shine, overgenerous. I googled "panic attacks" and "anxiety" a lot. I touched the glacial glow of my phone screen. I kept trying to find a therapist of color, kept failing at finding a therapist of color. I touched my anxiety because it was, *is*, a part of me. My anxiety feels warm, elastic, and ridgelike. It feels like rice noodles, stuck together, the cold rinse forgotten.

A friend suggested I try out ceramics at a local community studio in Bellingham. The first time I touched clay, I felt its wet impression on my skin, the earthy mess of it. The mineral smell of it. When I sliced it with a wire tool, it felt like slicing tofu. When I wedged for the first time, I could feel the clay moving around like the knots constellating my back. It took me many months to learn how to center a pot on the wheel, to pull up the sides steadily. The centrifugal force of the wheel scared me. There was so much to be afraid of in the world. I touched the pedal too fast or too slow. I touched the wet clay that splattered all over my arms, hair, eyelashes. I marveled at how it dried and crusted, a new version of itself. I had to throw my whole body at the wheel, had to steady my hands and say: *Go where I want you to go!* Cylinders collapsed. Bowls flopped, lopsided. I scraped them off the wheel, spackle stuck in my fingernails.

I told my mother over the phone that I was learning pottery. She seemed confused. "Why don't you just buy a bowl?" But then I made her a spoon rest glazed in swirls of soft sea blue. Post shelter-in-place, when we reunited in June 2021, she hugged the spoon rest to her face. It curved along her sun-kissed cheek. "This is like me," she said, smiling. Could a pot be a poem? Years ago, she said the same thing when I read "Twenty-Four," a persona poem from my first book, to her. From the end of that poem: "Each time my father waves // across the shore, I dissolve / one part more." "Yup, that's me," she nodded, even though I wasn't her, couldn't be her. "I miss my father just like that. You understand."

I finally told my mother about the intensity and frequency of my panic attacks, after my panic attack on that Denver street in April of

2022. I told her the details. I told her about my breath, the tingling void, the dizziness, the siphoning terror, the thoughts of worthlessness. I told her how my body felt, how—in the bubbling center of it—I was sure I was going to die. When I told her that, I could hear her voice struggle over the phone. Was she crying? She doesn't cry. It took her some time to speak. "Jane, you're scaring me."

If I can't write, if I can't write *this*, what could I do? *Now the horse is dead. Walk.*

Mile after ancient mile, here I am, walking my ghost horse to the bus stop.

9

THE THIEF

THE THIEF DREAMT OF OPENING A SET OF ENCYCLOPEDIAS. She dreamt of the shiny spines like the foil of chocolate coins, the fresh metallic ink, the pages falling open like the wings of some newly discovered moth. The thief went over to her neighbor's house to hang out and there it was: the *World Book Encyclopedia* 1996 set, *A* through *F*. The encyclopedias were heavy enough to press four-leaf clovers or straighten out curling band posters or clobber a kingpin cockroach. Even though her friend was missing the rest of the alphabet, even though this wasn't the highly coveted *Britannica* set, she wanted it.

As her friend talked on the phone to some middle school crush, a boy with so much hair he was practically a yak, the thief lay down on the rug near the bookcase, touching the oxblood spines. She dreamt about devouring these books, gorging herself on facts about flying squirrels and tectonic plates and Romanticism, the pages stuck between her teeth like caramel. She would need to floss for sure. Did it matter that these entries were often wrong? Or that the books lacked entries that reflected who she was, how she grew up, where her ancestors came from? Did it matter that the whole thing was a marketing scam, brought door to door via a salesman in a tweed suit or a thick catalog that promised knowledge at your fingertips with a pay-in-installments plan?

The thief looked at her fingertips, glitter nail polish chipping like an old disco ball. The want was somersaulting inside her, an oil fire. The want was rollicking in her lungs, hay heavy. This is when it first happened. Yes, she thought about it, for a few brief seconds. Of tipping book *B* from its place like a trust fall, of letting it land in her hands and then slipping it quietly into her backpack. Of pushing the other books to the left, closing the ghost book gap. No one would miss the *B*'s anyway. Her friend could live without interrogating the beach, the barnacle, the beetle. Seconds of the thinking, of the longing, dragged on. The longing for what we can't have and what trouble this longing gifts us. The longing settled in her, the first firefly among decades of tall brush.

But the thief did nothing and, when her friend gave her the receiver to talk to Yak Boy, the cord dangling like a long ramen noodle, the thief hung up on him, her friend screeching, "OMGOMGJANEEEEEEEWHATTHETRUEFUCK!"

* * *

WHEN I WAS FINALLY caught, I cried because I thought I should cry. The tears were like glue, sticky with empathy. When I was finally caught, I lied and said it was my first time stealing, that my friends put me up to it, that I had never thought about stealing till now. No, I hadn't been here before. No, that wasn't me on the tapes, but some other Asian girl (and maybe it was, my thieving döppelganger). When I was finally caught, it was in the jewelry section of a big department store in the Monmouth Mall in Eatontown, New Jersey. I was trying on a pair of earrings and moved my head back and forth like a fish to see the cerulean stones shine. I did not put the earrings back. I just left them on as if they'd been mine to begin with. When he caught me, the security guard walked me through every single department— women's shoes, men's dress shirts, bedding, appliances, hosiery—like

154

I was on a grand parade of shame. I kept my eyes on my boots, which were wet with melting snow and sidewalk salt like blue Pop Rocks. I was then led into a back room that was dimly lit and had blurry gray security-camera televisions stacked atop each other. A chair swiveled behind a long steel desk and the manager was there with a goatee, looking at me with furrowed brows, and it was so much like a bad crime show, I laughed. "What's so funny?" the manager asked, placing both his hands down on the desk like he was pressing apples for cider. In response, I sat there amid the spectral glow of the security televisions and thought about how the earrings I stole were on sale, 65 percent off. I laughed again, thinking about how I only stole things on sale. That even in my deep sinkhole of indignity, I was a thrifty thief, a clearance red-sticker shoplifter. An immigrant baby, always. The manager admonished me again as he took my photograph for the wall of shoplifters banned from the store. I closed my eyes as the flash went off. I couldn't stop laughing and crying at the same time. "This is not funny, young lady."

* * *

"CHI SIN! DID YOU hear me? Put it back!" Like two Eeyores filled with deep ennui, my brother and I folded our bodies into the grocery cart and fished out boxes of Lunchables, Gushers, and Quilted Northern Ultra Plush toilet paper. We sighed dramatically in each aisle, returning them one by one. We put our heads against the plush three-ply like it was a pillow. My mother mocked us: "You have it so tough. I should send you to China!"

She was right. We were jerks, true brats. We dreamt of congealed turkey against the buttery flake of Ritz Crackers, of name-brand fruit snacks coloring our mouths peacock blue, of toilet paper that didn't scratch our asses one-ply raw. We were at BJ's Wholesale, the Costco no one's heard of. Our "American" grocery trip was always after our trip to AFC, the Asian Food Center, and we were here only to pick up a potting-soil-sized bag of knock-off Frosted Flakes and a brick of cheddar cheese large enough to clobber a mouse. Just 30 minutes ago at AFC, we'd been rich with 39-cent scallions and discounted oxtail thanks to our mother's beauty queen smile.

On the outside, no one knew about our credit card debt or the gaping hole in our kitchen ceiling, dripping dirty water from the upstairs bathroom. No one knew my mother went to illegal Chinese dentists and no one knew Ngin Ngin shoved ketchup packets and oyster crackers into her pockets because they're so utterly free. I was always dressed to the nines in GapKids, Tommy Hilfiger, Express, and Limited Too—freshly plucked from the final sale rack. The rack always had the styles that were a little too weird for basic Jersey consumption. Only we could pull off pink overalls with too many zippers and yellow velour turtlenecks. Mixed with hand-me-downs and worn in a variety of ways (a button-down dress was now a jacket), my mother saw the sartorial vision.

* * *

THE DESIRE TO STEAL was like terrible metals, fastening themselves to any glittering thing, swaying in wicked delight. The desire was almost romantic, almost swoon-worthy, akin to the crush I had on the homeschooled punk kid who also worked at the public library with me, stamping dates on newspapers in the Periodicals section. During my year of stealing, I wanted so badly to be bad. I wanted to shake loose all the expectations placed upon me—quiet, sweet, "good." In my 30s, a man will say to me, after shoving his cockroach tongue in my mouth, "Are you a good girl or a bad girl?" How was I supposed to calculate the length of time it would take to let loose what others thought of me? This man bit my ear and all I could think about was how I had eaten pig ears the night before, sliced thin and fried. "We both know you're a bad girl," he said.

At 17, I wanted to want, to be wanted, wanton in my wanting. I worked in the Children's section at the Eastern Branch of the Monmouth County Public Library, mostly reshelving dinosaur books, and I would sometimes stop by Periodicals like I had something to retrieve. A stapler maybe, a misplaced issue of *Highlights*. Because he was homeschooled, the punk didn't know that I was a nerd in high school, or that I'd never been kissed or asked out, or that I spent my weekends reading novels and short stories instead of going to parties. Once, in his oversized ripped-up hoodie, he looked up from the counter with basset hound eyes and said, "I want to check you out." And when I stood there, slack-mouthed in my ugly duckling stink, he quickly added, "Just trying out terrible library pickup lines. Did it work?" I hope you're wincing too.

* * *

I DIDN'T HAVE TO tell my mother. But what kind of immigrant baby would steal and then lie to her mother about it? I drew a line in my shame, a boundary in the dirt. I didn't have a car and so I had to wait for my mother to pick me up from the mall. When she arrived, she had to park far away because a large section of the parking lot was being paved with a fresh coat of asphalt.

When I told her, I said it simply. I said it without looking at her, for fear of seeing myself reflected in her face. "I stole something and got caught."

She said nothing. We walked back to the car, past the perimeter of the new asphalt, the dimpled potholes, the gasoline slush of January snow. My mother is not the quiet type. It's never a good sign when she has nothing to say. She's an extrovert, a total ham, someone who loves to talk and wraps you in the warmth of her talking. She will literally talk to anyone. Once, calling sick out of work, she thanked the automated assistant who told her to have a nice day. "You have a nice day too," my mother said and hung up. Aching with laughter, I told her she didn't have to talk to robots. My mother smiled and shrugged: "But the robot is nice." Here, in the stinging cold of my failure as a daughter, I was Pepto-Bismol nauseous with her silence. All I could hear was the sound of the car starting and snow crunching underneath the tires. I wanted any sound to come out of her—a tremble, a sigh, a growl. Nothing.

When we got home, she closed the front door behind us and locked it. The click echoed through the hallway. In the hollowed privacy of shame, she spoke.

"I give you everything you need! Food, a house, clothes, everything for school? How could you do this to me?"

I felt my body go slack from everything she said, everything that was true. The child of an immigrant single mother, how could I have slapped her in the face like this, ungrateful and greedy? When my mother arrived in this country, arranged to be married to my father, she had only $20 in her pocket. I thought about poorly packaged mail getting jammed in the machine at 2:00 AM (read: please stop putting candy in business envelopes), of her reheating rice, string beans, and steamed fish on her lunch break at midnight, whirring in the alien light of the microwave. The same food I'd eaten many hours prior, the black bean sauce delicious with the flaky white fish. How I funneled it into my mouth, scallion scented, mindlessly. At that moment, I touched my ears, which were no longer bejeweled, and started sobbing. I fell to the floor, a broken sprinkler, sputtering apologies. I knew how hard my mother worked, knew what it meant to live paycheck by paycheck, knew why there were no baby pictures of me, knew she was sending money back to the old country, knew I could go to college only if I got a huge scholarship. My mother's eyes were wild, disappointment flashing like telephone wires in a storm.

And finally, slowly, she said in both English and Toisanese: "You broke my heart." These words could have been stolen from any pop song, yet they stuck their spindle legs deep into my chest, finding footing for a kind of disgrace I couldn't bear. She turned away from me then, as if declaring we were no longer mirror images—our mouths, our noses, our eyes, our moles, no longer the same. Variations in goodness, in badness, in what happens in this country because of too much want.

That night, from my bedroom window, I watched my mother hack ice off the windshield of our old, busted car—the cold crystals flying off like fireworks. The car huffed in its attempt to warm itself, clouds of exhaustion. I worried about my mother slipping away from me, skating off in a frozen pond. I leaned against a wall to brace myself, to feel something holding me up. I closed my eyes, imagining each brick of our house falling away, tumbling into the bright blue distance, and there I was—still leaning against some invisible force resembling the face of forgiveness.

* * *

THE THIEF LEFT HER books at home one evening, piled like a poorly built fire in her bedroom, and drove to the library punk's show at the Stone Pony in Asbury Park. She went alone and pushed through the forest of tall teenaged boys, to the front of the crowd. The library punk was a bassist, his hair spiked with crusty gel, and to be honest, the band was absolutely terrible and the drummer kept losing the drumsticks. But he smiled at her like cracking the sugar of crème brulée. His friends and bandmates would tell him later to never smile like that because it was fucking cheesy and what was he doing liking a Chinese girl anyway unless he liked Oriental sluts? The fear of being a fetish overwhelmed her so much, she felt like she was going to tip over and fall face-first, and so she moved backward instead to overcorrect. Ever the nautilus, she moved so backward that she tripped on someone's Converse shoelaces and swiftly left the venue. The thief returned home to her books and, like heavy necklaces, she put them on top of her chest, one by one.

* * *

THE MANAGER PLACED ME in Customer Service at Marshalls on the first day of my job. It was the summer of my senior year of high school. "A smart girl like you can deal with stuff like returns and exchanges," the manager said, leaving me with a line of 10 customers, snapping their gum and shifting their screaming babies from one arm to another like judicial scales. I was still working at the library, only a few streets away, and my mother had decided I needed a job with "people skills" too. She was worried that I was just hiding in the book stacks like an awkward turtle. To be honest, she wanted the 15 percent staff discount. And to be honest, I was most definitely an awkward turtle and I fumbled about my shell daily.

"I'd like to return this rug," my first customer said, her hair piled atop her head like a chandelier of curls. She kicked open a 9-by-12-foot damask rug and it unfurled like a wave on the floor, forcing the people behind her to step back. I peered over the counter and took a look at the rug. It was covered in footprints, cat hair, and cigarette burns in the corners. The hell was this?

"You speak English? I said I'm returning this rug," the customer said, now gripping the counter with her hands. There are moments like this, when a white person asks me if I speak English, where one of two things happens: 1) I feel immediately defensive and enunciate every. single. syllable; or 2) I feel bad about the impulse to prove myself to white people and move quickly toward rage against the racist hierarchy of English and say absolutely nothing and go into side-eye hibernation.

The second option is where I am these days. I chose the first option when I was younger, swimming through the arteries of internalized racism. "I sincerely apologize. Let me see what I can do for you," I said, as A+ AP Lit as possible.

During my time working at Marshalls, so much stealing happened. But this time, it wasn't me. Customers would try to return random shit, retagged with a price maker at home. "This is from the dollar store across the street," I told one of them, lifting up a plaid cosmetic pouch. She kind of shrugged and didn't even try to disagree. Some people stole in the most blatant ways—shoving a pair of lacy underwear into their purse while tying their shoes. Or sometimes it was more subtle, like moving a red-tag clearance sticker onto a full-priced item, which I honestly felt fine about. If you need the sale, make it happen, I guess. Once, one of my co-workers got caught stealing money and items from layaway. During a break, she told me she'd upgraded to a queen-sized bed. She shared half of an orange with me, peeling it in a perfect spiral. Sweet citrus perfumed the air. One of the items on layaway was a headboard. When she was pulled out of the store in handcuffs, she looked only at the ground, even when a few employees called out *We got you* and *You didn't do it!* None of them knew I was in my year of stealing. That I had put on five pairs of Victoria's Secret underwear the day before, mesh boyshorts hidden beneath sweatpants. That I carried scissors in my purse, at the ready. As my co-worker passed by me, I thought about how sweet it was that she had shared that orange with me, cleaning off the pith with such grace, generosity.

* * *

AS A TEENAGER, MY mother rode her bike to the factory where she embroidered fancy birds onto silk. Peacocks with rich oceanic plumage, cranes with pearly ballerina legs. Twenty other young women worked there, entangled in embroidery thread and the hot hum of the machine. High school lasted only two years and she worked during it, with her two best friends. She'd tell me how, when she'd get off work, there would be this guy who brought her bread from his restaurant. "I thought you might be hungry," he'd smile, holding out the crusty top. Before finding out she was arranged to marry my father, this guy spent a year trying to talk to her. My mother told me that, after he saw her go to the movie theater with her friends, he got a job at the theater and always saved three tickets for them. He was from the city and Gung Gung said that if my mother ran away with him, he'd disown her. I ask her if she was interested in him at all. "No, no. He was so into me. It was too much!" she says, but with a huge smile on her face. She admits to eating the bread; she really was hungry. And it was delicious, milky, warm. "But I want to know why. I want to go back to the city and ask him. I heard he's still there. Why? Why me?" I wonder why she wants to know. Why it pleases her to remember this wanting, this old current of yeasty curiosity. Can we choose what kind of wanting we want?

Then she tells me about another guy from China, who finds her number 30 years later and tells her over the phone: "I had the hugest crush on you in high school, but I was too scared to tell you. So I'm telling you now." He's married with kids and says that she has a place to stay if she ever visits San Francisco. When she tells him that would be weird, he brushes it away: "We're all old now, it doesn't matter. We're old friends." But my mother insists that it is weird, that she can't go back in time. Why would she? I think about the different lives my mother could have lived, if she didn't follow my father to the U.S. These lives start to sprout roots in water, little soft tendrils of movie-theater life and Bay-area sea lions, but she cuts them short. Reels and fins recede back into my wanting imagination.

* * *

EVER SINCE I TOLD my mother I stole in high school, I haven't shoplifted. When I glimpse a group of teenagers at a store motioning to each other with their eyes, readying their moves, I can't bear to watch. I grow sticky with fear and unease. I have to leave the store immediately. These days, 20 years later, I keep thinking someone is going to catch me stealing something. Even if I'm not. Like putting shiitake mushrooms in a brown bag with cremini mushrooms at the grocery store. Like I'm-sorry-my-mistake. But then I worry: Was it really a mistake? I've begun to suspect myself.

* * *

GROWING UP IN THE countryside during the Cultural Revolution, my mother had so few clothes—threadbare hand-me-downs and a couple of hand-sewn separates. She wore the same blue high-collared button-down jacket mandated by Mao every day. Her clothes were simple, easy to work in. When she immigrated to the U.S. in the '80s and stepped into Macy's for the first time at 21, she glazed over like a doughnut. She reached out her hands and touched silky mannequin after silky mannequin. Scarcity can make you crazy broke with the things you never had. She discovered the immediacy of credit cards. Plastic magic. Free from utilitarian expectations, she was flooded with fashion. Remember, my mother is an extrovert. Lacking English skills, she expressed herself through her clothes. She delighted in every cuff, seam, color, texture, bead, cut, weight, movement.

And so I'd find leather gloves, pearl-studded sweaters, oversized silk shirts, flocked velvet leggings, off-shoulder floral dresses, confetti bodysuits—all with their sale tags still on—hidden in the strangest places: under the always-foggy fish tank, inside a large vase, shoved under the sofa, tucked away in a pantry by the dried tofu skin. Over the years, her closet would grow and grow, taking over numerous rooms. Whenever I urged her to clean it out, she'd always make up a reason for keeping something: "Oh yeah, that dress is good for grocery shopping," or "You can't get rid of that, I'll need lots of sweaters for when I'm 80," or "Those are good pants for cutting grass." Growing up, I was convinced there was an outfit for everything: the pants for your period, the tank top for trimming tomato plants, the blouse for when you want to make the bully at work jealous. And now—clothes for when you visit your daughter in rainy, gray Seattle: bright colors and bold cuts only. Magenta balloon sleeves, canary-yellow asymmetrical dresses. "Funky," she beams. "I like to be funky here."

Every time I go home to visit, I go row by row through her closet. It's like shopping through memories: the outfits she wore when going to illegal dentists, her return-to-the-village outfit, her rage-filled-Atlantic-City sequins. I "borrow" (okay, I take) her clothes and shoes often. Sometimes she'll look up and say: "Oh, I like that! Where did you buy that?"

* * *

WHAT THE THIEF WOULD like stolen from her: the tick her college boyfriend found curled up in her belly button; pairs of socks with holes in them that she can't bear to throw away; the moldy shower curtain from her first apartment in Seattle; her collection of broken sunglasses with one of their lenses popped out; the memory of the man who bit her nipple so hard he drew blood; the memory of another man who held her neck with his hands, stewing in the suet of power and violence; the vast flood of her period during history class and the non-memory of passing out in the hallway when she rushed to the bathroom; the swamp marsh of rotting herbs in her fridge; all her throbbing mosquito bites past, present, and future; her broken pair of flats that flapped about like a duck; her college debt, each loan piled atop another like a cairn; each rattling heartbreak in which men made it very clear to her that they did not want her—that no one would want a woman who wants so much and has too much to give.

* * *

PAU PAU BUYS ALMOST-ROTTEN fruits and vegetables because they're on super discount. A lot of the Asian grocery stores in Seattle's Chinatown-International District bag up all almost-rotten food into one giant bag and sell it for a couple of bucks. I tell her I can buy her some nonblemished, mold-free fruit. A sturdy orange, not about to collapse upon itself. But she waves me away. She tells me that, if she doesn't eat it, it will go to waste. She wants this orange in this two-dollar bag. She wants to pay with change. I sit in the discomfort of upward mobility, in my professorial bowl of fresh fruit. There's such good honeydew this week. What more could I possibly want?

I remember watching rich hipsters dumpster dive and raid free piles when I was at Bard. It didn't make sense to me. Your parents paid something like $60,000 for school for you this year and you really need that shoe with a hole in it? For them, it wasn't cool to be rich, I guess. They were trying to lob intergenerational wealth away from them like a wet rag; they didn't want it. At the end of my freshman year, I helped my dorm neighbor clean out his room. "Just throw it all away in this garbage bag," he said. I stared at his coat hangers, which were the good wooden ones. "What? No!" Even though he said I could take anything, everything, including stray dollar bills, I couldn't help but feel like I had orchestrated a heist. I stuffed it all to take home like a criminal squirrel, brimming at the cheeks.

* * *

ONCE, THE EX WHO promised to move to Bellingham for me drew a card with a raccoon holding a heart on it. It had been traced with a pencil and then filled in with a Sharpie marker and colored pencils. Written inside: "She stole my fucking heart." He told me he was dumbfounded that he could be with someone so beautiful and brilliant. He traced the corners of my mouth gently. He loved the shape of my upper lip, said there was something catlike about me. "I think about our babies. Don't you think about that? I can just see it, can't you?" he'd say, wild-eyed. He came so loudly during sex, I often blinked, startled by my own power. He wanted me from the very start, sitting front row at a poetry reading at a local bookstore, fixed on me. He was so handsome and so bearded and I was such a glutton. On our first date, I remember unbuttoning his shirt so slowly, I felt like I was chewing each button like it was Smarties candy. After he ghosted me and disappeared that summer, it took until December for me to realize he'd brought my space heater along with him. I sat in my Bellingham bedroom—which used to be an enclosed porch—bundled in blankets and a beanie, trying to warm myself with indignation.

I remember the exact moment when I first saw the look of desire pointed directly at me. I was 16 and my family was visiting China. This trip was my mother's return to her ancestral village. Before she sashayed down that dirt walkway, we took a two-day detour in Guilin to see the karst mountains. Our tour group was lined up to get into rowboats. From my boat, I noticed a guy, another Chinese American teenager, smiling at me. I looked back and felt the bud of want curlicue within me, a packed dahlia. He smiled at me so intensely that his foot missed the boat. Just like that, he fell into the water from the dock, his black hair disappearing into weeds and slime. When he stood up, drenched in river water, he wiped his eyes and opened them wide like a gorgeously eyelashed Furby. He winked at me. Who winks? His mother slapped him hard on the back, calling him stupid in Cantonese. But he kept smiling at me, even as our boats slipped away from each other, and I felt the imprint of that desire for months. Up until that point, no one had paid romantic attention to me. Heading back to school that fall, I reminded myself of his want. When I popped a pimple, white guts speckling the mirror, I said to my reflection: *You made him fall off a boat.*

Over and over, I rolled around in the greasy glut of being wanted. I longed for that look of theirs—that look where the besotted can't seem to make sense of me, can't help but flutter near me. I was a senior in college when I attended a writer's conference in Vermont on a scholarship. I met an older poet who clearly wanted me. He stared at me from across the dim wood-paneled room, whiskey glass in hand. He was a professor somewhere. He gave me his book, which I never read. I had no interest in him whatsoever, but at that time I wanted to be wanted and so I spoke to him. He thought I was such a Goody Two-shoes, asked me if I'd ever done anything bad. These men and their stereotypes, their fantasies. I told him I used to steal. "Did you ever lay out all the things you stole on your bed? That's sexy," he said, inching so close I could see his nose hairs. He reached out to touch my hand. I stepped back, suddenly uneasy. "I stole on clearance." I left him there, gawking, and never spoke to him again.

That ex of mine disappeared, his want disappeared, everything—my space heater included—disappeared, as if we hadn't been together for a year. There were so many men like this in my life that it became a sickening pattern, with varying degrees of cruelty. The obsessive, visceral want and then the sudden shutting down of that want. I was told so many things. That I intimidated them, that I wanted more than they could give, that I was worthless and ugly and stupid.

Over time, I grew terrified of want. I didn't want men to want me; I didn't want them. I slinked away from their looks, grew disgusted by their image of me and desire to seduce me. One of the things I "borrowed" from my mother was a '90s black flocked-velvet lingerie robe. I wore this everywhere in my late 20s and early 30s. It was sexy, effortless, and the perfect length and weight. It swooshed down a hill. It looked great with jeans and a minidress. My mother used to throw it on in the morning before putting her makeup on. When an ex of mine tore the back of it, eager to get my clothes off, I pushed him so hard, he fell onto the bed. He thought I was flirting, but I quickly moved away and caressed the robe, staring at the damage. It was nearly impossible to fix silk and velvet. "You ripped it. I'm going home."

At a restaurant, I'll catch myself staring into a bowl of beef noodle soup or tonkotsu ramen. What do I want? I'll ask this question, my face steaming with oily answers I can't decipher. More precisely:

What does it take to want myself? I stare deeper. I slurp noodle after noodle, ravenous. The noodles bounce back against my teeth, deliciously resistant to the bite.

*　*　*

THE THIEF'S HAIR WAS long. It grew way past her butt, and was as thick and coarse as horsehair or a straw broom that never quite swept everything up. Throughout the school week, her hair would grow dirty, full of dust and sweat and pencil shavings. She'd swat disheveled strands out of her face. Her mother's hands were rough from chopping vegetables and scrubbing dishes, so this meant she plaited the thief's hair with the strength you need to make a proper loaf of bread. She braided her daughter's hair each morning, the snap of the hair tie a daily alarm.

But this day was different. This was the day the thief's family restaurant would close. The door would be locked, the key given to some other family, some arguably better daughter. On this day, the thief's mother braided her hair one last time. The thief's father and brother were waiting in the car, the engine wheezing. The thief stood in front of the restaurant's door with her mother. It was then that her mother took a hair tie out of her purse and wrapped the top of the braid. It was then that my mother took a pair of kitchen shears out of her purse and, without warning, chopped my hair right off. In the storefront's reflection, I gasped. I saw my short hair. I saw my mother smiling back at me as I swung my head from left to right, right to left, weightless. She placed the scissors back into her purse. "Here, Jane," she said, handing me the thick braid like a rack of ribs, what was once a part of myself. "You can keep it. It's yours."

NOCTURNAL FORCES

PLEASE BE PATIENT WITH WONGMOM.COM'S REPLIES. BAL-ancing psychic energy and night shift at the postal service has been a challenge.

Though, as my mother likes to tell me, night shift is the perfect time to ask for guidance. She has trained numerous new employees. Whenever I call her when she's at work, she always pauses in the middle of a sentence to say: "Hey, did you get that bag of nuts I got you?" and "Let's talk later, I got an idea." She tells me her co-workers stop by her station often because talking to her relaxes them. "It relaxes me too," she says. "When we share about life, everything loosens up." She stretches her arms over her head like a big halo. She is in the flow of her powers.

My mother has worked night shift for almost 26 years, with just a few brief interludes of day shift. She's still on night shift and commutes an hour to the Trenton facility each day. When I tell people my mother's a postal worker, they assume she's in uniform behind the counter selling booklets of stamps or walking down the street, stacks of mail tucked under her arm. Most people don't know that there are thousands of clerks who sort mail in giant postal facilities, the whirring sounds of machinery surrounding them at all times. My mother has been one of those night clerks for decades, sorting millions of magazines, envelopes, postcards, flyers, and boxes. During night shift, employees eat lunch at 2:00 AM. Inside, the facility is brightly lit and abuzz with activity; outside, possums carry their babies down the street, their eraser-pink tails and car-headlight eyes finally free.

I think about my mother and Vinny driving late at night, sometimes carpooling with fellow night-shifters. A school bus that picks up in the pitch-darkness with Whitney Houston playing on the radio to make sure everyone stays awake. You can't fall asleep to "I Wanna Dance with Somebody (Who Loves Me)." How still the streets are when they back out of the driveway—no power walkers, no lost softballs, no guzzling lawn mowers. Even the neighborhood dogs are deep in sleep, twitching their legs, chasing porpoise-sized rabbits. The Parkway, usually congested with stop-go traffic and underlined with staccato honking, is empty and silent. It's as if the organs of the highway have been hollowed out, the ribs of the median flashing silver under headlights. I think about the wheels of their car crushing plastic bottles—litter is always harder to see at night. A scrap of tire here, a jug of AriZona tea there. How the drive home is always harder after working overtime. Sometimes Vinny will stay even longer and catch a ride home with another co-worker. I imagine my mother, driving alone in the plump darkness, popping another ginger chew into her mouth. She adds chew after chew, looping the sticky ginger like a rubber band ball.

I'm scared to even write down what I'm afraid of. Of who else might be driving during those hours. The awful stink of liquor on someone's breath, twisting into the dark sky like licorice. Wearing the amber-colored cologne my father wore when he crashed into the Parkway that one time. Or the rage-filled driver gunning it, tires squealing, because my mother's driving too slow. I'm afraid of what I can't control. *Get home safe*, I beg. *Don't work too hard.* I say this to my mother on the phone, but also out loud to the universe. Wongmom.com pipes up: "But that's what Mommy is supposed to say to *you*."

* * *

WHO IS WALKING BEHIND me? What was that noise from behind that thing I can't see? I can't help but be more fearful at night. What was that shadow under that shadow? What secrets does darkness hide? What do our dreams and nightmares say about our waking hours? Sometimes my dog howls in the dark. His silver fur spikes up, his tail tucks under. He thinks he sees something; maybe he does, maybe he doesn't. He's scared too, but he's also protective. *Everything's fine, go pee.* He looks at me skeptically with his soft fox ears. It takes him 10 minutes of staring into the darkness before he finally succumbs and pees, his urine steaming like hot tea in the cold. When we go back inside, he prances and rolls on the fuzzy carpet, paws up. He's excited to be warm, safe.

Night shift is a shift that is inherently more precarious, more unprotected. Beyond the late-night drive itself, I worry about the increased danger of harassment. I think about my mother's co-worker waiting by her car in the dark, yelling obscenities at her as she gripped her keys. Of how she couldn't see her harasser's figure until she got closer, under the yellow streetlight. I think about writing my mother's deposition down at the kitchen table, of her saying *How do you say*, *How do you say*, when trying to find the right words in English to describe a stalker who harassed multiple Asian women at work. What it took for her to stand up and tell her story, placing each encounter in the brightness of day, in the bluntness of record. This co-worker, after taking a mandatory mental health assessment, voluntarily "retired."

Aimé Césaire writes about "the nocturnal forces of poetry" in his essay "Poetry and Knowledge": "It is that mild autumnal nostalgia that threw mankind back from the clear light of scientific day to the nocturnal forces of poetry." For Césaire, poetry moves through the murky space of night, through the unknown, half-lit, unconscious space of our deepest selves. I find myself intrigued by these nocturnal forces, by what is dredged up from the darkness we often fear, which ultimately becomes a means of illumination. Poetry feels like that space before sleep, that liminal twitch of dreamy peculiarity in a very real world. A heaviness loosened like bats out for a hunt. This is the time when I feel the most powerful. Poetry as echolocation.

At a writing residency on the Washington coast, I woke up in the middle of the night and tongued the left side of my mouth. I felt a strange groove, a curved hollow, jagged along my tongue. I was missing a part of my tooth. Fumbling in the dark with my bad eyesight, I couldn't find my glasses. I searched around the bedspread, trying to feel my pebbled tooth. I recalled this one fact from first-aid training: you can put a lost tooth in milk, spit, or coconut water (not the flavored kind) to try to save it. But there was nothing around me to save, just the sweaty sheet. The gap in my mouth felt like an archway, my tooth an ancient crumbling building. It oddly didn't hurt. Why did I wake up? Where did the tooth go? Did I eat my own tooth? I tried to google next steps on my phone: "chunk of tooth missing, how, what to do." But it didn't really give me answers. As mosquitoes smacked themselves against my window, I didn't know what else to do but write a poem. Something was being dredged up and that something wouldn't let me sleep. I found my glasses and wrote until my anxiety burst open. I wrote about fear, about the flare of embodied trauma, about poetry itself:

> Flop into
> this poem, plead to this
> "clenched" (something inside of me,
> yolked) body: enough. Enough—I
> hear you howling

And then I fell back to sleep, a part of me still missing, my tooth chunk bobbing like a ship in my stomach acid. The poem wasn't very good and it didn't make "sense," but it gave me enough to know that something I'd overlooked was demanding my attention. Something was "howling" inside me—echoing off that hollowed tooth. This would be the night before I co-bought a house with a man who would later frighten me.

Further along in the essay, Césaire writes: "Poetry became an adventure. The most beautiful human adventure. At the end of the road: clairvoyance and knowledge." I keep returning to this idea that my mother is a poet. I think about that adventure being shared among her fellow postal clerks. How they take care of each other in the depths of the night shift with poetic advice, supplemented with midnight kimchi and pierogies and chaat. One of my mother's Korean co-workers gave her a jar with fermented fruit in it. "It's good for your skin, your soul. Leave it in a cabinet," she told her. And, like magic, once my mother drained the jar of juice, it filled up with more pale-yellow liquid the next day. I drank that tangy juice when I visited my mother in 2021, a ravenous fruit bat. When I kept asking for the Juice, she texted her co-worker: "Jane <3 juice. Jane need juice." Every day, her co-workers nourish each other, keep each other awake—literally and spiritually. And in turn, they nourish me. This force, this spark, is a relationship. I'm beginning to understand that clairvoyance is communal. I'm beginning to understand Wongmom.com needs you too.

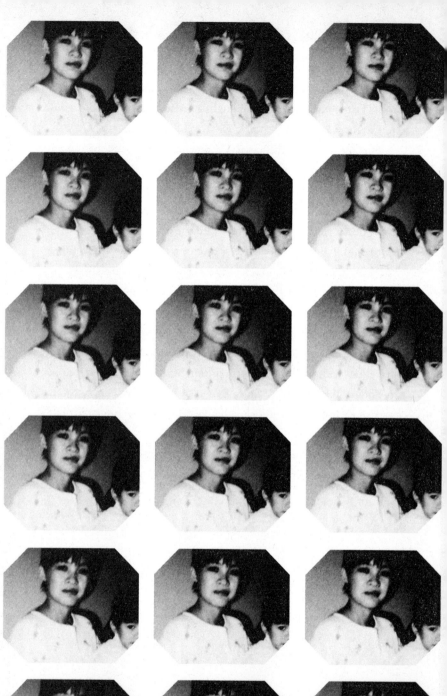

10

SNOW, RAIN, HEAT, PANDEMIC, GLOOM OF NIGHT

THE POST OFFICE DOESN'T HAVE CLOCKS.

Waiting in line, I can feel everyone's tension and anger stewing, leaking out of their pores like sewer grates. The air fills with the acrid scent of impatience. Compost and rotten designer perfume. I'm that type of person that ingests other people's tension, so my heart starts to race. I sweat my secondhand anxiety out and plead to no one: *Please stay calm.*

There are five people ahead of me. I take it all in: the tapping of a high-heeled shoe, the exaggerated checking of a watch, the shifting of packages from one arm to the other with a prolonged sigh. The line moves and a woman steps up to the counter with her face mask on wrong. It flops down below her nose like loose pantyhose. She keeps touching her mask. Not to adjust it to cover her nose and mouth, just to touch it, as if she's making a point. Then she slams her giant pocketbook down on the counter and shouts at the clerk: "Do you know how long I've been waiting in this fucking line?" I stew in my damp face mask. I want to puncture her bubble mailers with my claws. Carrier pigeon her entitled yoga face away. *You will meet people like this later in life.* I wish my younger self would have told me how frequent this would be.

*   *   *

IN 2020, A WHITE woman in a California post office was recorded screaming, "Can you just do your job? It's simple," at an Asian American employee, calling them a "chink" multiple times. Realizing she's being recorded by other customers, she says "chink" again—directly at the phone screen recording her. When she says this word in the video, I am transported back to grade school and the corner of a stuffy Jersey classroom where I'm standing with my back against a wall, the pushpins from posters that read "You Matter!" and "Division as Sharing!" digging into my back. A white boy is singing "ching-chong-ching-chong" and pulling at the corners of his eyes. This happens more than once, of course. And with different future variations. Men yelling, "Love me long time!" and "You need some white dick!" from apartment balconies and revved-up cars. Years later, as a 20-something, I will run into that classmate when I'm checking out from Lowe's. Years later, he will scan my light fixtures and then glance at me, the bags under his blue eyes like ejected airbags. He will smile wide, looking me up and down. "Hey, you look familiar. Did we go to school together?" Was he hitting on me? The light fixtures will clang together, percussive brass instruments, in my shopping bag.

In 2022, in a car outside of La Guardia Airport, the driver starts talking to me about the deterioration of American culture. He is an older white man and there's a medley of crosses and pine-scented air fresheners along his rearview mirror. "I heard the Chinese are going to take over the economy. Gonna put us out of business and jobs. The poor kids over there, working in sweat factories. They don't care about them. They don't care about anything. The Chinese are power hungry.

I mean, look at all this corona mess now. All because of them. It's so sad." He looks back at me via the mirror. "You aren't Chinese, are you? You don't look Chinese. Filipino? Thai? Korean?"

This is a leading question, I know; his look is suspicious. I don't want to answer him, but I do. "I'm Chinese American. I was born in Jersey."

"Oh," he says, suddenly careful with his words. "I do like the food. Sweet-and-sour chicken. I'm big on trying all types of things. I make stir-fry myself, you know."

Why did I feel the need to prove my Americanness? Why did I keep talking to him, telling him I grew up in a restaurant? Telling him I was the first in my family to go to college? *They don't care about anything.* He was and wasn't talking about me. I didn't owe him anything. But I was trapped in this car for at least the next half hour.

I called my mother at the start of quarantine in 2020. I told her that I was worried about her working conditions, worried about COVID safety precautions, worried about how much sleep she was getting, worried about her hour-long commute to the mail-processing facility and reckless drivers at night, worried that she worked too much overtime, and couldn't she just reduce her hours? She didn't have to work this much anymore. Steven and I were doing okay in our jobs, we could help her out. And was everyone wearing a mask? Over their nose and mouth? Gloves? Screens? Enough distance? Enough wipes? Enough hand sanitizer? Were the bathrooms clean?

"Don't worry about me! I worry about you. Teaching on the computer sounds bad. No circulation and it's bad for your eyes," she said. "Did you eat yet?" Lay sik jor fahn mei ah? Translation: How are you? Are you okay?

I was 2,935.4 miles away from my mother in Jersey. Because I missed her so much, I looked this up on Google Maps and learned it would take me approximately 44 hours to drive home. The blue route line on the map looked like a vast river. As if I could row my way home, paddle myself amid mud and snow and rain and eye-splinter-ing drought to her doorstep where she would be, hot pot boiling in the kitchen, giant ladle in hand, saying "I just put the fish balls in, so you're just in time."

"I'm going to eat soon, I promise," I told her, staring at my email inbox, which dinged like a doorbell every few minutes. Emails like *I can't find the link* and *best practices for breakout rooms* and *re: climate assessment update*. There was a splotchy, overripe banana on the couch where I was sitting. My back was curled like I was the overripe banana itself, smushing inwards. I wore my wrist brace and kept fidgeting with the Velcro strap, pulling it open and closed, open and closed. The sound was oddly pleasing. Could carpal tunnel care be an ASMR video? Was this my ticket to fame?

"You better eat now," she said. On her end, I could hear muffled voices in the background. "What? I'm talking to my daughter. One minute." I looked out the window and saw my mail carrier, waving hello. I waved back slowly, readjusting my position on the couch.

"Are you busy? Do you need to go?" I asked her. My inbox kept dinging, a xylophone.

"What? No. They're moving me to help with packages, that's why. Too many packages. New station. Let's walk over there together. Mommy will put headphones in."

* * *

THE POSTAL SERVICE HAS an unofficial motto, which origi-nates from Herodotus: "Neither snow nor rain nor heat nor gloom of night stays these couriers from the swift completion of their appointed rounds."

When I'd come back home from college during Thanksgiving break, my mother would take me to the postal facility on Thanks-giving Day to help her hand out meals to her co-workers. She loves feeding people. Even though my father was the chef at the restaurant, we all knew my mother was the *real* chef. She cooked without recipes and measurements and with a deep love for balanced flavors. One time, she brought roasted turkey, fresh corn, mashed potatoes, and some Toisanese cooking too: garlicky long beans and wood ear mushrooms with pork belly. I carried a teeming stack of aluminum food packets and met all her friends, who were starting their workday at 9:00 PM. *Nor gloom of night.* The majority of my mother's co-workers are people of color. Our local facility—which would close down years later, leading to significant layoffs—was massive, and the floors echoed with the sound of machinery, yelling, and blips of garbled announcements (replete with a thick Jersey accent) via the intercom. "Study hard," one of her friends told me, tearing the meat from a crispy turkey leg, as if saying: *We work this much for kids like you.* "Damn," he told my mother. "Jin, this is better than my granny's."

My mother regularly works overtime, especially during the holiday season. Or when her boss begs her to help out, because so-and-so has called out or there's-no-way-we-can-get-to-all-this-mail-can-you-please-come-in? "There's always overtime," she tells me. "If you want to work, the post office will give you work." Her giant work bag is always stuffed with Tupperwares of food, ginger to keep her awake during night shift, Tiger Balm, ChapStick, and Band-Aids. There are always coupons stuffed in there too: 15 percent off at Bed Bath & Beyond, a free Clinique gift bag with purchase, sub sandwich upgrades. Later, when I'd publish my second book, she'd stuff that in there too, to show off to her co-workers. The pages would fill with coupons as bookmarks. "My daughter was in the *New York Times*," she'd say. "Can you believe it?"

My mother's bouts of vertigo were intense. Her equilibrium was off cycle. She threw up and fell over. She was a tea bag spilled open, a rug pulled out from under a spinning world. When I'd express my worries to her, she'd wave me off: "I'm fine, I'm fine." Except she wasn't. I remember talking to her on the phone once when I was feeling nauseous: "Jane, you have to go get checked out. You never know. Remember when I hit my head and blacked out? What if Vinny didn't find me? I don't want that to happen to you." My heart sped up, my eyes nearly fell out of their sockets.

"What?!"

I could see my mother's face on the other side of the phone, squirming because she'd been caught. "Oh, I didn't want to worry you. You were so busy with school and work and writing. I just had vertigo, I'm fine. It was many years ago."

I said it again, this time furious: "Years ago? You have to tell me! You can't not tell me!" I forced her to tell me about it, about how she got so dizzy, she fainted and hit her head hard on the toilet seat. How she lay crumpled there, bruised, bleeding, and unconscious until Vinny found her. When she told me, I felt myself spiraling into my deepest fears, my innermost vortex of terror—even the slightest thought of losing my mother was unbearable.

Her vertigo is seemingly better these days. She stopped drinking coffee and red wine. "I'm telling you, yoga helps," she insists, popping another ginger chew. She knows how to find YouTube videos on her phone now, now that I installed the app. She does yoga every day. During the pandemic, I'd join her on the floor via FaceTime, stretching into downward dog. "Can you feel it!" she says this like a demand. She won't stop saying this until I declare "I feel it!" Via the camera, I can only see her left foot digging into the rug (she insists she doesn't need a yoga mat: too complicated). She makes ginger chews herself, drying out ginger along her kitchen windowsill and dusting them with a kiss of sugar. She likes them stronger and spicier than the store-bought brands. "Zing! You're awake!"

Can overtime have overtime? The pandemic has pushed my mother's and Vinny's hours to the edge. They basically live at work.

I think about the restaurant life, how I slept among those sacks of rice as my mother refilled soy sauce containers. Was it always going to be this way? Living to work? Working to live? "There's too much mail," they both tell me. "Some people don't care. But someone has to care." Twelve-hour, 14-hour days. And so they clock in, our dear essential workers, dreaming of sleep from under piles and piles of mail.

Teaching from home during the pandemic, I sit in the muck of my education.

* * *

YOU DEPEND ON THE postal service. It is the only mail-and-package-delivery system that has the universal obligation to provide service to every delivery point in the U.S.—even the most remote places. The most remote being the "Penguin Post Office" on Goudier Island in Antarctica, surrounded by hundreds of penguins, flapping their tuxedoed flippers.

Neither snow nor rain nor heat nor pandemic. During the pandemic, online shopping skyrocketed. In 2021, the USPS Office of Inspector General reported deliveries of over a billion packages during the last three months of 2020 and continuing customer interest in online shopping. I think about this too, as I guiltily scroll through my secondhand fashion apps, nostalgic for the thrifting hunt. Do I really need that silk dress? From a Vox interview with a postal employee in 2020: "But, yeah, seeing chair covers, Razor scooters, bathroom shelves, hemorrhoid cream, potato chips, cases of energy drinks—just a lot of nonessentials coming through."

Later that year, President Donald Trump blatantly opposed additional USPS funding—funding that would have made the delivery of mail-in ballots easier. Trump was quoted in the *Guardian* (brackets theirs): "If they don't get [extra funding for states and the USPS], that means you can't have universal mail-in voting because they're not equipped to have it." He was also quoted in *Politico* calling the USPS "a joke," but no one I know was laughing. In contrast, Rep. Gerry Connolly emphasized the necessity of supporting the USPS during the pandemic. Connolly on NPR's *All Things Considered*: "The Postal Service has been struggling for 14 years, and it is an essential service we all count on." He continues: "And if the airline industry qualified for assistance, it is time for Congress and the White House to address their needs." During the initial wave of shelter in place, alongside providers in health care, grocery, sanitation, transportation, etc., postal employees were deemed essential. Almost 40 percent of postal employees identify as people of color, with 21 percent identifying as Black.

In the midst of the early pandemic, my mother sends me massive Asian pears wrapped in paper towels, seaweed sesame crackers, and bags of salted pistachios and dried figs because she worries that I don't eat meals between teaching classes (she's right). I shake with joy when I cut open the cardboard, each morsel packed to the brim of this flat-rate Priority Mail package. She knows how to use every inch. I smell the box, as if I could smell her, sharp ginger lingering in each corner. When I slice open a pear, I lick the juice that spills from my hands, marveling at such sweetness.

* * *

WHEN IT'S MY TURN in line at the post office, I go up to the counter. Behind the plexiglass is a clerk, an older South Indian man. He could be my father's age. He immediately apologizes and doesn't look me in the eye as he moves mail into a slot: "I'm so sorry for the wait. Thank you for your patience."

I smile behind my mask and pass him my envelopes like I'm offering a slice of Asian pear. "Sorry for that angry woman before," I say. "How are you doing today? My mom's a postal worker too." He looks up at me immediately, his eyes crinkling into a smile as the customers behind me tap and groan and grumble and pout like, *Is she seriously chitchatting right now?*

"You know, I'm doing okay," he says, laughing, already reaching for the book of stamps he knows I'll order. "Where does your mom work? How's she doing?"

* * *

INSCRIBED INTO WHITE GRANITE at the Smithsonian's National Postal Museum is a poem. The first section reads:

> Messenger of Sympathy and Love
> Servant of Parted Friends
> Consoler of the Lonely
> Bond of the Scattered Family
> Enlarger of the Common Life

Several years have passed since the start of quarantine, and time feels warped, like dipping a hand into a river's unformed canyon. My mother processes next-day delivery mail, change-of-address mail, and midsize packages. There are so many people who need their mail immediately, so many people who can't afford rent, moving. These days, when I call her and ask her how she's doing, she tells me: "You know, the mail has to get there on time. Sometimes it's like mail over people." I think of how hard she's working, how worn her gloves are, how loud the machinery is, churning around her like the Atlantic Ocean we used to kick our sandy feet in. I think about her, over 25 years ago, studying for her postal exam at our kitchen table, the zip codes blurring in her massive textbook. Her blunt pencil poised to answer. *What if I fail,* she must have thought, but out loud she said: "I'm gonna get this one right!" Because she couldn't fail. The restaurant had closed and my father was unemployed. Maybe she felt the apparition of his leaving, fevered against her neck. She needed this job. She needed the employment benefits, her teeth and gums aching. We traded the floppy test book back and forth as I marked up her score. She failed the practice test again. "Again! No! How?" When she passed the real exam, there should have been a bottle of champagne resting on ice. Should have been a bamboo steamer plumped to the max with peachy lotus buns. Someone get this woman a gold congratulations banner! A floral arrangement, no fillers! Maybe we ate a slice of strawberry cheesecake that day to celebrate, or maybe we just washed dishes and went to sleep on pillows that suddenly inflated with benefits.

I think of all the angry people who don't get their mail on time, complaining about their backlogged deliveries. I think about the people who slam their pocketbooks down at the service counter. I think about the impatient men I've dated. The men who would mutter *Do they even see us here* under their breath at a restaurant, but loud enough to hear. My ex-fiancé who would spend hours on the phone about a return order for the tiniest thing like a meat thermometer, because it was *the principle of the matter, they couldn't do their job right.* He would take pleasure in making the customer service agent apologize profusely. "Sir, we will rectify this situation immediately." He would make sure to get his way. He told me he would do this for me, if I ever needed someone to demand what was due to me. He hated it when people took advantage of me. I'm sure he meant it lovingly, like *I will look out for you.* But what it all boiled down to, then and after it ended: he had power and he was going to use it.

"There are no islands in the Postal Service. All of our processes are linked. If you do one well, you're going to do well in another, and another, and another," says Pat Donahoe, the 73rd Postmaster General, on the USPS's blog, quoted in a post that stresses the need for interconnected mail operations, keeping each letter, each parcel moving continuously through the day and night. It's not New York City that never sleeps, it's the postal service. When I call or FaceTime my mother now, she tells me about her postal service family. How her close friend Frank passed away in 2021 and how they used to joke around about his messy haircut. She's known Frank for 26 years— ever since she started working at the USPS, after our restaurant failed and my father left us without child support. The camera is shaking on her phone as she wipes away tears. It's hard to watch her like this. Even during her father's funeral, my mother focused her attention on tending to her crying siblings, reassuring them of his beautiful afterlife. In this unraveling knot of grief, I can't help but cry with her. She tells me she misses Frank, tells me that he shouldn't have been alone when he passed. He was so sick. He should have reached out for help. "I didn't know it was that bad. I walk by his station and he's not there," she weeps. "Frank, where are you?"

Nearly every day for the last 26 years, for upward of 14 hours during the roughest night-shift overtimes, my mother has been with her fellow co-workers. They share every ounce of life: gossip, news, worries, hopes, love. They are that "bond of the scattered family." They come together in the loneliest of times. When my grandfather passed, they sent flowers, food, and cards; they covered my mother's shifts. When we FaceTime in the break room, she moves the phone to show off her co-workers behind her. The video is glitchy; service isn't the greatest in the facility. But I can see them all, opening up their Tupperwares and sharing their bags of chips. "Everyone, say hi to my daughter!" They wave at me from behind their pixelated face masks.

They've never read poetry before, but they go online and order my book. Someone else—their USPS kin—processes my book first-class to their home address. When my second book came out, I held a virtual launch at Elliott Bay Bookstore on Zoom. I was worried my mother wouldn't be able to go; she's never used a laptop before. But she reassured me: "Oh, someone at work is gonna set it up for me!"

As attendees filled the online room, there were names I didn't recognize. In the chat, they tossed heart emojis like horseshoes. "Hi Jane, you don't know me, but I work with your mom! We love you!" There are no words to fully express my gratitude to these strangers, yet not strangers. It would take a million postcards, stamped forever.

At the end of the reading, the host unmuted my mother and Vinny so they could say hi. In the background, I heard a chair move, glasses clink, and Vinny's thick Jersey accent: "Is that Jane? How old is she again?" I imagine my mother nudging Vinny over to the side, even though the camera wasn't on. She called out from the black void. "Can you hear me? I'm Jane's mommy," she declared to an audience of over 100. "I learned the Zoom at work. We're eating plum wine!" From the chat thread:

> _____: Eating wine
>
> _____: Plum wine <333
>
> _____: plum wine is the best
>
> _____: drink well!!!!!
>
> _____: This feels so healing for me to witness.
>
> _____: OMG Jane's family <3
>
> Steven Wong: lol im here

GHOST ARCHIVE

(LOOK AGAIN)

THERE'S SOMETHING EMBARRASSING THAT I CAN'T SHAKE as an immigrant baby. Once, a friend who read one of my essays said: *What's up with all the shame?* It wasn't cool to be worried about your family's honor, not very modern to be concerned about saving face, especially when your face is smeared with last night's gin-laden eyeshadow and some random date's crystalline fluids. Why couldn't I let go of what it means to be a "good Chinese daughter"? Why couldn't I let that word, "daughter," loosen into the sky like some rich girl's "dirty 30" balloon? I type into Wongmom.com: "Are you proud of me?" And then I delete it immediately, backspacing my stupidity. I'm almost 40. Why am I worried about whether or not my family is proud of me? And yet, even though I delete it with the thick fastidiousness of Wite-Out tape, Wongmom.com catches the query. She doesn't just catch it; she scoops it up with netted glee. I flail around, pinkish wet trout.

Wongmom.com asks if I've been at the cemetery lately. "But not like Halloween," she adds.

"I know what you mean!" I say, folding my arms.

In early 2022, I visited my Gung Gung's grave north of Seattle's city limits. My mother, aunt, and cousin Evan were with me. We brought fresh bouquets, mostly marigolds, the flashes of orange and yellow brilliant against this city's shadowy blue weather. I remember walking to his headstone, my flats softening in the wet grass. Just like Yeh Yeh, Gung Gung was so proud of his honorific title. *Look at all of this*, he'd wave his arms around while smoking his old Chinese pipe that looked like an elephant's trunk. *Look!* He was waving at us, his children and grandchildren. *Gung Gung is rich*, he'd declare as puffs of tobacco swirled around him like a carcinogenic cinnamon bun. I thought about taking a picture of his gravestone. I didn't want to forget his name; I hadn't thought to take a picture when I saw Yeh Yeh's name at the hospice facility. I started to take my phone out of my purse. But my aunt admonished me immediately, on the verge of tears: "No! No! Don't do that." I felt like a disrespectful child, slapped on the wrist with a stick. I should have known better. When I was on tour for my second book, I remember a fact-checker asking for my maternal grandfather's name for a magazine interview. A seemingly harmless question to ask. But I couldn't give it to her. How could I explain the wormy depths of my ghostly archive?

"Gung Gung is so happy we're here," my mother said, planting the gleaming marigolds by his grave. She fanned the flowers out neatly like rays. When my aunt cried, my mother held her by the shoulders. "Trust me, Daddy's doing well. I talk to him every day." My aunt took out a plastic package of cleaning wipes and began scrubbing his headstone, the stubborn moss rejecting the Clorox. The fake lemony scent permeated the air. I joked that I could hear Gung Gung's teeth-sucking curmudgeon voice, telling my aunt to stop cleaning, *Chi sin! It's useless, don't waste your time.* Evan laughed, "Yup, Gung Gung would say that for sure."

I grew up celebrating Grave Sweeping Day, also known as Qingming. As a child, I would pile with my family into our busted black-and-white Grand Marquis every year and drive to the cemetery—Celine Dion's "It's All Coming Back to Me Now" always, inexplicably, on the radio. I can't remember exactly when we went, but I knew it was around spring—late March or early April. In Jersey, my father's side would show up to honor my great-grandparents. There were probably 30 of us, including the kids—many of the adults in aprons, straight from working at various restaurants. Flower bouquets, plastic lawn chairs, Peking duck, chicken wings, longevity noodles, wontons, all kinds of bao, rice wine, oranges, incense, funeral money, buckets to burn said funeral money, and lots of shouting at everything and nothing in particular. We went all out for the dead. We wanted the dead to know we were there. We burnt so much funeral money, our ancestors might—for one otherworldly moment—forget the lived poverty of their lives. Wisps of burnt paper filled the air, haunted insects. Once, I mixed up Easter with Grave Sweeping Day because we drew bunnies in puke-colored pastel crayons at school. And so I painted eggshells to offer to my ancestors. I was sweaty in a too-frilled dress, and the colors rubbed off and stamped my arms. Each time I placed a painted egg on the ground, it rolled down the grassy cemetery hill, goddamn Jack and Jill. One of my uncles laughed, chopping chicken leg after chicken leg, the crispy skin shining like new money. "Gweilo," he said, "what kind of daughter doesn't know what to bring for the dead?"

In 2019, I had the opportunity to create a solo art exhibition at the Frye Art Museum in Seattle, entitled *After Preparing the Altar, the Ghosts Feast Feverishly*. A couple of years prior, I had won the James W. Ray Distinguished Artist Award for Washington artists, which changed my life. I don't say this dramatically. I mean, it literally changed my life. I screamed so hard when I found out, completely baffled, that a colleague in a nearby office almost called campus security. I couldn't even talk to the woman on the phone; I was too busy screaming and ugly sobbing and crawling out, at least in part, from under the gargoyled boulders of my college debt. Couldn't Pau Pau agree to a fresh orange now? I could buy her 100,000 oranges, a burgeoning pyramid of sweet citrus. I could go back in time and pay for my mother's fake teeth. I could go back in time and sneak my ancestors fatty pork belly and keep them glossy and alive. The prize also included the opportunity to show at the Frye Art Museum, with the support of a top-notch curation and installation team. I had never experimented with visual art before and I was trilling with the nocturnal forces of terror and play.

I set up an altar at the front of the exhibit, with my ancestors' favorite snacks. They had to be nonperishable items, though (I know it's not supposed to be cute to imagine mice roaming the museum at night, but it is). Among other things, I offered a bucket of Sky-Flakes, rice wine, haw flakes, and golden Taiwanese pineapple cakes. My poems were projected onto the altar, with photographs of my grandparents who had passed into the spirit world. The poems faded in and out, spectral in intestinal pink light. Other sculptural poems included the title piece: a large golden table full of poem bowls with a thank-you-bag chandelier, overflowing with fake oranges and flowers. You had to walk around the table to read the poem; unlike when I co-wrote it with my ghosts in that café, it had no beginning or end. I was nervous about what my family on my mother's side would think, especially my Pau Pau, aunts, and uncles—they all lived nearby in the Central District, Beacon Hill, and Renton. They didn't read my poetry because of the language barrier. This would be the first time they would experience anything creative I'd done.

The opening was packed, buzzing with artists, critics, and community members. Beautiful young Asian American folx took selfies with my neon sign. Was this really happening? I was just a restaurant baby. Wasn't it yesterday that I was squeezing the head of a mop, slopping its tendrils under a dirty booth? What were all these people doing here? I didn't know what to do with my hands, so I used them to shove my face with the free pulled pork sliders and puffed pastries from never-ending trays. And then they all arrived, dressed up in their best clothes, swapping out fish-gut-splattered aprons for pressed button-downs. My mother arrived in the lobby first, followed by her mother, four siblings, nieces, and nephews. She chose her dress because it looked like a painting, with large strokes of bright pink and an asymmetrical hem. I didn't know if I would shame them by making their stories of hunger and poverty so public. Once, I remember walking around Seattle's Chinatown-International District with a random date when I heard *Hang Neoi!* coming from an alleyway. I turned around and it was Gung Gung waving me down. *I think that old Chinese dude is trying to talk to you. You know him?* my date shrugged. Gung Gung had been playing cards outside with some of the other Chinese grandpas. He grabbed my arm and led me over to a park bench away from the game, making it clear with his eyes that my date should go the fuck away. *How can you walk around like that? We can afford clothes with no holes! We're not poor!* he said, pointing at my tights. They were a lacy fishnet pattern. I wanted to tell him it was fashion, or it was true that Urban Outfitters tights were trash and only worth buying on sale. I wanted to tell him anything really, but my language skills failed me once again. I felt the sharp October air smack itself against the lace. *Deoi m zyu, Gung Gung.*

What could language do? What could art do? Messy poems, plastic flowers, clownish eggs? What failures, what odd transmissions. But when my family turned the corner at the Frye Art Museum and saw the photographs by the altar—one image: Gung Gung's bemused face as he sat in my childhood home, relaxing in a puffy jacket in front of a crayon-covered wall—they all held hands and began to cry. It was as if the crowded museum disappeared. Pau Pau went up to the altar and touched each photograph of her husband, her fingertips trembling. In another portrait, Gung Gung's handsome jawline echoed the sharpness of his collared shirt. I could see a security guard head over to stop her, but I shook my head, and they nodded. Let them touch the art, because this wasn't art. This was our lives.

My family didn't say much to me, but they didn't have to. They patted me, smiled through their tears, and just a few minutes after, they said *It's time to go to dinner now, you know where.* I couldn't tell them that I had to stay the whole evening for the opening, that I'd rather suck the milky sea juice out of a shrimp's head. I may not know what to offer, but I can say this: I am listening, trying. Across so much distance and so much warbled life, I am tuned into all that came before and its thick, sugar-gilded deluge. I think I am waking up to my powers.

Wongmom.com pauses to reflect on that evening: "Proudest Mommy day." Blush, blush!

P.S. Look again: the museum staff told me that the pineapple cakes were stolen from the show. They apologized profusely and reassured me they were checking with security about it. They were in the process of replacing them right now. Was there a particular brand I preferred? I laughed so hard: "Oh, I don't care! Maybe that person really needed some pineapple cakes." Or maybe my ghosts finally crossed over and feasted on the buttery tropical fruit with the museum mice, wrappers and all.

11

FINDING THE BLOODLINE

HEART (FIRE):

There is something about cutting up slivers of ginger, little matchsticks of sharp love. I'm making jook for the first time in my life at 36. It's 2020 and the beginning of the pandemic. I pile the ginger up like little molehills on the cutting board. Smashing garlic with the flat of my knife, I think about inheritance and hands. The paper peels away like birch bark, like sheaths of lingerie. My mother's hands: bubbled-up burn scars from the restaurant days, arthritis from sorting endless mail, hardened muscle from farming in the countryside. Mine? Chipped blue nail polish, cracked and dry fingertips, and in my right hand, the constant thundering of carpal tunnel. Regardless, the chopping feels intimate, feels sexy. The scent of ginger and garlic fills the kitchen, creamy and winter warm. I wrap myself in it, in the sharp lines of the knife. I fight the urge to shove the cloves and slivers into my mouth and eat them raw. The spicy heat radiating in my entire throat. I don't know if I'm doing it right. I've called my mother at work twice already. But it doesn't matter: I need jook now. My body is wildly out of balance, shocked by anxiety and panic attacks, and I grasp at the one thing my stomach demands.

"Congee" has been showing up on bougie foodie menus everywhere. I cringe every time I hear it being called "congee," an anglicized version of the Tamil word "kanji." I don't know this "congee." I've only heard it called jook, though it goes by many names in different Asian cultures. As a child, it was my version of chicken noodle soup. Comfort soup, morning soup, healing soup when you're feeling sick or when you've let the haughty ventricles of heartache open and ooze. My mother made the meals we ate during the workday at the restaurant, often jook because it was the easiest. I remember her pouring it, steaming, into a little Styrofoam cup for me, making sure to get a few pieces of my favorite topping—thousand-year-old eggs. I love those salty, funky eggs so much—geodes gleaming in a blur of rice. Once, in high school, I fainted in the hallway from the worst period ever. Right on the linoleum floor, on my way to the bathroom during history class. When I came to in the nurse's office, pain surged through my abdomen like all the fire ants on earth decided *Yes, we'll bite right here!* Because I was a teenager, my thoughts vacillated between *Oh my god, how embarrassing* and *Wait, am I alive?* and *Shit, I missed the test and she'll never let me make it up.* I tried to breathe and unstick myself from that cursed roll of waxy paper on the old gum-colored cot. My mother arrived at the school with a Tupperware of jook, thick and heavy on the scallions. It was so hot, the plastic started to bubble and melt. "Let's go home," she said, holding my sweaty, shaking hand in hers. Blood poured out of me, ruby and viscous and unstoppable. "Eat this in the car."

LUNGS (METAL):

Jook's earliest known documentation occurred during the Zhou dynasty, the longest Chinese dynastic regime, around 1000 BC. In the summer of 2021, Michelle texted me: "Have you heard about the white lady who improved congee lol." A small-business owner made headlines for her take on jook, calling it the Breakfast Cure. A white woman acupuncturist, she gave herself the moniker "Queen of Congee" and wrote an essay on her website originally titled "How I discovered the miracle of congee and improved it." The blog post, since removed, speaks about how she modernized congee with a Western palate in mind. In an interview on YouTube, she calls congee "this sort of weird thing" and that it was her "calling to bring [congee] to America." Words like "improved" and "weird" fit the definition of Orientalism a bit too perfectly. This was a white woman speaking about a dish that swam through my family's veins for centuries and centuries. As if my Ngin Ngin's and Pau Pau's jook was not as good as hers, was deemed strange and alien. And wasn't I American? Wasn't I already eating jook? Immigrants brought this dish to America—not her. Despite being called out by the media for appropriation, Breakfast Cure is still in business, continuing sales. I couldn't help but take a closer look at the current website, which includes the Breakfast Cure's owner in a black cheongsam top posing with her former Chinese professor. What did he think about her Breakfast Cure? In the section where you can gift congee samplers, I found fake Asian-ish names such as Lisa Lu and Boo Bling referenced as example messages. Lisa Lu? Boo Bling? Add Cho Chang from the Harry Potter series and *Sixteen Candles'* Long Duk Dong. As if our names—that which makes us human, individuals—were pure imagination, pure joke. Mashed up, made up, a transliterated amalgamation. Also, as if Asian people would actually eat this? The copy for congee with pineapples keeps suggesting that eating this will transport you to a tropical paradise.

I'm never surprised when white people try to "elevate" or "modernize" Asian food—we all know what those dressed-up words really mean. It's not hard to link them to words like "clean" and "classy," not hard to link them to words like "cheap" and "dirty" to make a distinction, a separation. When I teach Asian American literature, I bring in Aimee Nezhukumatathil's poems, where she creates found poetry out of one-star reviews of the Great Wall of China and the Taj Mahal. From her poem "One-Star Reviews of the Great Wall of China": "The crowds are crazy! / The pollution is crazy! / No one can speak English!" In class, we speak about the Othering, exoticism, and stereotypes in these found poems. We look up negative reviews of Chinatowns across the country. And, unsurprisingly, a common theme always arises, tied to Yellow Peril—the fear of Asians as harbingers of disease and filth. Lifted from a series of Yelp reviews from 2014 to 2016:

> Dirty and disgusting low quality place with peddlers . . .
> Trash strewn everywhere, baskets overflowing, various
> juices on the street, and snot/spit from people of all
> ages. . . . Seriously you cannot go far without someone
> in front or back of you making that hack sound . . .
> People are not friendly, sometime don't try to speack [sic]
> english with you and some time try to sell you shitty
> stuff for expensive prices . . .

The reviews my students find for Chinatowns and Asian family-owned restaurants in the U.S. repeat the same painful racist stereotypes, up to the current day (I invite you to look it up yourself): it's dirty, you'll get sick, and the people are monstrous. "People are not friendly," "snot/spit," "peddlers." These are just a select few, but there are tons of reviews like this, some of which are more subtle in their Yellow Peril tint. The expectation: that these places are meant to serve white tourists and their "experience." That people didn't actually live in these places. My students are always horrified, shaking their heads with vigor, and I shake my head along with them. "It's [insert current year here]," they say. "Like, really?"

Elevated and modernized? When I was interviewed for KUOW/NPR about my Frye exhibit, I went to town on the word "elevated." I broke the heart of every foodie/tattooed white chef in Seattle who always swiped right on me. Over the radio, I said: "Why would you add lobster to something, or truffles? You can't gild a potato." Every time I hear the word "elevated," I feel my stomach lining flare. Which makes me think of how delicious tripe with winter melon is, how I slurped that up as a baby at yum cha on Sundays—the one day our restaurant closed. I love the spongy intestines, the plush chew, how the winter melon soaks up all that succulent brown gravy. The yum cha place (no one in my family calls it dim sum, which is, again, an anglicized term) we went to in Jersey was always full of Chinese people motioning intensely, meat bones and bao wrappers piled on the table like a game of Jenga. When the Chicken Bone Man was alive, he'd always be there walking the entire stretch of the dining room, gathering bones from everyone's table into a bucket. "Am I seeing what I'm seeing?" I'd ask my brother, who giggled so hard, tau foo fah drooled out of his mouth. For the record: the Chicken Bone Man did not work there. There was always the occasional white couple who ordered egg rolls, sesame balls, walnut shrimp, and sipped at their ice water silently. I can imagine their Yelp review now: "We felt ignored, the waiter rarely checked in on us. They barely knew ANY English, and the egg rolls were tiny. It was so loud in there and wild children were running all over the place!!! What a disappointment since we love Chinese cuisine and had wanted to try dim sum for years."

HEART (FIRE):
You're supposed to remove the bloodline. The bloodline is a blood-rich muscle that bisects many types of fish. If the bloodline is bright red, red like the first day of your period, the fish is fresh. Many recipes assume you don't want the bloodline because it has a discernably "fishy" taste. It's not, as they say, delectable. To remove the bloodline, feel for its bones, for red meat. Slice it all out. Cut crosswise on both sides and gently extract the red strip like a game of Operation. It's recommended that you take it out right away, so it doesn't stink up your house—seeping into your cupboards, your rugs, your own body. You don't want to smell like fish, brine along the underside of your wrist, do you?

"Fishy" is often code for nose-scrunched-up-gross. "Fishy" brings me back to the iconic "lunch-box moment"—that moment when Asian kids are mocked for the food their parents made them, heavy on fish sauce and oyster sauce, and whatever funk is the most pungently delicious. Like, umami is cool, but not *that* umami. Nose-scrunched-up-gross as in *What* is *that?* or *Why does it smell like that?* or *Is that rotten?* or *God, how poor are you?* or *Get it away from me* or [just the something-smells-bad face with the sidelong glance, trying to find an escape route]. There were so many variations on this lunch-box theme that I had to stop bringing my mother's food to school. This is why I coveted Lunchables, why I was perpetually obsessed with Pizza Hut and enrolled in their Book It! reading challenge within five seconds of hearing about it. I won so many Personal Pan Pizzas— puffed in oily, crusted glory—that they had to gently tell me to stop reading. The "lunch-box moment" isn't just for grade school either. As an adult, co-workers have asked if I could microwave my lunch elsewhere: *No offense, it's just that it lingers and I'm sensitive, sorry.* How many times have I sniffed my fish-scale sleeve, wondering if the stink was me?

Chef Tiffani Faison on *Top Chef: All Stars* got eliminated because she didn't take out the bloodline of her bluefish. After being eliminated, Faison defended herself in an interview, saying that there wasn't a bloodline to begin with. It was just fat content. She was surprised by the judges' critique. The term "bloodline" itself is particularly misleading. It suggests an internal arterial structure that doesn't exist. It's simply dark meat, just like the dark meat of chicken or turkey—powerful muscle that allows for continuous swimming. And yet, in trash bin after trash bin, bloodlines are discarded. Heaps of thick, blood-rich garbage. One instruction video suggests you feed it to your cat, if you don't want to waste it.

I've never seen my family cut out the bloodline. And I will never see them do such a thing. I can imagine what Gung Gung would say, huffing with annoyance under the soft earth, ladybugs punctuating his point with their shiny shells: *Chi sin! That's meat. How can you waste meat like that?* Growing up, the only fish I ate was whole. Its entire body was steamed on a plate in a wok with ginger, slivered scallions (sometimes a few sprigs of cilantro), oil, soy sauce, and pickled vegetables. That perfectly balanced mixture of smells—fishy aromatics—wakes me the fuck up! Literally. Once, I fell asleep after taking a red-eye from Seattle to Newark, and my mother steaming fish woke me up. I crawled out of bed, drawn to the fish cloud. She always gives me the honor of taking the spine out when we finish one side. I pick it up gently with my chopsticks like pulling out a tick. My family and I eat it all—the fatty bits, the cheeks, the eyeballs, the skin, the tail, the bloodline. The juice too, oozing with sea broth and sesame oil, is perfect over a mound of dimpled rice. We eat it slowly, for fear of swallowing bones, plucked like eyebrows onto a nearby napkin. When we're done, we use whatever is left to make fish head soup, throwing the bits into a tea bag of sorts. When I was little, I remember staring into a fish's little foggy eyeball, a psychic's swirling crystal ball, and thinking, *This fish knows the future.*

What if the bloodline is the most prized and sublime piece of all? What if "fishy" is what fish is supposed to taste like? (Shocking!) What if assimilation is akin to throwing away the bloodline, cutting it out in diagonals—my Toisanese lifted from me in timely movements? What if I want that bloodline, need it, will dig through teeming trash heaps to slurp up its red locomotion? The bloodline, of course, is also your line of descent. It is your ancestral genealogy and all that comes with it. The metaphor is too easy here, but it's also easy to make steamed fish, and I want both.

LIVER (WOOD):

It's one thing to appropriate food cultures and attempt to "discover" exotic dishes like jook with declarations of superior recipes and ingredients, and it's another to make money from it—when white businesses capitalize on and profit from ancestral knowledge not theirs. It happens so often, coinciding with whatever Asian culture is currently trending (i.e., McDonald's 2021 BTS Meal, with South Korean–inspired sauces called "Cajun" and "Sweet Chili," though it's unclear what Cajun has to do with South Korea). There are so many examples, it's impossible to gather them all. Let's not forget the food truck named White Girl Asian Food in Austin, Texas. Via a viral post on the *Angry Asian Man* blog, White Girl Asian Food purports to serve "deliciousness from all over Asia." I'm imagining it had a lot of canned baby corn. Trisha R. wrote on her Yelp review: "Being Asian I thought it would [be] comical. I wasn't expecting much. I ordered the Bahn Mi tacos and the cook actually asked my help in how he should make this. I felt like I was getting punked. Where is Ashton Kutcher? Very disappointed."

In 2016, the *New Yorker* published a poem called "Have They Run Out of Provinces Yet?" which featured Calvin Trillin, a white poet, making fun of various Chinese cuisines in a limerick form of verse (a rhyming form that is meant to be funny, meant to be a roast). Just a few select, cringey lines: "So we sometimes do miss, I confess, / Simple days of chow mein but no stress, / When we were never faced with the threat / Of more provinces we hadn't met." The blatant Orientalist and Yellow Peril use of words like "threat" and "we" vs. "they" are hard to ignore. He keeps returning to this idea of pleasing the white palate: "Long ago, there was just Cantonese. / (Long ago, we were easy to please.)"

There's a lot to unpack here, and I don't want this poem to take up that space. But the mere fact that this appeared in the *New Yorker*— as a poet myself, as a Chinese American poet myself, as a Chinese American poet who grew up as a restaurant baby myself—makes me feel invisible, disrespected, and dehumanized. What kind of person jokes about Cantonese food—the foodways of my family—being out of style? Who was laughing here? How did the editors of the *New Yorker* at that time allow a poem with "they" and "we" to run, as if their readership only included white people as that "we"? And how, most of all, did this poorly written "satirical" poem—even stripped from its ignorant underpinnings—get published? If poems like these were being published in top journals, what hope would there be for me? I think about the epic mound of rejection letters I received for two years after I finished my MFA from Iowa. I moved some of my poems into couplets, to un-weird them, and lo and behold, I finally got a poem accepted. *We were easy to please.* Trillin's "we" expands like relentless mold: white editors, white institutions. In the formative years of my education, change was slow. Change was like a cold, congealed pâté. It wouldn't be until I was rising into a position of (some) power—as a tenured professor—that journal after journal, institution after institution, would be called out for racism, tokenism, toxicity, performative allyship, and resource hoarding. It would take a community—led primarily by queer Black folx—to demand tangible and radical change in the literary world. To demand to not be at the mercy of white editors and board members, but to be the change makers.

In the film *Always Be My Maybe*, there's a scene where Marcus (played by Randall Park) tells celebrity chef Sasha (played by Ali Wong) that she's committing cultural betrayal by catering to white people. He tells her that Asian food isn't supposed to be elevated. That it's supposed to be authentic. Sasha wrestles with that comment. Who is she cooking for? What is her responsibility as a chef? But there it is, that other uneasy word that keeps popping up: "authentic." Growing up, our takeout restaurant had "authentic Cantonese style cuisine" printed on the menu because we were told that magic word would draw in people who could brag to their family that "it was as authentic as you can get." The word "authentic" leaves me with an egg-drop vortex of questions. Who declares something "authentic"? Is "authentic" cuisine also for the Western imagination? Can "authentic" food ever exist in the tumult of migration, capitalism, imperialism, we-have-to-make-do-ism? What happens when you can't get the ingredients you had back in the old country? Can't we add something more lived in, something more fluid? Am I authentically Chinese? What does it mean to be authentically Chinese American? Was it authentic when my mother used zucchini instead of winter melon because it was easier to pop over to her local Safeway than drive 30 minutes to AFC? I think of all the people in my life who are surprised that I am illiterate in Chinese—who point and ask: *What does that say?* And the subsequent: *Oh wow, you don't know Chinese? My [insert family member] did a study abroad and speaks fluent Chinese now [no indication of which specific language].* At the end of the day, at the end of the restaurant shift (which is all the shifts), I'm not interested in "elevated," "modernized," and "authentic" food. I'm interested in the stories food tells, sauced in gurgling comfort, marrowed connection, and fermenting bloodlines.

SPLEEN (EARTH):

For a long time, up until 2020, I didn't cook. Or rather, I barely cooked. I cooked basics for myself like pasta, eggs, and roasted vegetables. But I didn't *actually* cook and certainly not for others. And, other than cracking an egg and throwing some scallions into Shin Ramyun, I didn't cook Asian food. Ever since I was little, my mother has made me promise to never work in a restaurant. Even when I begged her to let me take on a waitress job as a teenager, because tips!, she refused to allow it. The restaurant life is hard, she reminded me—physically and emotionally. The long hours, the heat, the prep, the close quarters, the rude and dismissive customers. I did prep, a lot. You can't be a restaurant baby without working, for free of course, at the restaurant ("Your friends said what? Allowance? BAHHAHAHAHAHAH chi sin!"). Classic prep: folding wontons, cutting string beans, and cleaning that cursed black poop vein from shrimp. I was a well-seasoned sous-chef.

My mother would shoo me out of the kitchen, even when I begged to learn as an adult. I was always cooked for, in a language of love I blanketed around me like the softest white sugar sponge cake. Days before I'd come home to Jersey, my mother would tell me the week's entire menu over the phone. She always plans it all out, knowing my favorites of hers: tomato and egg, pan-fried eggplant, chicken with garlicky scallion sauce, watercress soup, steamed whole fish. I let my mother baby me, feeding me with her fatty love, one glistening rice grain at a time. I got into college because of a personal statement about her seasoned wok, which shines like a beetle's shell. Her wok as armor, as ardor, as a door to another world. She cooks everything in there, including spaghetti and meatballs for Vinny (which have a pinch of soy sauce). Maybe her wok is her ancestral portal. It's as if you can reach your hot hand into that steel and come out the other side into a persimmon grove. My Asian American friends and I joke that we begin the day by talking about what we're going to eat for dinner. While eating one meal, we're always scheming up another. I didn't know how to cook, but I did know how to eat.

Beyond my family, several of my ex-boyfriends cooked for me. They tended to my stomach like their existence depended on it. They watched me eat, spooning more noodles into my bowl and scooping that piece that fell on the floor. I ate it, dirt speckles from the floor and all. They swelled with disgusted love. They declared it a marvel—how could I eat more than them? Once, some guy I was seeing wanted to cook me a seven-course bacon meal, and he did—with the final course being candied bacon and a dollop of vanilla ice cream. I ate everything slowly, carefully, imagining the fat lining my organs like a frosted lake. When he kissed me at the end of the meal and tried to move me into the bedroom, I remember thinking I didn't like him. In fact, I wasn't attracted to him at all. I just wanted the meal. And so I pushed him away and said my stomach hurt. When he left, the whole apartment smelled like bacon, and I furiously opened the windows, letting the mossy air in. It wasn't balanced. My lips felt parched by grease. I left to get some lettuce and lemons from QFC to cleanse myself.

KIDNEYS (WATER):

When I was a toddler, Ngin Ngin would peel grapes for me. This slow and lavish act of taking away any bitterness was her way of telling me that my life—this life—would be sweeter. The naked grapes would rattle in a red plastic bucket by her sandaled feet, tan and wrinkled. She'd pour them out into a small bowl for me, translucent marbles of plump care. This is how she liked to spend her time as I played. She'd eat the peels, of course. You can't waste that. She never ate the grapes themselves. She watched me with glee as I plopped a seafoam jewel into my baby mouth, *Mmm ho hek!* They were so juicy, it was as if I became a bursting ocean Ngin Ngin swam in.

LUNGS (METAL):

The early days of the pandemic were reminders that this country was full of fear, inequality, and greed. Shelves were empty of rice, beans, toilet paper, bread, and flour. Hand sanitizer and disinfecting wipes were long gone. People who could afford to stocked up and up and up, leaving nearly nothing for others, and this left my stomach feeling like a pitted olive. Food insecurity soared, particularly impacting Black and Brown neighborhoods. A friend of mine texted me a photo of a nearby grocery store where there was literally nothing left except a single sad-looking pineapple, its scales pruning from rot.

What would I wipe my ass with? I kept telling myself: *It's okay, this is in your blood.* I was raised to be resourceful. I was raised to eat what most people throw away. To dry and reuse paper towels, plastic bags, and cookie tins. I did not panic. I did not go out there and stock up. I split two-ply into one. Over the coming months in Seattle, my aunts and uncles—the majority of whom work in the restaurant and grocery industries—were laid off. We worried about how to get food to Pau Pau. She waved us away, *Don't worry, I'm old, I don't eat much.* The Chinese businesses my family worked at were being boarded up one by one. They started to pool together resources, scrounging up whatever was left (no one had a savings account). My aunt sold face masks she sewed, and my uncle drove for Lyft. The two older siblings—my mother and my eldest uncle—helped out the most, as postal employees. I begged them to take my money, but my aunts and uncles shush-shamed me away. They wouldn't take money from someone who still sits at the kid's table.

Meanwhile, according to *Crosscut*, a white nationalist group posted stickers all over the Chinatown-International District with phrases like "America first" and "Better dead than red." Pau Pau told everyone she was afraid to go outside, even to walk. Her elderly friend had been attacked in the street, pushed down by a stranger who yelled something at her. Her friend was okay, but she broke her arm. Still today, Pau Pau rarely leaves her apartment in the city. She peers out of her window, the wet air offering a tiny breeze. As I'm writing this in 2022, my mother calls me to tell me that my uncle was pushed on the street by a stranger near Uwajimaya in the International District, left unconscious and bleeding in the parking lot. He was alone and no one in my family knows how long it took for someone to call 911. He didn't see it coming; he still doesn't remember what happened or if the person said anything. He suffered a severe concussion and though he's stable for now, we're all waiting to hear updates from the neurologists and physical therapists. My aunt feeds him home-cooked broth, one fearful sip at a time. Lots of Chinese medicinal herbs and tonics. Pounds of goji berries, ginseng, ox bones. He keeps throwing up; he doesn't have an appetite. He is so dizzy and so frustrated that he can't go back to work.

It's hard to explain how helpless I feel sometimes. How can I dress and heal the throbbing wounds of grief and violence? This *was*, *is* real. This *was*, *is* immediate. This *was*, *is*, will be. In 2022, a white man allegedly shot and killed a Chinese delivery employee because the restaurant shorted him on duck sauce in an order placed many months prior. My friend Anastacia and I text each other often: "tell me what you ate today." It's not a question anymore, it's a demand. Like, *Oh, you didn't eat yet when you got this text? You better eat and show me the proof, so I know you're okay.*

It's hard to not be afraid. But we have to eat. Everything became a clear broth: I needed to learn how to cook.

SPLEEN (EARTH):

Once a vegetable or fruit is harvested, it becomes detached from the sources that gave it life. In other words, it starts to die. Cell walls begin to break down, impacted by factors like air, temperature, and light. Microorganisms and molds lick up the water within, fueling decay. Since landfills don't have conditions ripe for healthy decomposition, there have been reports of 25-year-old grapes.

For years, I was obsessed with watching videos of fruit rotting on YouTube, particularly oranges. I couldn't stop thinking about Pau Pau refusing my fresh oranges, how she unpeeled the rough, leathery skin of an almost-bad orange to eat. How the vesicles started to dry up, parched and flavorless like a ruined glue stick. I wrote a poem, "What Is Love If Not Rot," where I stay with a rotting orange, up to 85 days: "how can I—liquefy by 45 days, wolfish in citrus murk—ever-shrinking like every grandparent I've ever held hands with—at 85 days, how to hold this slush of glittering bees—trapped in no worldly amber."

I am that person who thinks that the compost bin is beautiful, in all its swirls of color (jade mold, chocolate slime—why is no one hiring me to name nail polish?), surprising texture, and piquant death. The very fact that I am privileged enough to watch something go to compost is miraculous. I have to admit, I struggle to compost. Meaning I have this habit of using almost all of a vegetable, leaving one-eighth of a sliver just in case I might need it for something. It's this constant act of saving and forgetting, saving and forgetting, the package of meat gone boulder-gray sour, cement oxidation. I still struggle with not being able to eat something, rinsing the black goop off cilantro stems, scraping the fuzzy mold off bread. There have been too many times where I'd insist *it's still good*, with someone else (not in my family) shaking their head *NO*. I google "is it okay to eat" often, sticking my nose deep into the still-there thing. How was I supposed to tell if something went bad? Was that a "bad" smell? I mean, it was just fermenting, right?

I can't stop thinking about rot and love. About trashed bloodlines and ancestral knowledge brewing in my stomach lining. Where does this come from, my devotion to not waste? To save food at all costs? And was it a marvel that I ate more than my ex-boyfriends, or was I voracious for some other uncanny reason? What was I hungry for? What gustatory ghosts did I inherit?

Mao Zedong's favorite dish was red-braised pork. The dish is Hunanese, where Mao is from. Mao's nephew Mao Anping said: "Men eat it to build their brains and ladies to make themselves more beautiful." The Shaoshan communist party secretary reported to NPR that Mao devoured two bowlfuls of red-braised pork each day to ensure his intellect remained in tip-top shape, feeding his vision. The dish is overtly succulent—featuring huge chunks of pork at one and a half inches long. As if the decadence of meat isn't enough, the dish is centered around its rich red color, which comes from caramelized sugar and soy sauce. Due to hours of braising, the sauce is intense and thick like the interior of a molten lava cake.

I keep coming back to my family's history of hunger again and again. This hunger refuses to loosen its hold on me, gripping my organs. My family lived, or rather some ancestors didn't live, during the Great Leap Forward, when an estimated 36 million people died. This estimate is often higher; the *Independent* states that 45 million people perished. As I researched, it became harder and harder to reconcile the personal and the collective history. In the countryside, under the watchful eye of the Red Army, forced labor and daily torture were commonplace. Local officials consistently overfulfilled their grain production quotas—declaring surpluses that simply didn't exist. Propaganda posters during this time showed bountiful bumper crops, including squash larger than the people themselves. Millions of people starved to death as the grains that were harvested rotted away in facilities or were exported abroad. Despite blatant widespread starvation, Mao was determined to convince other countries of his successful agricultural plan. Officials pointed to bad weather conditions as the culprit and did nothing. A year earlier, in 1957, Mao had said: "We are prepared to sacrifice 300 million Chinese for the victory of the world revolution." And just a few years after the Great Leap Forward, Mao launched the Socialist Education Movement and then the Cultural Revolution, shifting the disaster of famine in another (disastrous) direction.

I spent the majority of my second book of poems and art installation work on this history of mine—something that took me almost 15 years to engage with after learning about the Great Famine in a Chinese politics class in college. In that classroom at Bard, we were watching a documentary on the Cultural Revolution, and there was a brief segment on the famine. The propaganda posters of children standing on wheat, the images of pots and pans being melted, the dates. The dates. When I put the dates together, when I realized Gung Gung's family didn't "disappear" as he said, when he was adopted by an older man in the village whose family also "disappeared," when this wasn't homework, when this was my bloodline. My body compulsively reacted. I ran out of that classroom and had a panic attack in the bathroom, heaving tears as thick as wheat. I knew my family had survived poverty, but I didn't know this. No one talked about it. Why speak about something so horrific, so inhumane, when you survived what your beloveds didn't? *Look at all of this*, Gung Gung says instead. *Gung Gung is rich.* I didn't come back to class for two weeks. My family had starved to death. Their bodies, their real bodies, perished from the bloated pit of nothing to eat. And my mother grew up on the edge of famine, hungry for bare nutrients. And I grew up gluttonous, spooning peeled grapes into my greedy mouth. In just a few generations, so much had changed.

Yang Jisheng's book *Tombstone*, banned in China of course, was brutal to read as I researched for *How to Not Be Afraid of Everything*. I honestly couldn't fully read it because my body reacted with psychic terror once I opened the book—arrhythmia, breathlessness, tightness. I could read only brief selections at a time. Yang wrote about the visceral realities of starvation, cannibalism, widespread death, violence, and corruption. His own father had died as a result of the famine in 1959. He wrote about villagers being tortured or executed for reporting the actual harvest data, and for trying to get food that they desperately needed—either by harboring the small amounts that remained or pilfering scraps. Millions took their own lives. Parsing through archived files, Yang reported that 22 million tons of grain were left to rot in public granaries while famine spread across the country.

What happens when your archive is a ghost? I couldn't possibly ask my grandparents about this. It would be completely disrespectful of their chosen silence. I wanted to honor their survival, their determination to live and be here—in the plentiful present before they passed into the spirit world. Instead, I listened deeply to what they said and didn't say. When my mother said she grew up vegetarian when I was dating a vegetarian, I listened—*An egg for my birthday!* When she used to nurse a single yam all day. When Gung Gung had his first battle with cancer and said he wanted to die, I listened when my mother revealed to me that his adopted father had committed suicide. Little bits and pieces of my history bobbed up from the murky depths of the ocean floor. For years, I listened so deeply, I felt tectonic plates shift underneath me.

I think about Mao eating red-braised pork during the famine, holding a gleaming chunk in his chopsticks like a flag. Can you imagine? I did what Gung Gung asked me to do, the one thing he's ever asked of me: I ate and ate and ate. I stuffed my mouth with the food I was given until every inch of me swelled like a scallion-scented balloon. From "When You Died," which is a series of epistolary poems, or letters, to my lost ancestors: "I have this strange feeling. / I've written this before. I've always been writing to you, even before I was born." And it did feel like that. When I finally spent time with this bloodline, from starvation to gluttony, time collapsed. I had this urge to go back to feed them, to transcend the boundaries of time and space. From another section of that poem, watching deer outside of my home in the Pacific Northwest: "I want to slice their bellies open, to gather this otherworldly meat. To feed you until your eyes shine back and the slugs recede from your mouth." I still have this desire in me, every time I eat almost-rotten cilantro. Or when I devour an entire pizza by myself. Whenever I see someone leave uneaten food at a restaurant. Whenever a waiter comes by to try to take my plate and I yank it back like a snapping turtle—there was still a morsel left. I am feeding my ancestors. I am certain of it. With every soup dumpling, every taco, every cheesecake, every yam, every bowl of jook. Everything I eat is a reminder that I am alive. I have no choice but to let food haunt me.

HEART (FIRE):

Tommy Pico writes in *Feed*: "Being protective / of yr recipes is only natural. Things get stolen." I remember being protective of my favorite childhood dish—Cantonese-style tomato and egg over rice. This was home cooking. Deceptively simple, but difficult to execute. You'd rarely find it in a restaurant. My mother's craving for tomatoes when she was pregnant with me couldn't have been a coincidence. She devoured tomatoes, eating heart after heart, knowing that red foods heal heart pains. Such sweet, acidic preventative care for my future of constant heartbreak. When this homestyle dish appeared in a major food magazine, I felt a surge of bursting tomato rage. I thought about white chefs making their version of the dish. I imagined them selling it as fusion cuisine, as chic "peasant" food. Of them calling it the "Chinese" spaghetti sauce. Ezra Pound's mantra of "make it new," meaning stealing what's very old and not yours. "Elevating" and "modernizing" the dish but promising to keep its "authentic" roots. Pulpy tomato seeds spewed out of me, terrified that this dish—something I craved before I was even born—would no longer be ours.

LIVER (WOOD):

During the early days of the pandemic, my hair grew longer and longer. I could feel grease slicking down from my crown, anointing my white hairs. The unspooling shine of it was unstoppable, this matted riverbed of black-gray hair. I ran my hands through it, my seaweed strands, and wondered if my hair could coat a pan on high.

I come from grease. I've scraped grease like old wallpaper from pans and griddles and plates. I've tasted grease, its tingling lacquer, on my peppered tongue. I've saved grease—warm and congealing—a galactic buttery balm to use for later. I like the fat, the spackle. My mother drains grease in brown paper bags, splotches like continents. My Pau Pau has a grease tin, repurposed again and again, layered like a trifle cake. A spooned dollop to start a new meal. To save fat that was so rare just a generation ago. Pau Pau begged for grease, for fat, for anything really, in a time of bone-dry bones. I grew up in a restaurant where customers stood behind the counter, saying to me, "I don't want grease." I was 12 years old. Were they speaking about the food? Or about me?

KIDNEYS (WATER):

In 2020, food critic Helen Rosner published an essay in the *New Yorker* called "The Joylessness of Cooking." In it, she writes about making dishes like Sichuan-style cumin lamb and slow-roasted per-nil asado. She declares how bored she is, how she enjoys cooking in theory, but in reality she's so sick of it. I can't help but wonder if being bored while cooking is a privilege. The meals that Rosner mentions, in her boredom, are notably ethnic. An exotic gustatory distraction from the dailiness of the pandemic, as if someone could travel while being in lockdown—a foodie tourist right in one's own home. I can't imagine my mother telling me she was bored of cooking Chinese food because that's just what she does. And during a time of very real food insecurity, how could you declare being sick of cooking decadent lamb and pork? Whenever I'd flop around as a preteen in the summer, crying about how utterly bored I was, my mother would snap back at me. *Boredom*, my mother always said, *is for rich people*. I was not allowed to be bored.

While Rosner was sick of cooking, I was finally learning to cook. When I made jook for the first time, the smell of rice toasting along-side ginger and garlic was warm, soft, and enveloping. When I poured in the broth, which I'd made from chicken bones and vegetable scraps, I kept thinking: How would all this liquid evaporate? How would it thicken? I could see my fear of failure growing like slime mold, and immediately tried to push that fear—of whether I was good enough, "authentic" enough—away. I just let the jook go, trusting in my sense of time: I listened to the humming simmer, I breathed the grains in like a steamy bath. I let it cook. It did its thing. I scrolled through Instagram and watched houseplant videos. I stirred sometimes. It thickened to that glorious soupy spackle I needed in order to see and feel clearly. My anxiety loosened from me in that pot. That first time, I added dried Chinese black mushrooms and scraps of chicken thighs and a single thousand-year-old egg. It was luscious. I ladled it into bowls, topped with scallions and white pepper and the tiniest splash of soy sauce. Since we were in lockdown, I shared some servings of soup via porch stoops. I also sent my mother and brother a picture.

My mother hearted it from night shift, said it looked pretty good and that she wished she could taste it. My brother, surprisingly, called me. "Wanna know something weird?" he said. "I just made jook for the first time today too." It was weird and it also wasn't. We are cosmically connected, after all. Or, across all this distance, maybe we were both in need of healing at the same exact time. When I asked him for a photo, he said he ate it too fast.

As I ate the jook, creamy and soothing, I thought about how I could finally feed those I love. I could make jook for my grieving friends, for the fight and exhaustion ahead. In inheriting this, in my mother finally talking to me about her recipes (which, of course, aren't really recipes—just generally *this, that, little bit, throw in, see how it tastes*), I felt like I could do something. I could take this soup to Seattle, once lockdown was over, and share it with Pau Pau. To make basic jook, you don't need much. At its simplest core, it's just rice and water. My family knows that. With much of my Toisanese gone, this was a new language I could unfurl. Maybe, just maybe, Pau Pau would leave her apartment and eat it with me on a picnic bench at Sam Smith Park nearby. I could spoon her the gelatinous egg. I could keep her safe.

LUNGS (METAL):

I spent some time at a writing residency in Butte, Montana, in 2021, eager to find out more about the famed "oldest continually family operating Chinese restaurant in America," the Pekin Noodle Parlor. Having opened its doors in 1911, the Pekin stands as one of the few remaining vestiges of Butte's Chinatown, which used to be bustling with immigrants. The owners, the Tams, were from the same province my family is from—Guangdong. Though, unlike my family, who came to the U.S. in the 1980s, the Tams emigrated in the 1860s. For over a century, their family served Chinese American food to those living in this historic mining town: chow mein, chop suey, and egg foo young. Not much has changed since then—including the menu.

When I visited, the restaurant was packed and full of white people. I looked around desperately to see if there was another Asian person. Where were the restaurant babies? I wanted so badly to meet Jerry Tam, who owns the restaurant now, but couldn't find him. I sat at a booth—a privacy booth—with my friend and former Missoula room-mate Dawn, surrounded by salmon-pink walls and a paper lantern. We ordered iced teas and barbecue pork with hot mustard. As we caught up, I was struck by how out of place I felt, despite the restau-rant connection. I couldn't help but notice people looking at me, like I was a real Chinese person here in Butte—a relic from Chinatown's past. But mostly, I felt out of place because I was not in the back of the house, not in the hissing heat of the cacophonous kitchen. It was strange to be a customer.

At the Mai Wah Society Museum nearby, housed in the Wah Chong Tai building and the Mai Wah Noodle Parlor building, I wandered the exhibits and preserved spaces. "Feel free to peek into anything," the person at the front desk said. "Oh, and the cat, she's friendly." This calico cat, which I'm pretty sure was someone rein-carnated, took me on a tour, starting with artifacts that had been in existence during the Chinese Exclusion Act. Her tail flicking back and forth, she led me through each dusty room, each secret crevice under each creaking step. She led me to places that felt oddly familiar: the tiny "storage" room where workers slept and the till at the medic-inal shop, which was lined with thick jars of herbs and a receipt pad. We stopped in front of old Chinese calendars the color of tea, pinned up with rusty nails. Was this cat Chinese?

I had come to Butte to research the Pekin, to trace the lineage of Chinese American restaurants in the U.S., delving into the different lives of other restaurant babies. But I found something else that res-onated with me, something I still can't help but be drawn to. Before we went to the Pekin, Dawn made a joke about her partner's dog looking like the Auditor, and I asked her what she meant. "Oh, you don't know?" she laughed. "Wong, you have to see this. He's called the Auditor because he comes when you least expect it." Dawn pulled up photos on her phone, and there he was: a massive, ghostly Puli in a barren wasteland. The Auditor lived in the toxic dumps and old mine roads outside of the Berkeley Pit—which was deemed a Superfund site in the 1980s—for over 17 years. I couldn't believe it. I zoomed into photos of his tangled white hair. Where were his eyes? Once an open-pit copper mine, the Berkeley Pit is nearly 2,000 feet deep, teeming with poisonous materials and heavy metals like sulfuric acid and arsenic. It has roughly the same pH as gastric acid. In 2016, over 3,000 snow geese died in the Pit due to exposure to toxins. When I visited, you could hear the sci-fi sounds of bird determent from the speakers, buzzing and spinning and fake cannoning. The cavernous pit itself was almost beautiful, a serene baby blue. As I was leaning against the railing, a strand of my hair fell in, and I imagined a cartoon sizzling sound. People first encountered the Auditor in 1986, wandering the mine. He, quite simply, shouldn't have survived. Before the Auditor died, tests conducted by an environmental engineer revealed that his fur contained 128 times the expected amount of arsenic.

Despite it all, the Auditor lived a long life and died in 2003. During his days in the Pit, he wouldn't let anyone touch him. I think about the Auditor, refusing to leave this place he made his home—no matter how toxic and inhospitable. Somehow, when no creature could survive there other than microbes, the Auditor lived. "I don't even know what to say," I told Dawn. "I love him so much." I asked almost every person I met in Butte, all of whom were generous and had working-class roots, about the Auditor. They told me about his commemorative bronze statue and guessed how heavy a single dread-lock of the Auditor's might be. After leaving Butte, and now still, I can't stop thinking about this ghostly dog. I keep zooming into his photographs, each grainy pixel of matted hair radiating.

There's this one photo where the Auditor is standing by a pipeline in the desolate rocky space on the edges of the Berkeley Pit—another planet. He almost blends into the tan dirt. What was he looking at? Where did he come from? How did he spend his days? And most importantly, what did he eat?

HEART (FIRE):

Ever since I started to make jook, I can't seem to stop. After I make a big pot of it, the whole house is perfumed with rice and aromatics and I can't help but feel pride in this very Chinese scent. Even though I've made other heritage dishes, leaving my bao dough in the just-run dryer to rise, this is what I keep coming back to. Healing food, filling food, food that is both poetry and medicine. Chinese cuisine, in all its different regional approaches, is centered around balance, harmony, the elements, and the body: the heart (fire), the lungs (metal), the liver (wood), the kidneys (water), and the spleen (earth). Whenever someone got sick in my family, it wasn't pills that we looked for, it was ginseng, vinegar, dragon fruit.

When I packed up my things to leave my ex-fiancé, he tried to pressure me into buying his mattress. He accused me of damaging his property with my period stain while we were together. He demanded that I redress the damage and pay him for my blood. He demanded that I scrub it out, taking before and after photographs to document. This was the same mattress he had slept on with another woman while we were dating. I had shared this bed with another woman, alternating weeks or maybe days, and neither of us knew until we did. And here he was, demanding payment for literal blood. Blood he couldn't even prove was mine. I felt disgusted. I felt unearthed, unbalanced, sick. I had planned a future and a family with this person. How could this be? How had I found myself here?

I didn't reply. I thought back to when I fainted from my period in high school, how eating jook in the car immediately eased my aches, how my grip on the car door loosened with each spoonful. When I got those toxic emails (yes, plural) about the mattress, I decided to cook. I started to chop ginger and garlic. I started to wash the rice, swirling my hand into the milky water until it became clear and clearer. I turned on the heat to boil water for tomatoes—the couple small romas I had on hand. My mother taught me to quickly dip them in boiling water, to make them easier to peel. My hands shook, my breath wavered, my period was on the verge of starting its flood of being alive. I wasn't hungry. I had no appetite and wanted nothing. But I knew I had to feed myself. I had to feed the blood that has no shame, that loved even in leaking grief. I had promised my grandparents and my ancestors. I had promised more than my survival. Fuming with fire, I ladled the tomatoes in slowly. Their skins began to split and curl like tissue paper. Even if I didn't want to, I had to start with the heart. My hands were hot with this cardinal knowing. I was always the one the heart wanted.

WONGMOM.COM
(FERTILIZER)

WONGMOM.COM IS PASSIONATE ABOUT FERTILIZER. IF SHE could gild her website with fertilizer, she would—a mosaic of eggshells around the URL's border. When I ask Wongmom.com what to do about people who bully and manipulate me, she tells me: "Make fertilizer!" Her special elixir: mixing shrimp shells with fresh orange peels. Mix them with lukewarm water and wait for a few months. Pour this fertile brew into your soil and compost, and let the magic happen. When composting was labeled "eco-friendly" and trending with fancy steel bins and worm bin recipes, my mother shrugged. She'd been burying scraps in the yard her whole life. Once a farmer, always a farmer.

My mother sends me a video of her garden in full bloom. It's so verdant that it's hard to tell which vegetable is which: a tangle of tomatoes, a bouquet of shiso, mint, and basil, all the greens you can ever imagine in their darkest, leafiest, crunchiest glory. There's lotus root and kohlrabi and Chinese broccoli and zucchini and eggplant and figs and carrots and the list goes on. Her garden spills over and deer paw at the fence with furious desire. They try to stick their tongues through the grooves, and it's cruciferously vulgar. Each vegetable has its own zone, but they all grow wildly—the fronds of one plant linking to another, making a pinky promise. She shares her bounty with her co-workers at the post office, the fleshy pink interior of figs shining under fluorescent light in the break room. My mother has a knack for sending me videos like this when I'm having tough days. The day my mother sent me this video, my sciatica had flared up like a poorly threaded needle and I'd received yet another anxiety-inducing message from my ex. I saved the video of my mother's Jersey garden on my phone to watch again, for future tough days.

I currently have around 80 houseplants, some of which are over a decade old. I started getting into the habit of purchasing plants off Facebook Marketplace, from college students who can no longer take care of them. I scoop up sad discount plants from Fred Meyer too, thirsty and dying on a store shelf. I bought this one massive elephant ear (Alocasia 'Regal Shield') from a college student; it was most certainly not thriving. Usually velvety, its leaves were crispy and brown. I repotted it with the tenderness of changing a baby, spooning dirt around its hungry roots. Within a week, a new leaf started to unfold, so glossy it looked like spun silk. Whenever a new leaf starts to open like a Pirouline cookie, I do a cheerleader move, my arms pom-pom out. New growth! New growth! My mother's indoor plants resemble a glorious jungle too, her fiddle leaf growing horizontally now, having hit the ceiling. *It wants to keep going,* she says, *I can't stop it!*

I think about fertilizer. About the intense pungency of shrimp shells and orange peels, and the loud orange of such nutrients—a color most people find ugly. And I think about being called "intense" by many of my exes. Everything about me was "too much." How they always seemed to want less of me: less plants, less time for me to write, less discussion of race and feminism, less with all its hissing sibilance. I keep thinking about being stunted, about growth in reverse—contorted in past boyfriends' images of me, a pleasing and curated bonsai tree.

These days, I live alone, in a place right on a lake. On my new porch, I leave a plastic water jug of shrimp shells and orange peels, rotting in the generous sunshine. My neighbors must think I'm disgusting. This putrid slush, freshened slightly by fruit, will be what saves me. Or at least I hope it will. I sow seeds into planter boxes: some bok choy my mother gave me, some holy basil Nick gave me. The dirt clings to my nails like cake crumbs, soft and delicious. My dog tries to bury his yak cheese treat in it. Together, we sit on the porch and watch massive egrets swoop fish into their streaming gullets. Then he jumps into the lake to fetch his ball, a repetitive motion that gives him so much panting joy, and I vow to be that happy.

During a writing conference in Boston in 2013, I was hanging out with my friend Sally. We were at a Kundiman event uplifting Asian American literature and dressed to the nines, of course. I was wearing my mother's vintage white fur shawl and warm red lipstick. As we talked, I felt a tap on my fur shoulder and turned around: it was Marilyn Chin. She was gorgeous in a satin bomber jacket, her hands on her hips. She looked at me and Sally, petting my mother's fur. "Are you wild girl poets?" she asked us.

We looked at each other. "Yes! That's us!" Though we didn't know exactly what Marilyn was asking, we knew. When I met Sally in 2012, we were crossing paths on the stairs; we didn't know each other, but we knew each other's poems. And just like that, stopped in our midstair tracks, drawn to each other's creative orbits, we became wild girl poets together. Being a wild girl is about resistance, about taking risks, about not being afraid of being too loud or too quiet. It's about listening closely to what moves underneath, about cultivating your own power and the power of the people you love deeply. It's about fertilizing community, one fecund orange jug at a time. I want to grow and guzzle the flora myself. Wongmom.com reminds me I have farmer blood in me too and that it's time to get dirty.

素香 素香

素香 素香

素香 素香

素香 素香

12

ASTONISHED ENOUGH?

I write. I write you. Daily. From here.

—THERESA HAK KYUNG CHA, *Dictee*

MAYBE POETRY WAS THE PORTAL THROUGH WHICH MY POW-ers *came alive.* Sometimes I sit in the bathtub, the water so hot it stamps my ass red like a medium-rare steak. I lie there, letting the Epsom salt dissolve around me. I'm a boiling pot with a heaping scoop of salt. They say to always season your water for pasta like the ocean. I twist back and forth in this gracious sea, the creaks and cracks of my body unleashed in submerged quiet. I don't have a pen. I don't have a notebook. But it is here that I am writing, lines looped around in my brain like coils of clay. Poems fall out of me in the bath, each syllable sloshing. What arises out of this hot murky water, half-formed. I slough off caesuras like curls of dead skin. I lie like that for about 20 minutes before something else demands my attention—grading, teaching prep, organizing readings, drafting a letter demanding living wages for graduate students, dirty dishes, replying to a problematic colleague, academia red tape, heaps of laundry, walking the dog, persistent bills, a vengeful ex. When I pull the stopper, water gulps downward, a literal portal. I arise from the bath drowsy, plump as a harbor seal. Sometimes I write lines and ideas down afterward. But sometimes I let them leak away from me and trust them to return.

Did I write a poem that day? Did I write? Maybe I was always writing. Before I was born. Before language could exist. Before opening my mouth. Before touching paper, before "I" became a tangible thought, a declaration of existence I had been taught to erase for years. How did I become a poet? What does it even mean to be a poet? From Audre Lorde's "Poetry Is Not a Luxury": "Poetry is not a luxury. It is a vital necessity of our existence. It forms the quality of the light within which we predicate our hopes and dreams toward survival and change, first made into language, then into idea, then into more tangible action." I didn't become a poet in school. If anything, much of my formal education pushed me away from the roots of poetry. I became a poet from my mother, from her own powers of lyrical divination. I became a poet from my ancestors before that, from the poetry of freshly cut scallions, the interior slime spicy along our tongues. Poetry as synesthesia. Poetry as what moves within us, pulled out with a fishing lure. I also wrote from the absence of those scallions; I became a poet due to deprivation. I needed to fill voids and plant gardens. Poetry pulled me in with its bewildering fate, with its yellow custardy "quality of light." Poetry as dan tat, a flaky egg tart funneled into my mouth. Poetry as tangible nourishment. I became a poet because I am a voracious, greedy restaurant baby.

Sometimes it feels like I don't have a choice. Even if I pursued something else in life, poetry would follow me like the smell of the restaurant's fryer—chicken grease congealing behind my ear. Maybe I was always writing because I wanted to live. I didn't want to disappear. I wanted to be, right here. Maybe I compose in the bathtub because it's like being birthed again, sleek and steaming, into this world and whatever world is next.

I became a poet because of my literary lineage too, which took me too long to discover. Later in life, I had to search for this lineage, this linked connection. Growing up, I didn't even know there were Asian American writers. There were only two books by Asian American authors that we read in high school: Maxine Hong Kingston's *The Woman Warrior* and Amy Tan's *The Joy Luck Club*. I remember my English teacher's multiple-choice pop quiz on *The Woman Warrior*, how I got five answers wrong, like: How old was Fa Mu Lan when she started her training? This was a quiz on random details in the book. We never actually talked about the book. We never engaged with what sparked our thinking, what moved us, what the stakes were. When my teacher handed back my terrible quiz grade, she gave me this disappointed look like but-you're-Chinese-shouldn't-you-ace-this. As a high school senior, I was selected for a free summer camp called the Governor's School of the Arts, held on the College of New Jersey's campus. I had never been around other peers who were as passionate as me about writing. I wondered if this was it—I was finally going to meet people who made sense to me. Did they also dream about a snail's life in the undergrowth, weave a story from its lush slime? The vast majority of the high school writers there were white. At large camp functions in the dorms, I kept being mistaken for a violinist and was asked whether I was first chair; most of the musicians were Asian American. During one outing, the creative writers went to the bowling alley, and one snarky writer typed my name into the roster as "Amy Tan." After a while, the teacher who took us there noticed and tried to erase it, but it was too late. The game had started and we couldn't go back. For three hours, I was Amy Tan. I remember giving up at the very start, tossing the marbled ball into the gutter whenever it was my turn. With each gutter clunk, I felt more and more invisible. I rolled down that grate with my ball, into the void's moldy maw. Everything was telling me that I didn't belong there. We read Allen Ginsberg that day, and I remember looking at this skinny, bearded white guy chanting on the projector's screen. Was this what poetry was? His poems fell flat for me, nothing stirred within me. But

I looked at everyone nodding around the room and wondered if I was missing something (I was. I was missing Lucille Clifton, Audre Lorde, Theresa Hak Kyung Cha, June Jordan, Sonia Sanchez, Joy Harjo, Marilyn Chin, Kimiko Hahn . . .).

Even if I wanted poetry, did it want me?

In *Dictee*, Theresa Hak Kyung Cha writes: "The memory is the entire. The longing in the face of the lost. Maintains the missing." Like many Asian American poets, Cha was formative in my creative life. I was 31 and working on my critical dissertation at the University of Washington when I visited Cha's archives at the Berkeley Art Museum and Pacific Film Archive. I saw her book arts and film work such as *Pomegranate Offering* and *Exilée*. Her voice—soft and intimate—reverberated throughout the tiny black viewing room. There was a small jar with a line of poetry dangling outside of it, a cloth book with screen-printed poems. The special collections handler wore white gloves as she showed me piece after piece. As if one's bare touch would make them disintegrate immediately. Dust to dust, just like the opening image of *Dictee*, which features a barren, rocky landscape without a caption. To begin in rubble. It looks a bit like the Berkeley Pit, where the Auditor lived and survived. "Do a lot of people come in to see her work?" I asked the woman. She peeled back a layer of protective material like a cocoon. "Not that many. But she has so many pieces, I'm surprised there aren't more people who come by." Though I was there to do research for my dissertation on the poetics of haunting, visiting Cha's archives felt like visiting her grave and paying my respects. I wanted to offer incense, oranges, and some muscat gummy candy, but I knew I wasn't allowed. My offerings would have to be ethereal.

When I first read *Dictee*, which was on my own during an independent study in college (there were no Asian American literature classes offered at Bard at that time, so I made my own syllabus), I had a hard time describing the book. Instead, I felt through it. *Dictee* asked me to float through Cha's ghostly desires, via her offerings of fragments, images, and documents. Her mother, as was my mother, was at the center of it all. Alongside her mother, she wrote about Korean freedom fighter Yu Gwan-sun who protested during the Japanese occupation of Korea. I read *Dictee* waywardly: I read a section, skipped another, and went backward to reread. I'd sometimes dwell with one word or phrase for a long time, like "interrogation mark," as she subverts grammar—a system of linguistic privilege and colonialization: "open quotation marks / How was the first day / interrogation mark / close quotation marks."

During college, I was struggling with writing fiction and couldn't figure out why I couldn't write a linear narrative. I kept criticizing myself for it: Why can't I just begin and move forward, scene by scene? Why couldn't I make up a plot? *Make something happen!* Cha's art made me realize that storytelling was hardly a linear act when you come from a history of trauma, war, and migration. Reading *Dictee* gave me permission to create constellations of speculative memory. It gave me the permission to break down genre boundaries. Time collapsed. Fact and fiction intermingled into some hopeful alternate universe. My poems—or whatever hybrid amalgamation that occurred—unraveled my desire to know the unknowable. In my failure to write clearly, something else arose, like a bioluminescent creature from the deep. I was lured by its anglerfish light, grazed by its needling jaws. My college mentor, Mat Johnson, always told me: "If you fail, fail beautifully." Once, when I told him how frustrated I was by another professor—a white professor who didn't "get" my work and refused to write me a recommendation letter—he closed his office door and shoved a pillow under the bottom, as if that would magically shut out sound. His face changed, furrowed with frustration. "Don't let those white folks get to you. Those people will make you stop writing. And you can't stop writing."

How many times had I wanted to give up? How many times did I think: *Get me out of here. They don't want me here.* And: *That will never be my name on that shelf.* (There were so few names that looked like mine.) Each time I faltered, each time a white writer dismissed me or tried to kiss me, each time I got rejected, each time I was mistaken for another Asian poet, I returned to Cha. My visit to Cha's archives was timely. Cha and I were both 31 in that cold museum room in Berkeley. When taking notes on her work, I turned to a blank page in my notebook and noticed that there was a large piece missing from the top corner. This jagged tear took me by surprise. It was as if she had eaten a chunk of my notebook, ripped it out with her hungry teeth. What happened? I looked under my seat for the sliver of paper. I paced the room trying to find it. Nothing. "Maintains the missing."

In 1982, two years before I was born, Cha was raped and murdered by Joseph Sanza in New York City. *Dictee* had just been published and she was on her way to meet her husband on Lafayette Street. In Cathy Park Hong's essay on Cha, "Portrait of an Artist," she goes into detail about Cha's case, speaking to her radical creativity and distinct vision, as well as the gruesome details of the racialized and sexualized violence that links us all. I learned about her death after reading *Dictee* in college, when I tried to find more to read by her. A recent report from Stop AAPI Hate found that, of the more than 9,000 reports of hate incidents they received over a 15-month period, "incidents reported by women make up 63.3%." Nearly a year after the Atlanta spa shootings, 35-year-old Christina Yuna Lee was murdered in February 2022 after being followed into her Chinatown apartment. Her memorial, which is overflowing with flowers and messages of love, has been repeatedly vandalized, and an article in Hyperallergic notes that "Asian femmes have reported experiences of being stalked upon visiting the site." Even her altar—a glowing, sacred space—was not safe. Hypersexualized, objectified, and reviled, it terrifies me to think about the violence that will continue to occur. Have our bodies ever known safety? It would take until January 2022, two years after Hong's *Minor Feelings* came out, for an obituary for Cha to appear in the *New York Times*. The opening phrase of the obituary's title: "Overlooked No More." I was taken aback by that title. I *had* looked for Cha, *had* searched for my literary lineage in her undeniably powerful voice. I had looked into her open mouth, in her video piece "Mouth to Mouth," attempting to speak Korean amid static, darkness, water, and birdsong. Overlooked by whom, exactly?

Recently, I met a new acquaintance who also teaches Asian American studies. She told me she didn't know what to do with poetry. "What if a student asks me about a poem? Like, what does it mean? I can't teach it because I wouldn't know what to tell them!" But that's exactly it, I told her. That's exactly why I love poetry, why we *need* poetry. It asks us to come to it on our own terms, to let go of our structures—clock and calendar, email and spreadsheets, clarity and aboutness. We need bewilderment. We need transformation: "then into idea, then into more tangible action." Maybe it's one line. Maybe it's just the sound of a word. Maybe it's the shape. Or the flush of feeling that overwhelms you after listening to a poet read, so you must beg: again, again. It's incredible: how one poem can expand your entangled mind and heart, borderless. A poem can stay with you your entire life. When I teach *Dictee* in my Asian American literature and hybrid poetry classes, I ask my students: "How did it feel to read this? How did you 'read'? What is reading? Where were the heart spaces for you? As Cha writes: 'beginning wherever you wish, tell even us.'" In workshop too, I always ask for heart spaces, for the ventricles of pumping blood. Like an octopus, poetry has multiple hearts. Like an octopus, it changes color through metaphor, form, music. *Dictee*, for me, was a Russian doll of hearts—hearts within hearts within hearts. If we want to understand resistance, we must turn to poetry.

When I met Maxine Hong Kingston in 2018 and awkwardly asked her for a photograph (her white hair entwined with mine like a string of lightbulbs), I wanted so badly to tell her she was the first

Asian American writer I had read. I wanted to push aside those empty pop quizzes and ask her what was really on my mind. I wanted to ask her about demanding to be seen and resisting the white gaze, about joy and humor and epic love—which was also ours. I wanted to ask what her favorite dish was, if she used fertilizer in her garden, how she started a new piece of writing. From *The Woman Warrior*: "We're all under the same sky and walk the same earth; we're alive together during the same moment." Here was that present moment, as we walked together on a sunny day in Portland. But I was too shy to say anything, and she probably got fangirled a lot. As if she knew what I wanted to say, she simply hugged me and my friend Sally. It was a strong hug. I felt my ribs contract, an umbrella opening and closing. "It was for you. The next generation and you will do the same," she said to us. *And you can't stop writing.*

> Say to them,
> say to the down-keepers,
> the sun-slappers,
> the self-soilers,
> the harmony-hushers,
> "Even if you are not ready for day
> it cannot always be night."
> You will be right.
>
> —GWENDOLYN BROOKS, "Speech to the Young:
> Speech to the Progress-Toward (among Them Nora
> and Henry III)"

When I was at Iowa, I had a secret admirer. Someone would leave me beautiful floral arrangements by my apartment stoop—fuchsia roses, minty eucalyptus, orange lilies, pink peonies, and striking calla lilies. There was always a little sliver of a note with the arrangements.

For Jane, because spring is coming. For Jane, because poetry. There was also a handful of chocolates and candy. Nick, my boyfriend at the time, was annoyed. *Who is this?* he kept asking. *Why do they know where you live?* And: *Don't eat that candy,* when I held it to my mouth, the chocolate already melting on my fingertips. There were at least four different bouquets in vases, and I carried each one into my apartment. As Nick side-eyed the bouquets, I changed their water every other day, dumping out the browning liquid. I never found out who left them for me. I still have no idea. In the tumult and awfulness of my time at Iowa, when my professor said my poem was like "going to Ikea for cheap furniture and not knowing how to put the shit together" during workshop, I welcomed this tiny gesture. Sure, maybe it was creepy. Sure, it pissed Nick off. But if I held that daisy's bright face for one moment, I felt like I was doing something right. *For Jane, because poetry.* It was as if I left the bouquets for myself.

Wake up to your powers! When I was a kid, my mother would drop me off at the public library, which was conveniently close to the strip mall where the restaurant was located. I'd stay there for hours on end, reading book after book. My mother packed me wontons and I ate those, licking sesame oil off my fingers as I turned the pages. The librarians, who kept an eye on me, were unwittingly my free babysitters. But as I read, I couldn't help but grow frustrated. I hated how these stories ended, how they never included characters that reflected who I was (with the exception of Claudia Kishi from *The Baby-Sitters Club*, whose mixed-pattern and velvet wardrobe I coveted). I wrote alternative endings and new scenes. I drew Asian American girls on strips of scrap paper meant for call numbers and secretly slipped them into books. I wonder if some of those children's books still have my writing in them, or if some other young writer of color added to them too. I've always dreamt of that—creating a timeless friendship over notes in library books.

I almost quit Iowa. A few months into my MFA, I called my mother in Jersey: "I can't do it. I don't know anything. I feel so stupid," I cried.

And this was exactly how I felt: like I knew nothing. I didn't know the terms everyone was using: "anaphora," "spondee," "anapest." Words that sounded like the name of a bougie coffee shop that sold drinks I never ordered (just plain drip). I didn't know how to scan, didn't know anything about feet except that mine were two different sizes. A classmate of mine who went to an Ivy League school had just laughed at my poem during workshop. He didn't say a single thing, just let out a haughty, dismissive laugh after I read my poem out loud, shaking in that suffocating room. My professor would spend the next hour lecturing on the poem: why this one line felt too vague, why there should be one wolf instead of two. We were all stuck in that room for hours, our stomachs growling. Outside, it was starting to snow and it stuck to the ground, one snowflake at a time. I wanted to leave.

"No one can make you feel stupid. They're not allowed," she said sharply. My mother, like Mat, demanded that I keep writing. She didn't know what writing meant and didn't read my writing due to a language barrier, but she knew it mattered to me. "They're jealous," she insisted. "They know you have something in you. And they are scared. Look how scared they are." From the lonely cornfields of Iowa, from my bleak puffy coat huffing it begrudgingly to the Dey House, I kept showing up. Later, when that professor who called my poem Ikea furniture (he also said one of my poems was like Poetry 101) refused to write me any feedback the entire semester, I wrote a note on my last workshop poem: "This time, please read it and comment ahead of time." This professor only wrote notes for poets he liked, and I was clearly not one of them. Everyone in the Writers' Workshop saw my comment in the packet as we grabbed copies from the packet cubbies. My friends were proud of me and told me so when we went through the packets on Wednesday night, as we always did, with Pabst and Thai food Nick cooked. "Oh shit, Jane's mad," as they spooned curry into their mouths, and "You fucking tell him. He doesn't even do the bare minimum." And lo and behold, for the first time all semester, he actually wrote a few comments down. Even in the maelstrom of impostor syndrome, I started to stand up for myself. And even though I had spent three hours going back and forth as to whether or not I should write that note, it felt necessary that I did. I'd feel that way often in the near future—calling out racist practices at work, demanding payment that was mysteriously "forgotten about," the list goes on. I fretted for hours, days, weeks, with my anxiety spiking up and out, but I had to say something. I didn't want to disappear.

The entire time I was at Iowa, I didn't write a single poem that I was actually in. If there was a speaker, which was rare, it wasn't me. I hid away from my poems, ran off into the thick cornfields with no scythe to speak of. I wasn't myself. I wrote obliquely. I wrote from a distant past. I wrote after the white poets I had read during my MFA: Dickinson, Oppen, Keats, O'Hara, Howe. And I clung to the few poets of color who were "experimental" enough to be taught. Poets like Claudia Rankine, Mei-mei Berssenbrugge, and Myung Mi Kim were chosen, but they also didn't choose to be tokenized. When I had the opportunity to take a class with Myung Mi in 2009, during a summer fellowship at Naropa University, she opened me up to so many Asian American poets I had never heard of. She told me more about Kundiman, a literary nonprofit for Asian American writers, which eventually changed the entirety of my writing life—toward community and radical expansion. In her workshop, I wrote my first lyrical "I" poem, the first poem where the "I" was unabashedly me. This seven-page poem, "House of Accident," which can be read both across and down, was my first memoir.

Now, looking back, I realize I didn't have a single poetry professor of color at Iowa, including the visiting professors. When I finished in 2010, I didn't apply to any of the third-year post-grad fellowships, which offered more funding to write and teach. I wanted to get the hell out of there. And so I did, selling all of my thrifted furniture (I miss that baby-blue writing desk, though!) and packing up my books for media mail. My rhetoric students apparently made a Facebook photo album of our class (including bar crawls at the Ped Mall post-class) and, after I graduated, they tagged me. It was funny to see myself, this blurry image of me waving my hands above my head. Two of my students who met in that class got married. I'll never forget that last day of class, when no one showed up for 15 minutes. I sat there with the doughnuts I had brought, perplexed and kind of pissed off. I had spent $30 on them. I started to eat a stale bear claw when I heard chanting from the yard. That's when I saw them: my entire rhetoric class in single file with their final projects in hand, chanting "RHETORIC! RHETORIC!" They came into the classroom through the side door and drummed on the tables together, this time adding my name: "JANE WONG RHETORIC! JANE WONG RHETORIC!" I remember thinking: *Were they freaking high?* It was noon. Afterward, they devoured my doughnuts and took turns giving random persuasive speeches, including why incoming freshmen should take my class (I tried to tell them I was leaving Iowa). I was charmed. At that very moment, I knew I wanted to teach forever. A future student hand-knit me socks: "To keep you warm when you're writing poetry! Thank you for changing my life!" Fourteen years of teaching later, in a department where there are so few of us professors of color, it will always be my students who remind me who I really am: a total nerd, a weirdo, a goofball, someone who wants everyone to love writing as much as I do, someone who knows her worth—despite everyone who doubts me.

Some things some white people have said to me about my writing and scholarship, beginning wherever I wish:

After a class presentation during my PhD coursework: "That was actually really good. I'm surprised. No offense."

On a dating app: "Oh, you're tenure track? Really? How did you get that?"

After letting a "friend" know that I was a finalist for the Ruth Lilly Poetry Fellowship: "You know only one Asian can win."

On a dating app: "You're too cute to be a professor. What do you actually do?"

During one of my job talks, which made it clear this faculty member didn't read my file or care about the fact that this was quite illegal to ask: "How old are you? How did you learn all this pedagogy in such a short time?"

A DM on Instagram, an hour before a poetry reading: "[Insert another Asian American poet's name here] cancelled and I thought you'd be perfect to fill in. Can you read?"

On Twitter, after my first book came out: "Congrats to [insert another Asian American poet's name here] on *Overpour*!"

On a dating app: "I bet you can teach me a few things ;-)"

During an interview: "Your poetry is beautiful and spare, it feels like a skeleton doing tai chi in the glistening sun."

After a first date, in which I let him know I wasn't interested in a second: "But I bought your book, so you sure we can't go on a second date? I can bring it for you to sign!"

Via an email following up about an invitation to read: "No, there's no honorarium or travel funding. But you should know that poetry is a labor of love."

During a Q&A after a reading: "Have you read the ancient Chinese poets? I think you can learn a lot from them."

During a Q&A after a reading: "I have a question [it is always a comment]. There are so many poets these days who can't shut up about race. Everything is about race. I've been writing for over twenty years. Can't we just talk about the poems?"

During a Q&A after a reading: "My son's Chinese girlfriend wrote a novel inspired by their love and I brought it to give to you. Here, it's called *Chopstick Love*."

As I'm trying to get off the stage after giving a featured craft talk: "What do you have against clichés? They work for a reason. I hate metaphors." This MAGA hat–wearing man nearly hit me with his cane on the exit stairs.

During a writing conference, after my name was mixed up with the name of another Asian American presenter, I pointed out how problematic that was, #WrongAsian (there's a lapel pin), that this was a constant experience of erasure: "I see that we need to be better about copyediting. And I want you to know that this [my anger? Me standing up for myself and that other writer?] won't impact our decision to invite you again."

Always, not the professor: "Are you a student here?"

Always, a hobby: "Have you published anything?"

When I was a part of *The Best American Poetry 2015* anthology, in the "Contributors' Notes and Comments" section: "After a poem of mine has been rejected a multitude of times under my real name, I put Yi-Fen's name on it and send it out again. As a strategy for 'placing' poems this has been quite successful for me. The poem in question . . . was rejected under my real name forty (40) times before I sent it out as Yi-Fen Chou (I keep detailed submission records). As Yi-Fen the poem was rejected nine (9) times before *Prairie Schooner* took it. If indeed this is one of the best American poems of 2015, it took quite a bit of effort to get it into print, but I'm nothing if not persistent." These lines were written by Michael Derrick Hudson, a white poet who pretended to be Chinese. Hudson had taken the name of a former high school classmate, Yi-Fen Chou, in this act of yellowface. Chou's family demanded that he stop and apologize, but he never apologized. Ellen Chou, Yi-Fen's sister, was quoted in the *New York Times* saying that Hudson demonstrated "careless disregard" for the Asian community. Sherman Alexie, the editor who selected the poem for inclusion, kept the poem in the anthology despite persistent demands to remove it. Years later, Alexie would be called out for unwanted sexual advances and harassment by the women he preyed upon—several of whom are Indigenous. News of Hudson's act of yellowface appeared on all the major news outlets, yet there was no reporting on his claim. None of his rejection letters or submission logs were shown or verified. As Alexander Chee stated during a PEN America roundtable: "The only reason I can think no one has made him prove it is that he is a white man, and when white men in America say they are discriminated against, people just say 'oh, ok,' and do not ask them to prove it. Meanwhile, this case will be thrust at us as the sign that we are lying whenever we claim we're discriminated against."

I find it strange how I had forgotten that this had happened to me—at the start of my poetry career. I had forgotten the horror of this erasure, this blatant and unethical act of yellowface, right near my own name in the table of contents. I had shoved this memory down deep in my gut like freezer-burnt corn, but recently it all sprang back up in nauseous disbelief. Like, did this really happen? Did this really happen to me? This was my first time being in the Best American series. I remember buying used copies for $1 as a college student, dog-earing my favorite poems. How could I ever imagine that I would be in one of those copies? When I got the acceptance email for the anthology, I marked it as spam and didn't reply. But I got a follow-up a week later, asking if I could confirm permissions. I blinked over and over, rereading the email, trying to find anything strange about it— misspelled words or send-me-your-SSN. But no, this was very real. I was going to be in *The Best American Poetry 2015*. I hadn't had many publications yet, and the ones I did have were mostly in small journals. The poem of mine that was in the anthology, "Thaw," was published online by a lovely indie journal, *Birdfeast*. This poem was from my first book, which would be published the following year. The poem ends the book, offering a future free from the terror that surrounded me. It was written to leave the Bad One. It's a hopeful poem, a poem that desires softness. From "Thaw": "A planet fell out of my mouth /

My organs bloomed, parachutes in the night," and later, "The fish sitting too long in the sun melted / Into a sea, cell after cell / My prized imperatives, my root words: gone / Long live the day." I think about how much I still love this poem, how I wrote it to demand kindness, to demand a new, surreal beginning. How the poem delights in living, in being alive. I think about the soft organs of this poem, up against Hudson's starched suit-and-tie words: "(I keep detailed submission records)" and "it took quite a bit of effort to get it into print, but I'm nothing if not persistent." When this act of yellowface happened in 2015, so many media outlets asked me for a quote, for a comment about the "kerfuffle" (a word one writer used, tricking me into a question about Hudson's actions under the guise of an interview for my forthcoming book). I felt dizzy, sick. I tried to hide away. I wanted the sweaty spotlights off of me. No one was talking about the actual poems in the anthology, which included numerous ones by real Asian American poets and other poets of color. Everyone was reading his poem and dissecting it like a gilded frog. The names of the real Asian American poets in the anthology—all of whom I hold dear as friends: Chen Chen, Rajiv Mohabir, Aimee Nezhukumatathil, Monica Youn, Jane Motherfucking Wong.

I think about Hudson's words—his aggressive "persistence," bemoaning the plight of white male poets who are used to getting what they want. Hudson was on a crusade to push out writers like me. My ex-fiancé also harbored this type of entitlement, this obsession with letting everyone know how he was slighted. He, too, let me know that he kept records. He makes his own records—manipulating every word and insinuating threats from my refusal to engage. He, like Hudson, was going to win at all costs. That smirk of "persistence." *You'll meet people like this later in life.*

When I was invited to read for the anthology's celebration at the New School in New York, I was going to say no. I didn't even open the anthology when my copy arrived in the mail. It just lay there atop the bubble mailer, untouched on my desk, his fake Chinese name too near my real Chinese name. But I was going back to Jersey for the holidays and my mother perked up when I mentioned the invitation. This would be the very first time she'd hear me read. "I'm so proud of you! You have to read! We will all come to see you—Ste and Vinny! We can take the train!" I didn't have the heart to tell her about what had happened. She was so excited; she had already picked out an outfit and turned on her hair curler. When we got to the reading, I saw Chen, whom I hadn't met before. We kind of wordlessly hugged each other and laughed—our joy of connecting pasted over such brash erasure. We took cute pictures in the stairwell and talked about each other's poems. Of course, during the reading, people brought up Hudson again and again, and rightfully so in their outrage. When I read "Thaw," I made my mother stand up in the audience. I asked everyone to clap for her, and the entire auditorium echoed with the flapping sounds of gratitude. She waved to everyone, from all sides, like royalty, like *Yes, it's me.*

Afterward, when I asked if she liked it: "Oh, your poem was good. I don't get it, but Mommy liked it. Some poems put Vinny to sleep. He was snoring. I had to poke him. And why was everyone so angry? Who were they talking about? Who is this guy? I don't get it."

I still couldn't tell her, so I just told her to forget about it. She'll never know—she's never "googled" anything in her life. She has never even used a computer. And telling her wasn't worth it—Hudson cannot take away my mother's right to celebrate her daughter.

"I'm glad you liked it, Mommy. Come on, let's go get some mai fun." And so we all left, arm in arm, to eat noodles. My contributor's note from the anthology: "I wanted the feeling of impossible warmth and potential, hurling us into each new day." I would be featured in another Best American series later—*The Best American Nonrequired Reading 2019* anthology. Hilariously, it would be for a piece called "Curse for the American Dream." From that piece: "Hex the executives who can't see beyond their golden watches." People like Hudson pilfered gold, refusing to see the very real Yi-Fen Chou. I think about the fact that Hudson works at a library. I imagine going to the library where he works, making him watch me as I check out my own books. I want to scan my books slowly, the barcode buzzing under sweet laser light. I want him to see what I've made and tell me to my face that I didn't deserve it. *Say it to my face.*

> When you turn the corner
> And run into yourself
> Then you know that you have turned
> All the corners that are left

—LANGSTON HUGHES, "Final Curve"

When I write poetry in the bathtub, there is nowhere else to go except through the heat. There is always this sense of terror in writing, this dip into vulnerability that can unearth something you've worked so hard at burying. That's the risk—the fleshy interior. When, as Langston Hughes writes, you "run into yourself." Poetry hasn't taught me to make better decisions. It hasn't taught me to better assess danger. But it has taught me a lot about myself and what that "I" can do. As Sharon Olds writes in "Take the I Out": "I love the *I*, / frail between its flitches, its hard ground / and hard sky, it soars between them."

When I arrived at Iowa, I had been living in Hong Kong for a year. After being home in Jersey for just one week, I packed my things to move to the Midwest. On the flight to Cedar Rapids, I had no idea where I was going. I opened the flight map from the backseat pocket and stared at the intersecting dotted lines. Looking out the window, all I saw were squares of farmland—a patchwork quilt. When I arrived at the airport, I immediately felt unmoored. I had just spent a year living in a place where almost every face looked like mine. I blended in for once in my life. The smell of soy sauce eggs and sweet gai daan jai had filled the muggy city air. Here, in this small Cedar Rapids airport, I smelled nothing except old carpet and recycled air. I was the only Asian person there. White people stared at me, looking me up and down. Outside at passenger pickup, a truck rolled down its window and a middle-aged white man with a trucker hat said "konnichiwa" to me. This is how I started my MFA. I was most definitely back in America.

When I applied to MFA programs, I applied to just four schools, since the application fees were so expensive. I only applied to ones that didn't require the GRE (which cost even more money. Also, I was a terrible test taker and grew anxious at the very thought of anything timed). When I applied to Iowa, I knew it was a long shot. Didn't everyone apply? I had written mostly fiction throughout my time at Bard and applied in fiction for all my schools. At that time, Iowa just happened to be having what I like to think of as a two-for-one deal: you could apply to both genres for the price of one. And so, I put in one singular poetry application, which contained mostly prose poems. I was in Hong Kong when I applied and didn't think too much of it. If I didn't get into any of my schools, I'd try to stay abroad longer. I loved the MTR and its snack vending machines, loved walking around the big trees in Victoria Park, loved wandering the streets full of goldfish, songbirds, flowers, and skewered fish balls. Tipsy on cheap wine, I often stumbled upon art speakeasies—the one I frequented was a barbershop by day and a poetry open mic bar at night. The Barbicide, with a suspended comb or two, was not to be mistaken for Bombay Sapphire. The speakeasy was in a cobblestone alleyway notorious for midnight cats—almost a hundred would show up to be fed by this one woman. Her back was hunched from carrying bags of kibble. Poetry, whiskey, and petting staticky feral kittens in the moonlight. Maybe there was a part of me that wished that I wouldn't get in. Maybe my Cantonese would get better, maybe I didn't have to go back to the U.S., where people gawked at me, boring a hole of their fantasies into me, asking me the same question that was really a statement: *You're not from around here, are you.*

I was on the other side of the world, so far from Jersey. The local time in Hong Kong was over half a day ahead, but my mother was up at 3:00 AM her time because of work. She called me and told me someone left her a message at home, said that I had to call back as soon as possible. "Where did they call from? Who were they?" I asked her.

"Something called Iowa," she said matter-of-factly. My mother's international calling card was running out of minutes. "Did you eat breakfast yet?"

My mother had never said that word, ever, so it took me some time to figure out what she was saying. "Iowa!" I scribbled down the number my mother gave me and asked her to check the mail and call me back later.

"Okay, but did you eat breakfast yet?"

After punching in a bazillion digits, I finally got an answer on the other line—from Hong Kong all the way to Iowa City, the Writers' Workshop's program administrator answered the phone. "You're Jane. Okay. I need you to fax me your recommendation letters today. Or you can't get financial aid," she said, flatly. We all loved Connie and how blunt she was. Right before I graduated, during the annual poetry vs. fiction softball game (Flowers of Evil vs. Crime and Punishment), the poets had T-shirts that read "Connie loves us more" spray-painted on the back.

"What? Wait, I got in?" I was so confused. My roommate had just come back from running and I could hear him panting outside my bedroom. The smell of his sweat leaked under the door. I moved over to the window, my drying underwear smacking me in the face with each gust of wind.

"Yeah, yeah. Anyway, today. Fax them. Bye."

And that was it. I never got an official call, which I discovered later was what most people got. I had somehow gotten into Iowa and my recommendation letters had somehow never made it there. I didn't even have time to celebrate or squeal or stomp or shove celebratory har gow into my face. I emailed my recommenders with a subject line in all caps: I GOT INTO IOWA, NEED YOU TO FAX RECS TODAY, PLEASE! And, after many apologies, all three of my professors replied immediately. They sent faxes, they called Connie, they were so excited for me: Jane, the budding fiction writer, the future novelist.

When my mother called me back, she told me she had forgotten to open some mail because it was under a pile of bills that were overdue.

"Okay, okay, I found it, sorry." I could hear paper shuffling all around her and the ripping of envelopes. I'll never know how long they'd been sitting there.

"Columbia, looks like from New York. It says dear Jane Wong. That's you! *Congratulations...*" But then there was Iowa: "You have two letters! That's good, right? Two is better than one!" I had forgotten that I had also applied in poetry. With one rejection came something else. Iowa had rejected me for fiction but had accepted me for poetry. It was that two-for-one deal that would send me into an overgrown future of poetry, tumbling into the tangled unknown. A future that somehow had always been there, a lurking lyric I was afraid to sing.

After I stopped screaming with disbelief, leaving the realm of fiction for now, my mother shared her thoughts: "Iowa? What is that? Don't go there. I don't know what that is. Are there bears there?" She will forever ask me if there are bears. Are there bears in Montana? In Washington? Where are you going? Are there bears?

> If I dip my hand in,
> I will change history.

—VICTORIA CHANG, *Dear Memory*

When I was an undergraduate at Bard, I couldn't afford to purchase the books for class. I discovered the interlibrary loan system, which is this magical gift of books delivered from school to school. With one click, I could request a copy from Vassar. It was through the library that I was able to be present in those classes, able to read *Dictee* during my independent study. One English professor, in the middle of a class on theory, stopped discussion. She stared directly at me across the long table. "Is that your writing? Did you write in a library book?" I flushed flamingo pink, awkwardly covering the penciled notes and underlining with my arm. I looked like a dog that had snuck a slice of pizza and then was like *No, no, I didn't eat that pizza*, dried cheese on my mouth. "Don't ever write in library books," she chastised me sharply, before continuing her lecture on Derrida. I wanted to tell her that I couldn't afford the book, wanted to tell her I was trying to practice active reading—just like she'd taught us. And that I'd erase the markings later. My classmates stared at me, probably thinking I wasn't dedicated enough to buy the book. *How lazy*, they probably thought. Or worse, with pity: *How poor*.

In my formal education, it was always like this. Being judged for how I was reading and what I was reading. All the hipsters I took classes with would smoke cigarettes beside the ivy-covered buildings, talking with lilting voices about Lydia Davis and Cormac McCarthy and L=A=N=G=U=A=G=E poets and Neutral Milk Hotel lyrics. They were so over vests. They wanted more bike shorts. One day I was delivering a package to a faculty member's office and loitered, listening. I nodded as if I was a part of the discussion. "Hey, aren't you in my fiction workshop?" one of them asked.

"Uh, yeah. Just delivering a package," I said awkwardly before squirreling away into the building, the heavy wood door slamming behind me. Majoring in English and creative writing seemed terrifying to me as someone who was a first-generation college-goer. What would I do after graduating? Unlike some of my classmates whose parents were professors or doctors, I had no net. I *was* the net. I didn't just want writing to work out. I needed it to work out. As the oldest of my cousins, I had to change the direction of our lives, away from moldy oranges and piles of overdue bills. So what was I doing writing stories, writing poetry?

I worked five jobs during my time at Bard, one of which included babysitting for a favorite professor of mine. She was headed to the opera with her husband and I watched her two little kids, who went to bed at 7:00 PM, so it was a pretty sweet gig. I remember her telling me it was "picnic night," which meant rolling out a gingham picnic blanket for dinner in the living room. And tossing some ham and cheese cubes on it, with Ritz Crackers. I watched these children chomp up the cubes on the floor like that game Hungry Hungry Hippos. "Jane," they called out to me. "Picnic with us!" and it was there that I finally ate the Lunchables I had coveted my whole childhood. The ham was so pink and salty and eerie in its perfect squareness. Another job included being an usher for the American Symphony Orchestra on campus, at the Richard B. Fisher Center for the Performing Arts. I got to dress up in a twirly black dress and take people to their seats. One time, a middle-aged white man needed help finding his seat. He waved me down with his pocket square, smiling a bit too broadly. When I showed him to his aisle, he looked at me *that way* and said: "Are you from Hawaii?" When I said no, he replied: "I can take you to Hawaii." How many times have I wanted to say "ew" and didn't? Was my "ew" worth $5.25 an hour? In addition, I worked as an administrative assistant at the dean's office, as an attendant at the Hessel Museum of Art, and as a delivery person for the Bard Publications Office. Some work study highlights include: a biology student bringing a tiny albino frog that was no longer "needed" to the dean's office (I was to "set it free" in a pond); being told by a security guard at the museum that I should apply for the CIA and that he had an in; Jamaica Kincaid, a.k.a. one of my ultimate fiction idols, calling the dean's office, and instead of putting her on hold, I accidentally hung up on her and cried about it like a fool; and falling asleep at the publications office while reading *Dracula* and waking myself up screaming from a vampire nightmare—to the horror of my stoned co-workers.

A month before graduating, I was chosen by *Monocle* magazine as a featured senior for a story they were doing on Bard being a thriving arts destination. When they took my photo, I smiled a giant Jersey pageant smile, my hands on my hips and my head tilted slightly to the right. I showed lots of teeth and made sure my baby hairs were matted down. "No, no!" the photographer waved me away like a fly. "Don't smile. You're a writer. Look serious." He told me to push my long bangs, which were always to the side, into my face. When the issue came out and I scooped it up from Barnes & Noble, I turned to my profile. I looked at my unsmiling face and my artsy bangs covering my eyes. I looked sad. I poked at the glossy paper. *Who. Is. That.*

While I was in college, my little brother was working at Pizza Hut and lobbing dough in the parking lot when his co-workers and friends were bored. His friends dared him to eat a ghost pepper and he did, his guts spewing sickness for days. All he ate was Pizza Hut pizza because he was always at work, and he was starting to feel terrible. When I came home during winter break once, he stood up straight like he was being measured and said, "When you come back for summer, it'll all be different." I barely recognized him when I returned. He told me he'd quit Pizza Hut and that he was learning to be a personal trainer. He'd just started working at Work Out World (yes, WOW) and Bruce Springsteen had come into the gym the other day. "I wanted to put on 'Born to Run,' just to see if he'd run faster." When I published "To Love a Mosquito" as an essay, I sent Steven a copy. I wondered what he thought. Was it okay? Was it too cheesy? "It's like you know me," he said softly. "It was always hard with dad." When the editor at *Shenandoah*, where the essay was published, asked me to dream up a fun side project to support the journal, I asked my brother to read a scene from the essay and share his thoughts. A week later, he sent me a YouTube link. In the opening minutes, he is sitting at his computer's gamer chair. He talks like he's an Esports announcer, his keyboard lighting up like a galactic rave. "This is my sister's essay. Again, I did not write this. My sister did. Let's begin."

Later, in his reflection, he talks about how he wants to be a great dad, to loosen the weight of his own relationship to his father. It was all too much. The video was too tender, too generous. I couldn't share it. This was the first time my brother had read something of mine. And it had opened a vulnerable portal I wasn't expecting or ready for.

Once, after a particularly awful meeting at the university where I teach, I called my mother while walking off campus. The rain swirled around me like a vortex. I told her that a colleague of mine had been bullying me for quite some time. That I felt like, no matter what, that colleague didn't think I belonged here as a professor. What do you do when a white person tries to force impostor syndrome on you? It bubbles up your worst fears, all the things you've been told growing up: You won't amount to anything. You are here only because we needed a token. That, no matter how many poems and books you publish, no matter how exemplary your teaching evaluations are, no matter how much labor and heart you put into your job, you simply don't belong here. Years later, there would be a few colleagues who would not rate me highly on my tenure file. They offered no written comments. They couldn't substantiate their ratings. It was as if they just wanted me to know that they didn't like me. As I cried on the phone, transformed back into an insecure 20-year-old self, my mother said calmly and carefully: "You know how to fight a bully? Make more friends."

My writing life is anything but solitary. Even though the sting of someone trying to stop me from writing is wasp sharp, there are so many writers who have bolstered me over the years. Peers and mentors, dreamers and karaoke laughers. My friends joke around about making a podcast called "We Don't Talk about Poetry," where we invite poets to talk about anything but poetry—thrifting, kitchen utensils, pet food, sex toys, houseplants, lipstick, stretches for lower back pain. Because we realized that, even though many of our friends happen to be writers, we rarely talk about writing. Wasn't poetry in all those everyday things around us, in the creamy swipe of purple lipstick? I do what my mother tells me: I make more friends. This is what she does too, when someone at work makes fun of her accent or says her pants are too tight or tells her she's too loud (because the expectation is that she's quiet). After *Best American Poetry 2015*, it was rage and resistance and beauty that brought Chen, Aimee, Rajiv, Monica, and I together, wasn't it? Rage in solitude is one thing; rage in community is another. The latter is fertilizer, is transformative.

After Iowa, I went to Kundiman—the Asian American poetry retreat at Fordham's campus that Myung Mi had mentioned. My friend from Iowa, Hannah, also got in and we were going to go together. But at the last minute, she couldn't go. I went, but with my guard up. When I arrived, everyone was hugging each other and holding hands like they had known each other for centuries. I kept hearing "I'm so glad you're here" and "I can't wait to read your poems" and "I love your outfit, you're stunning." What was this place? Why was everyone being so nice? I moved around like a Komodo dragon, my tongue flicking out with poison at the ready. After my time at Iowa, after years of internalized racism and the assumption that there can "only be one" (the *Highlander* syndrome), I was a beast of unease. I tried to smile, I tried to gently shake hands, I tried to back into a corner and stay there against the wall. During one evening exercise, we were working in small groups. As we brainstormed, I felt this terrible churning of fear within me. And I blubbered some sort of quick apology and got up and ran away. I literally ran, my flats paddling the squeaky floor. I ran to my single dorm room and locked the door. After I made sure it was locked, I lay in bed and cried. I cried so hard, for what I didn't know yet. I texted Hannah and told her I wished she was there. I didn't know why everyone was so nice. What did they want from me? We had been taught to be suspicious of each other, and it was debilitating; I wanted to leave and planned to leave in the morning.

As I cried, I heard footsteps. I hid under my sticky sheet in the muggy heat. One after the other, little notes were being slipped under my door. It was around 1:00 AM when I got up the courage to pick them up. They were love notes. "We love you, Jane" and "Hope you're okay and "I'm here for you!" and "You are my sister! What do you need? I can bring you snacks!" There were Sanrio stickers and hearts. I held these notes in my sweaty raccoon hands.

When I returned the next day, during breakfast, I was met with hugs and gentle check-ins. When I opened my mouth to try to explain, someone stopped me: "You don't have to explain. I'm just glad you're here. Let's eat this damn quiche, haha." I had entered some sort of bizarre paradise, after years and years of searching for my literary lineage. And here I was, surrounded by my lineage in the present. With my Kundiman fellows, it wasn't weird or novel to speak about ancestral altars, about my desire to reach across time and space to alter the present. As Victoria Chang writes: "If I dip my hand in / I will change history." This is what poetry felt like—that enveloping touch, that liquid portal, that possibility of radical astonishment. Later that evening, at a karaoke party, there was a huge order of takeout noodles—but no utensils. Wordlessly, we all got cups and scooped the noodles into our mouths. Saucy noodles dangled from our mouth corners like we were transmitting messages via telephone cups. I was with family.

> Placing different languages in proximity removes
> them from their prescribed roles, jostling them into
> new possibilities.
>
> —SOLMAZ SHARIF, "A Poetry of Proximity"

As part of their final project, my students write poetics—thinking about their own writing and what poetry means to them. Why do they write? What obsessions keep circling around them? To return to Lorde, what action do they want poetry to catalyze? I've had so many beautiful poetics over the years—one woven into a basket, another buried in a pot of dirt, another that glowed from within a lantern. These are not metaphors. To read the one in the pot of dirt, written by a poet whose family are migrant workers, I had to dig, dirt seeping into the cracks of my hands. My office is not an office, but a poetry art gallery, buzzing with curiosity.

I ask my students to do this difficult task of reflecting on their writing, and I struggle to do it myself. Even now, thinking about my life through poetry, I flail in the lake weeds that tickle my dog's feet when he swims. Poetry defies explanation and stasis. So much and so little has changed in my writing life, which started before I was born. As Solmaz Sharif writes in "A Poetry of Proximity," as the "caretakers of language," poets refuse calcification. Language is powerful, as we know. Language is used to dehumanize, to enact war, to denigrate, to extol empire. How something is said makes us feel something, makes us act in both beautiful and terrible ways. Knowing all the damage language can do, we must "jostl[e] [language] into new possibilities."

My mother jostles her fertilizer jug, sloshing it back and forth. Pau Pau jostles a cookie tin and stores free ketchup packets and hand sanitizer wipes in there. My brother jostles his tomato plant from the bottom of the pot, shaking a persistent squirrel away. His plastic-fork method, which lines the pot like castle ridges, is not working exactly. Poetry as trying something and then trying something else. I jostle my poem "The Long Labors" and cut out lines from sheets of rice paper. I fold these rice paper lines into my mother's dumpling recipe—pork, shrimp, and chive—and my words disintegrate as I fold. I read, I scoop, I read, I fold, I read, I seal, I read, I steam, I eat my poem. How did I get here, glistening with all this nourishment? *Powers, portal me. Poetry came alive, through the maybe—*

MANGOES FOREVER

THERE'S SOMETHING ABOUT LEANING ON MY MOTHER'S shoulder as she slices into a mango like filleting a fish. She waves a mango spear in the air, a sunlit sugar torch. Chewing on the fibrous pit, mango thread woven in our teeth, we watch reruns of *The Fresh Prince of Bel-Air* in our underwear. The fan flaps our hair around, sticky with sweat and juice. It's Jersey July heat. The tomatoes are bulbous and ripe.

Wongmom.com is melting, so I tuck some ice cubes into the browser. She thanks me, reassures me that I have, indeed, taken the bus. "You're going places," she types, as ice crackles and pools around her. "You know what I mean?" I really do.

When I ask my mother why mangoes are her favorite fruit, she tells me she likes the colors. "They're all different colors. Yellow and pink and green. It's like you open your heart to enjoy it. I like it because it takes time to eat it." And it does take time to eat. When my mother cuts off the skin, she hands it to me, and I eat the tiny bits of remaining pulp. I scrape the skin with my teeth until it curls like a cupped palm. We pass the hairy pit back and forth, gnawing under the television's glow. We make the mango a desert.

When she was 15, my mother saw a mango in the city where she worked, after her factory shift. "What is that?" she asked her friend.

"Don't eat that," her friend swatted her away. "I heard they're no good for you." My mother didn't buy it—and certainly couldn't afford it anyway—but she stared at the sunny fruit, mesmerized by its glowing striations and fleshy weight. In 1968, Mao became enamored by mangoes, intrigued by their decadence after receiving them as a gift from Mian Arshad Hussain, the Pakistani foreign minister. Mao, in turn, regifted these mangoes to workers after an uprising during the Cultural Revolution, and the mango cult exploded. Mangoes became divine relics, became Mao himself. Workers tried to preserve the rare fruit in formaldehyde and wax. Despite rot, they cooked it to make "holy" mango water. The BBC reports that workers drank a spoonful each. That year, there was a parade float filled with papier-mâché mangoes through Tiananmen Square in Beijing, the air pickled with summer salt and nectar-flushed obsession. In another province, a villager remarked that mangoes looked like sweet potatoes and that was all it took for the villager to be executed as a counterrevolutionary. Dangerous language, dangerous fruit.

But this wasn't what the mango meant for my mother. Or for me. In this cosmos of ours, it was shared tenderness and care. It was decadent because it was withheld. We waited all year to eat this together. When my mother buys a whole carton of mangoes, she is letting me know that survival is done and it's time to thrive, grow, and devour. We eat mango after mango, no limit, until we turn the color of a broiled sunset. We blush with sweet yolky gold, ripening on windowsills stippled with dead flies. When her boss calls and asks if she can please come in to cover, she tells her: "Nope, sorry, my daughter and I are eating mangoes on my day off, bye bye!"

My mother tells me that mangoes are good for cooling down, for nausea, for seasickness, for clearing your system. It feels like everything we eat is good for clearing our systems, and maybe it is. There's a lot of clearing to do. Wongmom.com blinks on-screen and wants to join the mango feast. She says Buddha meditated under a mango tree, but meditation can be too quiet and it's just not her thing, so she starts shouting with gilded glee: "Mangoes forever! Mangoes forever! You know what I mean!"

Jane:

Quick q: did Bruce Springsteen really come into the gym you
worked at

With a bodyguard

Brother:

Well that was a random as hell q

But ye he did

Jane:

Many random q ahead

Memoir writing

ACKNOWLEDGMENTS

PORTIONS OF THIS MEMOIR HAVE APPEARED IN THE FOL-
lowing journals, in different versions and forms: "Meet Me Tonight
in Atlantic City" in *Ecotone*; "Root Canal Street" in *Black Warrior
Review*; "A Cheat Sheet for Restaurant Babies" as "A Family Business"
in *This Is the Place: Women Writing about Home* (Seal Press); "Give Us
Our Crowns" in the *Georgia Review*; "A Jane by Any Other Name" in
Joyland; "Bad Bildungsroman with Table Tennis" in *Apogee*; "To Love
a Mosquito" in *Shenandoah*; "The Thief" in *Wanting: Women Writing about Desire* (Catapult); "Snow, Rain, Heat, Pandemic, Gloom of
Night" in *What Things Cost: An Anthology for the People* (University
Press of Kentucky); "An Ancient Chinese Saying" is a reworked ver-
sion of "How to Touch" in *Poetry Northwest*; and "Ghost Archive
(Look Again)" is a reworked version of "Offerings" in the *Common*.

PERSONAL ACKNOWLEDGMENTS

IF GRATITUDE COULD BE MEASURED IN BOARDWALK SHAVED ice, I would make a delicious lemon tundra for everyone who helped me with this vulnerable memoir. Thank you to Elizabeth DeMeo, my visionary editor, who believed in the book's twists and turns, offering insightful feedback at every stage; I wrote parts of this book during a tumultuous time in my personal life and I'm so grateful for her patience and unwavering confidence. Thank you to everyone at Tin House, the best team I could ask for, especially Becky Kraemer, Nanci McCloskey, and Craig Popelars. I'm honored to be one of your authors. Thank you to Jaya Miceli for the hermit crab dream of a cover.

Thank you to my dear friends and close readers who supported this book through heartfelt conversations, attentive notes, and endless snacks. Extra soup dumplings for Quenton Baker, Tessa Hulls, Brenda Miller, and Michelle Peñaloza for being early readers with generosity and insight. All the crispy chips to Naa Akua, Katie Anderson, Catina Bacote, Bill Carty, Paul Hlava Ceballos, Cathy Linh Che, Chen Chen, Darren Davis, Nicholas Gulig, Sally Wen Mao, Natalie Martinez, Diana Khoi Nguyen, Keenan Norris, Eric Olson, Anastacia-Reneé, Matthew Schnirman, and Keith S. Wilson for your encouragement and lightbulb conversations. A special thanks to Brandon Young for conjuring Wongmom.com. Extra boxes of Pocky for Dan Lau who lent me his noodle-filled apartment, where the memoir started to take full glutinous shape. Thank you to Mat

Johnson for the beginnings; I promised I'd come back to prose. As always, sticky-note stars for my students, who remind me of the goat in the attic. Endless boba tea for Victoria Chang, Elissa Washuta, Sally Wen Mao, Morgan Parker, Gina Chung, Tessa Hulls, and Kyle Lucia Wu for their generous simmering words about the book.

Thank you to all the fantastic editors I worked closely with on earlier versions of these essays, especially Margot Kahn Case, Anna Leahy, Crystal Hana Kim, Kelly McMasters, Soham Patel, Beth Staples, and Kyle Lucia Wu. Thank you for pushing me forward.

Thank you to the following writing residencies where many of these pages were written, in one form or another: Loghaven, Mineral School, Hedgebrook, Dear Butte, The Whiteley Center, SAFTA, Sou'wester, The Jentel Foundation, and Willapa Bay's AiR. I want to especially thank my fellow artists at Loghaven, where turkeys flew around this memoir: Daniel Corral, Kleaver Cruz, Alexander Gedeon, DaEun Jung, and Jennifer Wen Ma—your log is my log, always. Kundiman, you changed everything; thank you and see you on the dance floor. Thank you to Artist Trust, the Frye Art Museum, the Barbara Deming Memorial Fund, and Western Washington University for their kind support.

Thank you to my family, who have trusted me with their stories— one orange segment at a time. Thank you to my grandparents, my baby cheeks still bundled to their chests. Thank you to Vinny, whose big heart makes me laugh. Three XL thin-crust pizzas with all the toppings for my mother and brother—the mighty triumvirate, with lots of red-pepper flakes and parm. You two are my entire world and I wouldn't be who I am without you both. I love you so much. Foot race at Sea Bright? Oops, I cheated and already started (little bird feet running) . . .

BIBLIOGRAPHY AND CREDITS

MEET ME TONIGHT IN ATLANTIC CITY

AC Primetime. "Atlantic City Boardwalk: Wooden Way Steeped in History." March 4, 2015. https://acprimetime.com/atlantic-city-boardwalk-wooden-way-steeped-in-history/.

Associated Press. "Crash Highlights Chinese American Gambling Market." NBC News, March 16, 2011. https://www.nbcnews.com/id/wbna42113287.

Associated Press. "Officials: 14 Dead after Bus Traveling from Mohegan Sun Casino Crashes in Bronx." NJ.com, March 12, 2011. https://www.nj.com/news/2011/03/bus_traveling_from_mohegan_sun.html.

Atlantic City Free Public Library. "History of Atlantic City." Accessed February 6, 2023. http://acfpl.org/ac-history-menu/atlantic-city-faq-s/15-heston-archives/147-atlantic-city-history-22.html.

Brennan, John. "Construction Abounds, Atlantic City Rebounds." NorthJersey.com, May 5, 2017. https://www.northjersey.com/story/news/2017/05/05/construction-abound-atlantic-city- rebound/101151098/.

Chin, Marilyn. "How I Got That Name." In *The Phoenix Gone, the Terrace Empty.* Minneapolis: Milkweed Editions, 1994.

Cision PR Newswire. "Lucky Dragon Hotel & Casino in Las Vegas Opens Its Doors to the World with Grand Opening Celebration on Saturday, December 3." Press release. December 7, 2016. https://www.prnewswire.com/news-releases/lucky-dragon-hotel-casino-in-las-vegas-opens-its-doors-to-the-world-with-grand-opening-celebration-on-saturday-dec-3-300374283.html.

Collectors Weekly. "Vintage and Antique Mahjong Sets." Accessed January 10, 2023. https://www.collectorsweekly.com/games/mah-jong.

Fong, Timothy W., and John Tsuang. "Asian-Americans, Addictions, and Barriers to Treatment." *Psychiatry* (Edgmont) 4, no. 11 (2007): 51–59.

Glionna, John. "Gambling Seen as a No-Win Situation for Some Asians." *Los Angeles Times*, January 16, 2006. https://www.latimes.com/archives/la-xpm-2006-jan-16-me-gamble16-story.html.

Kozek, Barbara. "History of Atlantic City." City of Atlantic City, New Jersey (website). https://www.acnj.gov/page/history-of-atlantic-city.

Liao, Michael. "Asian Americans and Problem Gambling." *Problem Gambling Prevention: Technical Assistance and Training Project.* January 2016. https://docplayer.net/14740916-Asian-americans-and-problem-gambling-by-michael-liao-msw-nicos-chinese-health-coalition.html.

Linky, Don. "Atlantic City and Casino Gambling." Eagleton Institute of Politics, Rutgers University (website). Accessed February 6, 2023. https://governors.rutgers.edu/atlantic-city-and-casino-gambling-history/.

Louie, Sam. "Is Gambling Addiction in Asian American Community Rooted in Culture?" AsAmNews, July 10, 2014. https://asamnews.com/2014/07/10/is-gambling-addiction-in-asian-american-community-rooted-in-culture/.

Pierson, David. "Las Vegas Casinos Love Chinese Gamblers. So These Guys Built a Casino Just for Them." *Los Angeles Times*, October 26, 2016. https://www.latimes.com/business/la-fi-vegas-chinese-20161026-snap-story.html.

Press of Atlantic City. "A Look at Key Moments in the History of Revel Casino Hotel." January 9, 2019. https://pressofatlanticcity.com/a-look-at-key-moments-in-the-history-of-revel-casino-hotel/article_7a8abe14-e84f-5968-a5f8-1b1c74e087e9.html.

Pritchard, Mike. "Lightning Strike Kills Worker at Revel Construction Site, Injures Two More." *Atlantic City Weekly*, September 15, 2011. https://atlanticcityweekly.com/archive/lightning-strike-kills-worker-at-revel-construction-site-injures-two-more/article_db409ab2-ca87-5ae8-ad5a-ef3011197150.html.

Stapleton, Susan. "Meet the Dragon Alley, Lucky Dragon's Night Market." *Eater Vegas*, December 5, 2016. https://vegas.eater.com/2016/12/5/13833644/dragon-alley-lucky-dragon-night-market-eater-inside#4.

Voigt, Emily. "This Fish is Worth $300,000." *New York Post*, June 5, 2016. https://nypost.com/2016/06/05/this-fish-is-worth-300000/.

Weisner, Ken. "Interview with Marilyn Chin." *MELUS* 37, no. 3 (2012): 215–26.

WONGMOM.COM
Cha, Theresa Hak Kyung. *Dictee*. Berkeley: University of California Press, 2009.

ROOT CANAL STREET
Dental Implant Cost Guide. "Complete Dental Implant Cost Guide." Accessed June 25, 2021. https://www.dentalimplantcostguide.com/dental-implants-cost/.

Lee, Youngsub, and Hyoungsup Kim. "The Turning Point of China's Rural Public Health during the Cultural Revolution Period: Barefoot Doctors: A Narrative." *Iranian Journal of Public Health* 47, suppl. 1 (2018): 1–8.

Li, Diane, dir. *The Barefoot Doctors of Rural China*. 1975; Stanford, CA: Diane Li Productions. YouTube video, 50:03 min. Uploaded by PublicResourceOrg, December 12, 2009. https://www.youtube.com/watch?v=1YvwVFC-TJY&t=106s.

Martin, Dawn Lundy. *Life in a Box Is a Pretty Life*. Brooklyn: Nightboat Books, 2014.

Pierre-Pierre, Garry. "10 Held as Unlicensed Medical Practitioners." *New York Times*, August 9, 1996. https://www.nytimes.com/1996/08/09/nyregion/10-held-as-unlicensed-medical-practitioners.html.

Wilson Center Digital Archive. "Long Live Mao Zedong Thought (1968)." Accessed January 15, 2018. https://digitalarchive.wilsoncenter.org/collection/733/long-live-mao-zedong-thought-1968.

Yang, Jingyi, Ying Zhang, Xiaolong Ye, Cheng Xie, Xv Ge, Fan Lu, Qing Yu, Hantang Sun. "Dental Education Evaluation in China: A Systematic Review." *BMC Medical Education* 14, no. 178 (2014).

Zedong, Mao. "Directive on Public Health." *Long Live Mao Tse-tung Thought*, June 26, 1965. https://www.marxists.org/reference/archive/mao/selected-works/volume-9/mswv9_41.htm.

GHOST ARCHIVE

Cha, Theresa Hak Kyung. *Dictee*. Berkeley: University of California Press, 2009.

GIVE US OUR CROWNS

Amazon. "TOOGOO Nose Up Lifting Shaping & Bridge Straightening Beauty Clip." Accessed February 6, 2023. https://www.amazon.com/champper-Lifting-Shaping-Bridge-Straightening/dp/B00PTXA46S.

Chow, Yiu Fai. "Moving, Sensing Intersectionality: A Case Study of Miss China Europe." *Signs: Journal of Women in Culture and Society* 36, no. 2 (2011): 411–436.

Petersen, Barry. "Latest Trend Sweeping China: Lighter Skin." CBS News, October 14, 2012. https://www.cbsnews.com/news/latest-trend-sweeping-china-lighter-skin/.

Tomb, Devin. "China Women Go in for Western Features." *Los Angeles Times*, August 28, 2010. https://www.latimes.com/archives/la-xpm-2010-aug-28-la-adfg-china-cosmetic-surgery-20100828-story.html.

Village Green of Maplewood and South Orange. "Maplewood's Nyla Edwards Wins Miss Preteen New Jersey." November 28, 2016. https://villagegreennj.com/towns/maplewood/maplewoods-nyla-edwards-wins-miss-preteen-new-jersey/.

———. "Miss NJ Pre-Teen Nyla Edwards of Maplewood Hosts Coat Drive Nov 12." November 4, 2016. https://villagegreennj.com/community/maplewoods-miss-nj-pre-teen-nyla-edwards-hosts-coat-drive-nov-12/.

Yashoda Hospitals. "Niacinamide: Frequently Asked Questions Answered." Accessed July 16, 2022. https://www.yashodahospitals.com/medicine-faqs/niacinamide/.

You, Tracy. "Women in Asia Deliberately Insert Pegs Into Their Nostrils [...] Beauty Trend." *Daily Mail*, November 7, 2017. https://www.dailymail.co.uk/news/article-5055215/Women-Asia-insert-pegs-nose-look-European.html.

WHITE HAIR

Feldman, Margeaux (@softcore_trauma). "The Traumatized Urge to Change Your Aesthetic Instead of Feeling Your Feelings." Instagram photo, June 13, 2022. https://www.instagram.com/p/CewszhyPQ9y/?hl=en.

A JANE BY ANY OTHER NAME

Castelow, Ellen. "Lady Jane Grey." *Historic UK: The History and Heritage Accommodation Guide.* February 4, 2020. https://www.historic-uk.com/HistoryUK/HistoryofEngland/Lady-Jane-Grey/.

Chan, Anthony. *Perpetually Cool: The Many Lives of Anna May Wong (1905–1961).* Lanham, MD: Scarecrow Press, 2007.

Faye Wong Library. "Faye Wong's Career: Hong Kong Never Changed Her (2010)." Translated by Faye Wong Fuzao. Tumblr, October 21, 2020. Original source *Sanlian Lifeweek* magazine. https://fayewonglibrary.tumblr.com/post/632624975708307456/faye-wongs-career-hong-kong-never-changed-her.

Franklin, Chester M., dir. *The Toll of the Sea.* Technicolor Motion Picture Corporation, 1922.

Jordan, June. "Poem about My Rights." In *Directed by Desire: The Collected Poems of June Jordan.* Port Townsend, WA: Copper Canyon Press, 2012.

Liu, Nathan. "Why Do We Remember Anna May Wong?" Asian CineVision, May 10, 2021. https://www.asiancinevision.org why-do-we-remember-anna-may-wong/.

Martin, Ann M. *The Baby-Sitters Club: Claudia Kishi, Middle School Dropout.* New York: Scholastic, 1996.

Wikipedia. "Anna May Wong." Last edited November 20, 2022. https://en.wikipedia.org/wiki/Anna_May_Wong.

———. "Calamity Jane." Last edited October 15, 2022. https://en.wikipedia.org/wiki/Calamity_Jane.

———. "Faye Wong." Last edited October 23, 2022. https://en.wikipedia.org/wiki/Faye_Wong.

———. "The Good Earth (Film)." Last edited August 24, 2022. https://en.wikipedia.org/wiki/The_Good_Earth_(film).

———. "Jane (Given Name)." Last edited November 5, 2022. https://en.wikipedia.org/wiki/Jane_(given_name).

———. "Pearl S. Buck." Last edited January 23, 2023. https://en.wikipedia.org/wiki/Pearl_S._Buck.

———. "Streatham Portrait." Last edited June 26, 2022. https://en.wikipedia.org/wiki/Streatham_portrait.

Wiktionary. "Wong." Last edited December 5, 2022. https://en.wiktionary.org/wiki/Wong.

Wong Kar-wai, dir. "Faye Wong – Dreams, Chungking Express (1994)." YouTube video, 4:29 min. Uploaded by Van S, April 14, 2018. https://www.youtube.com/watch?v=H3VpC8x3wL8&ab_channel=VanS.

Wong Wayne, Gwen. "Lust for Life with Gwen Wong Wayne." *Playboy*, September 14, 2020. https://www.playboy.com/read/lust-for-life-with-gwen-wong-wayne.

BAD BILDUNGSROMAN WITH TABLE TENNIS
Anwar, Bisma. "Do I Have Daddy Issues? Ask a Therapist." Talkspace, March 28, 2022. https://www.talkspace.com/blog/daddy-issues/.
Beech, Hannah. "China's Sports School: Crazy for Gold." *Time*, June 19, 2008. https://content.time.com/time/subscriber/article/0,33009,1813961,00.html.
Brussat, Frederic, and Mary Ann Brussat. "Top Spin." Spirituality & Practice. https://www.spiritualityandpractice.com/films/reviews/view/28039/top-spin.
China Daily. "In Memory of China's 1st World Champion Rong Guotuan." April 4, 2014. https://www.chinadaily.com.cn/sports/2014-04/04/content_17409143.htm.
Chineseposters.net. "Table Tennis." https://chineseposters.net/themes/table-tennis.
Nusbaum, Eric. "The Lost Legend and Secret Legacy of Table Tennis Master Rong Guotuan." *Deadspin*, September 24, 2019. https://deadspin.com/the-lost-legend-and-secret-legacy-of-table-tennis-maste-1838346515.
National Museum of American Diplomacy. "Ping Pong Diplomacy: Artifacts from the Historic 1971 U.S. Table Tennis Trip to China." August 5, 2021. https://diplomacy.state.gov/artifact-collection-highlights/ping-pong-diplomacy-historic-1971-u-s-table-tennis-trip-to-china/.
Sakugawa, Yumi. "14 Practical Uses for Nail Polish Remover That Have Nothing to Do With Removing Nail Polish." Wonder How To (website), April 20, 2013. https://thesecretyumiverse.wonderhowto.com/how-to/14-practical-uses-for-nail-polish-remover-have-nothing-do-with-removing-nail-polish-0146460/.
Santos-Longhurst, Adrienne. "Yes, 'Daddy Issues' Are a Real Thing – Here's How to Deal." Healthline. https://www.healthline.com/health/what-are-daddy-issues.
UV Academy. "Table Tennis Fun Fact!!!" Facebook, July 10, 2018. https://www.facebook.com/uvacademy/posts/table-tennis-fun-factin-1993-two-players-named-jackie-bellinger-and-lisa-lomas-s/1966170373694562/.
Wikipedia. "Ping Pong Diplomacy." Last edited August 28, 2022. https://en.wikipedia.org/wiki/Ping-pong_diplomacy.
———. "Rong Guotuan." Last edited August 7, 2021. https://en.wikipedia.org/wiki/Rong_Guotuan.

THE WATCHER
Hirshhorn Museum. "Yayoi Kusama: Infinity Mirror Rooms." Accessed June 13, 2022. https://hirshhorn.si.edu/kusama/infinity-rooms/.
WebMD Editorial Contributors. "What Is Hypervigilance?" WebMD, October 25, 2021. https://www.webmd.com/mental-health/what-is-hypervigilance.

THE OBJECT OF LOVE

Brockes, Emma. "Toni Morrison Interview: 'I Want to Feel What I Feel. Even If It's Not Happiness.'" *Guardian*, April 13, 2012. https://www.theguardian.com/books/2012/apr/13/toni-morrison-home-son-love.

Chou, Elaine Hsieh. *Disorientation*. New York: Penguin Random House, 2022.

Emerson, Ralph Waldo. "Circles." In *Essays*. Edited by Edna H. L. Turpin. Urbana, IL: Project Gutenberg, 2005. https://www.gutenberg.org/ebooks/16643.

hooks, bell. *All about Love: New Visions*. New York: HarperCollins Publishers, 2018.

Internicola, Dorene. "Medicine Balls Are Ancient Fitness Tools That Keep Bouncing Back." Reuters, October 6, 2014. https://www.reuters.com/article/us-fitness-medicineballs/medicine-balls-are-ancient-fitness-tools-that-keep-bouncing-back-idUSKCN0HV0O020141006.

WONGMOM.COM (DON'T MESS WITH ME)

Clifton, Lucille. "why some people be mad at me sometimes." In *The Collected Poems of Lucille Clifton 1965–2010*. Rochester, NY: BOA Editions, 2012.

———. "won't you celebrate with me." In *The Book of Light*. Port Townsend, WA: Copper Canyon Press, 1993.

Yang Jisheng. *Tombstone: The Great Chinese Famine, 1958–1992*. New York: Farrar, Straus, and Giroux, 2013.

TO LOVE A MOSQUITO

Anderson, Bradley. "Komarno, Manitoba, Canada: World's Largest Mosquito." Roadside America, April 27, 2010. https://www.roadsideamerica.com/tip/25034.

Berliner, Hila. "On Family." *Chinese Idioms and Sayings* 汉语成语 (blog), November 17, 2011. http://sin-idioms.blogspot.com/2011/11/on-family.html.

Christopher, Dean. "20 Things You Didn't Know About . . . Mosquitoes." *Discover Magazine*, July 22, 2007. https://www.discovermagazine.com/health/20-things-you-didnt-know-about-mosquitoes.

Miller, Brad. "Tiger Father Begets Tiger Son – Chinese Proverb." Pinterest. https://www.pinterest.com/pin/163959242658279008/.

MosquitoNix. "7 Facts About Mosquitoes." July 2, 2018. https://mosquitonixatlanta.com/2018/07/02/7-facts-about-mosquitoes/.

Zieff, Howard, dir. *My Girl*. Imagine Entertainment, 1991.

AN ANCIENT CHINESE SAYING

CantoDict Project: Learn Cantonese. "馬死落地行." October 30, 2005. http://www.cantonese.sheik.co.uk/dictionary/words/13795/.

Guardian. "Georgia Officer Says Atlanta Shooter Was 'Having a Bad Day.'" March 18, 2021. https://www.theguardian.com/us-news/video/2021/mar/18/georgia-officer-appears-to-say-it-was-a-bad-day-for-atlanta-shooter-video.

NOCTURNAL FORCES

Césaire, Aimé. "Poetry and Knowledge." Translated by A. James Arnold. In *Toward the Open Field: Poets on the Art of Poetry 1800–1950*. Edited by Melissa Kwasny. Middletown, CT: Wesleyan University Press, 2004.

SNOW, RAIN, HEAT, PANDEMIC, GLOOM OF NIGHT

Del Ray, Jason. "Sneeze Guards, Toilet Paper, and Visits from Lonely Seniors: Running a Post Office during the Pandemic." *Vox*, April 1, 2020. https://www.vox.com/recode/2020/4/1/21199646/coronavirus-covid-19-usps-post-office-hours-postman-interview.

Levine, Sam. "Trump Admits He Is Undermining USPS to Make It Harder to Vote by Mail." *Guardian*, August 13, 2020. https://www.theguardian.com/us-news/2020/aug/13/donald-trump-usps-post-office-election-funding.

National Conference of State Legislatures. "COVID-19: Essential Workers in the States." November 1, 2021. https://www.ncsl.org/research/labor-and-employment/covid-19-essential-workers-in-the-states.aspx.

Naylor, Brian. "You've Got Less Mail: The Postal Service Is Suffering Amid the Coronavirus." NPR, April 8, 2020. https://www.npr.org/2020/04/08/828949609/youve-got-less-mail-the-postal-service-is-suffering-amid-the-coronavirus.

Page, Sydney. "World's Most Remote Post Office is Hiring. Penguin Counting Required." *Washington Post*, April 23, 2020. https://www.washingtonpost.com/lifestyle/2022/04/23/antarctica-post-office-hire-penguin/.

Pope, Nancy. "100th Anniversary of the DC City Post Office Building." Smithsonian National Postal Museum (website), September 4, 2014. https://postalmuseum.si.edu/100th-anniversary-of-the-dc-city-post-office-building.

Rahman, Khaleda. "California Woman Yells Racial Slur at Asian American USPS Worker in Video." *Newsweek*, July 27, 2022. https://www.newsweek.com/woman-caught-video-racial-slur-usps-employee-1520692.

United States Postal Service. "24-Hour Clock Keeps USPS Linked." Accessed March 10, 2021. https://about.usps.com/postal-bulletin/2006/html/pb22176/atworkl.html.

———. "About That Motto." Postal Facts. Accessed March 10, 2021. https://facts.usps.com/no-official-motto/.

———. "Workforce Diversity and Inclusiveness." Accessed February 8, 2023. https://about.usps.com/strategic-planning/cs09/CSPO_09_087.htm.

United States Postal Service Office of Inspector General. "The Pandemic, the Postal Service, and Public Perception." April 12, 2021. https://www.uspsoig.gov/blog/pandemic-postal-service-and-public-perception.

———. "The Postal Service and Its Obligation." November 17, 2014. https://www.uspsoig.gov/blog/postal-service-and-its-obligation.

Ward, Myah. "Trump: Postal Service Is a 'Joke' That Must Raise Price to Get Bailout Money." *Politico*, April 24, 2020. https://www.politico.com/news/2020/04/24/trump-us-postal-service-coronavirus-bailout-206851.

GHOST ARCHIVE (LOOK AGAIN)

Wong, Jane. *After Preparing the Altar, the Ghosts Feast Feverishly*. Exhibition. Frye Art Museum, June 1–September 1, 2019. https://fryemuseum.org/exhibitions/jane-wong-after-preparing-altar-ghosts-feast-feverishly.

FINDING THE BLOODLINE

Akbar, Arifa. "Mao's Great Leap Forward 'Killed 45 Million in Four Years.'" *Independent*, September 17, 2010. https://www.independent.co.uk/arts-entertainment/books/news/maos-great-leap-forward-killed-45-million-in-four-years-2081630.html.

Anderson, Brett. "With Chop Suey and Loyal Fans, a Montana Kitchen Keeps the Flame Burning." *New York Times*, Aug 3, 2021. https://www.nytimes.com/2021/08/03/dining/pekin-noodle-parlor-butte-montana.html.

Block, Melissa, and Fuchsia Dunlop. "Revolutionary Recipes from China's Hunan Province." NPR, February 28, 2007. https://www.npr.org/2007/02/28/7603457/revolutionary-recipes-from-chinas-hunan-province.

Branigan, Tania. "China's Great Famine: The True Story." *Guardian*, January 1, 2013. https://www.theguardian.com/world/2013/jan/01/china-great-famine-book-tombstone.

Breakfast Cure. Accessed February 8, 2023. https://breakfastcure.com.

———. "The Breakfast Cure Story with Karen Taylor, L.Ac., founder." YouTube video, 1:50 min. Uploaded April 21, 2019. https://www.youtube.com/watch?v=kRNiuFVhGfk.

Breen, Kerry. "Brand Selling 'Improved' Congee 'for the Western' Palate Stirs Up Controversy." *USA Today*, July 19, 2021. https://www.today.com/food/breakfast-cure-brand-sells-improved-congee-sparks-controversy-t225951.

Brown, Clayton D. "China's Great Leap Forward." *Education about Asia* 17, no. 3 (Winter 2012): 29–34. https://www.asianstudies.org/publications/eaa/archives/chinas-great-leap-forward/.

Chang, Jung, and Jon Halliday. *Mao: The Unknown Story*. New York: Anchor Books, 2005.

Chineseposters.net. "Great Leap Forward." Accessed July 6, 2022. https://chineseposters.net/themes/great-leap-forward.

Cooking in Mexico. "A Guided Tour of the La Cruz Fish Market with Tips for Buying Fish and an Easy Recipe for Pan Fried Fish." April 22, 2010. https://kathleeniscookinginmexico.wordpress.com/2010/04/22/a-guided-tour-of-the-la-cruz-fish-market-with-tips-for-buying-fish-and-an-easy-recipe-for-pan-fried-fish/.

The Culinary Pro. "Fish and Shellfish Identification." Accessed July 2, 2022. https://www.theculinarypro.com/fish-shellfish-identification.

EarthTalk. "Do Biodegradable Items Degrade in Landfills?" ThoughtCo., October 16, 2019. https://www.thoughtco.com/do-biodegradable-items-really-break-down-1204144.

Eva R. "People are not friendly…" Yelp review of New York City's Chinatown, March 24, 2014. https://www.yelp.com/biz/chinatown-new-york-4?start=80.

Facebook. "Pekin Cafe." https://www.facebook.com/pekinnoodleparlor/.

Fadulu, Lola. "Man Charged with Killing Worker over Duck Sauce Found Dead, Police Say." *New York Times,* August 8, 2022. https://www.nytimes.com/2022/08/05/nyregion/delivery-worker-duck-sauce-suspect-dead.html.

Fernando, Christine. "'What Is This White Nonsense?': So-Called Queen of Congee Accused of Cultural Appropriation of Chinese Food." *USA Today,* July 22, 2021. https://www.usatoday.com/story/news/nation/2021/07/22/breakfast-cure-queen-congee-accused-cultural-appropriation/8060424002/.

Gyimah-Brempong, Adwoa. "Have You Eaten Yet? Poet Jane Wong Prepares Her Ancestors a Feast." KUOW, August 8, 2019. https://www.kuow.org/stories/jane-wong-after-preparing-the-altar-the-ghosts-feast-feverishly.

Haupt, Melanie. "White Girl Asian Food Truck Draws Internet Ire." *Eater Austin,* January 25, 2016. https://austin.eater.com/2016/1/25/10829798/white-girl-asian-food-truck.

Jackson-Glidden, Brooke. "A White Woman from Oregon Is Getting Called Out for Claiming to 'Improve' Congee." *Eater Portland,* July 23, 2021. https://pdx.eater.com/2021/7/23/22589073/eugene-oregon-food-business-cultural-appropriation-congee-breakfast-cure.

Jerome L. "Dirty and disgusting low quality place…" Yelp review of New York City's Chinatown, November 22, 2017. https://www.yelp.com/biz/chinatown-new-york-4?start=50.

Johnson, Ian. "Finding the Facts About Mao's Victims." *The New York Review,* December 20, 2010. https://www.nybooks.com/online/2010/12/20/finding-facts-about-maos-victims/.

Kakutani, Michiko. "*Mao: The Unknown Story.*" *New York Times,* October 30, 2005. https://www.nytimes.com/2005/10/30/arts/mao-the-unknown-story.html.

Khan, Nahnatchka, dir. *Always Be My Maybe.* Good Universe, 2019.

Laskow, Sarah. "Even in a Toxic Pit, There Is Life." *Atlas Obscura,* May 7, 2015. https://www.atlasobscura.com/articles/even-in-toxic-berkeley-pit-there-is-life.

Lim, Lisa. "Where the Word Congee Comes From—The Answer May Surprise You." *Post Magazine,* November 10, 2017. https://www.scmp.com/magazines/post-magazine/article/2119163/where-word-congee-comes-answer-may-surprise-you.

Mason, Jane. "Surviving Butte: The Story of the Auditor." *Ohmidog!* October 21, 2022. https://web.archive.org/web/20101111115416/http://www.ohmidog.com/2010/11/02/surviving-butte-the-story-of-the-auditor/.

Mike M. "Trash strewn everywhere…" Yelp review of New York City's Chinatown, May 29, 2016. https://www.yelp.com/biz/chinatown-new-york-4?start=40.

Morales, Danielle Xiaodan, Stephanie Alexandra Morales, and Tyler Fox Beltran. "Racial/Ethnic Disparities in Household Food Insecurity During the COVID-19 Pandemic: a Nationally Representative Study." *Journal of Racial and Ethnic Health Disparities* 8, no. 5 (2021): 1300–1314.

Nezhukumatathil, Aimee. "One Star Reviews of the Great Wall of China." In *Oceanic*. Port Townsend, WA: Copper Canyon Press, 2018.

Pico, Tommy. *Feed*. Portland, OR: Tin House, 2019.

Rosner, Helen. "The Joylessness of Cooking." *New Yorker*, November 25, 2020. https://www.new yorker.com/culture/kitchen-notes/the-joylessness-of-cooking.

Scarpa, Gina. "Top Chef: All Stars, Conference Call with Tiffani Faison." Reality Wanted, January 13, 2011. https://www.realitywanted.com/newsitem/3964-top-chef-all-stars-conference-call-with-tiffani-faison#.YyOXZuzMKRM.

Shanfeld, Ethan. "BTS Meal Coming to McDonald's in May." *Variety*, April 19, 2021. https://variety.com/2021/music/news/bts-fries-meal-mcdonalds-1234955071/.

Stoops, PJ. "The Dark Side of Yield." CleanFish (website), September 4, 2019. https://www.cleanfish.com/blog/2019/9/4/the-dark-side-of-yield.

Times of India. "What Makes Fruits and Vegetables Rot?" January 29, 2019. https://timesofindia.indiatimes.com/life-style/food-news/what-makes-fruits-and-vegetables-rot/photostory/67735843.cms.

Trillin, Calvin. "Have They Run Out of Provinces Yet?" *New Yorker*, April 4, 2016. https://www.newyorker.com/magazine/2016/04/04/have-they-run-out-of-provinces-yet-by-calvin-trillin.

Trisha R. "Being Asian I thought it would [be] comical." Yelp review of White Girl Asian Food, October 14, 2017. https://www.yelp.com/biz/white-girl-asian-food-austin-3.

Vansynghel, Margo. "Seattle Artist. Fights Anti-Asian Racism in the Chinatown-International District." *Crosscut*, May 14, 2020. https://crosscut.com/culture/2020/05/seattle-artist-fights-anti-asian-racism-chinatown-international-district.

Wikipedia. "Auditor (Dog)." Last edited August 15, 2022. https://en.wikipedia.org/wiki/Auditor_(dog).

———. "Berkeley Pit." Last edited October 17, 2022. https://en.wikipedia.org/wiki/Berkeley_Pit.

———. "Great Leap Forward." Last edited November 11, 2022. https://en.wikipedia.org/wiki/Great_Leap_Forward.

———. "Pekin Noodle Parlor." Last edited November 9, 2022. https://en.wikipedia.org/wiki/Pekin_Noodle_Parlor.

———. "Red Braised Pork Belly." Last edited November 18, 2022. https://en.wikipedia.org/wiki/Red_braised_pork_belly.

Yang Jisheng. *Tombstone: The Great Chinese Famine, 1958–1992*. New York: Farrar, Straus, and Giroux, 2013.

Yu, Phil. "There Is a Food Truck Actually Called 'White Girl Asian Food.'" *Angry Asian Man*, January 14, 2016. http://blog.angryasianman.com/2016/01/there-is-food-truck-actually-called.html.

Zaru, Deena. "Outrage after Man Accused of Killing Chinese Food Delivery Worker Released on Bail." ABC News, June 19, 2022. https://abcnews.go.com/US/outrage-man-accused-killing-chinese-food-delivery-worker/story?id=85915540.

ASTONISHED ENOUGH?

Aiello, Antonio. "Equity in Publishing: What Should Editors Be Doing?" PEN America, October 24, 2015. https://pen.org/equity-in-publishing-what-should-editors-be-doing/.

Alexie, Sherman. "Sherman Alexie Speaks Out on the Best American Poetry 2015." *Best American Poetry Blog*, September 7, 2015. https://blog.bestamericanpoetry. com/the_best_american_poetry/2015/09/like-most-every-poet-i-have-viewed-the-publication-of-each-years-best-american-poetry-with-happiness-i-love-that-poem-je-1.html.

Brooks, Gwendolyn. "Speech to the Young: Speech to the Progress-Toward (among Them Nora and Henry III)." In *Blacks*. Chicago: Third World Press, 1991.

Cha, Theresa Hak Kyung. *Dictee*. Berkeley: University of California Press, 2009.

———, dir. *Mouth to Mouth*. Electronic Arts Intermix, 1975. https://www.eai. org/titles/mouth-to-mouth.

Chang, Victoria. *Dear Memory*. Minneapolis: Milkweed Editions, 2021.

Dean, Michelle. "White Poet Who Wrote as 'Yi-Fen Chou' Reportedly Took Classmate's Name." *Guardian*, September 10, 2015. https://www.theguardian.com/ books/2015/sep/10/white-poet-chinese-pseudonym-yi-fen-chou-former-classmate.

Hong, Cathy Park. "Portrait of an Artist." In *Minor Feelings: An Asian American Reckoning*. New York: Penguin Random House, 2020.

Hong Kingston, Maxine. *The Woman Warrior: Memoirs of a Girlhood among Ghosts*. New York: Vintage, 2010.

Hudson, Michael Derrick. "Contributor's Note." In *The Best American Poetry 2015*. Guest edited by Sherman Alexie. New York: Scribner, 2015.

Hughes, Langston. "Final Curve." In *Selected Poems of Langston Hughes*. New York: Vintage, 2011.

Ling, Isabel. "Commemorating the Life of Christina Yuna Lee." *Hyperallergic*, May 30, 2022. https://hyperallergic.com/735786/commemorating-the-life-of-christina-yuna-lee/.

Lorde, Audre. "Poetry is Not a Luxury." In *The Selected Works of Audre Lorde*. Edited by Roxane Gay. New York: W. W. Norton & Company, 2020.

Moses, Dean. "Public Memorial to Chinatown Murder Victim Christina Yuna Lee Senselessly Trashed." *Villager*, February 17, 2022. https://www.amny.com/ new-york/memorial-chinatown-murder-victim-christina-yuna-lee-trashed/.

Neary, Lynn. "'It Just Felt Very Wrong': Sherman Alexie's Accusers Go on the Record." NPR, March 5, 2018. https://www.npr.org/2018/03/05/589909379/ it-just-felt-very-wrong-sherman-alexies-accusers-go-on-the-record.

Olds, Sharon. "Take the I Out." In *Blood, Tin, Straw*. New York: Knopf, 1999.

Saltzstein, Dan. "Overlooked No More: Theresa Hak Kyung Cha, Artist and Author Who Explored Identity." *New York Times*, January 10, 2022. https:// www.nytimes.com/2022/01/07/obituaries/theresa-hak-kyung-cha-overlooked. html.

Schuessler, Jennifer. "Family Protests White Poet's Use of Chinese Pen Name." *New York Times*, September 10, 2015. https://archive.nytimes.com/artsbeat.blogs.nytimes.com/2015/09/10/family-protests-white-poets-use-of-chinese-pen-name/.

Sharif, Solmaz. "A Poetry of Proximity." *Kenyon Review*, Sept. 2014. https://kenyon review.org/kr-online-issue/kenyon-review-credos/selections/sharif-credo/.

Yellow Horse, Aggie J., Russel Jeung, Richard Lim, Boaz Tang, Megan Im, Lauryn Higashiyama, Layla Schweng, and Mikayla Chen. "Stop AAPI Hate National Report." Stop AAPI Hate, August 12, 2021. https://stopaapihate.org/wp-content/uploads/2021/08/Stop-AAPI-Hate-Report-National-v2-210830.pdf.

MANGOES FOREVER

BBC News. "China's Curious Cult of the Mango." February 11, 2016. https://www.bbc.com/news/magazine-35461265.

Gingrich, Jessica. "How a Fruit Basket from Mao Made China Mad for Mangoes." *Atlas Obscura*, November 4, 2019. https://www.atlasobscura.com/articles/does-anyone-like-fruitbaskets.

Greene, Nick. "How Mao Accidentally Turned Mangoes into Divine Objects." *Mental Floss*, July 22, 2014. https://www.mentalfloss.com/article/57937/how-mao-accidentally-turned-mangoes-into-divine-objects-cultural-revolution.

READER'S GUIDE

1. In chapters like "Meet Me Tonight in Atlantic City," author Jane Wong weaves in research about the high rates of gambling addiction among Asian American communities with her father's own experience in Atlantic City and its impact on her family. Where else does Jane intermingle different storytelling approaches? What is the impact of including research alongside personal narrative?

2. Throughout *Meet Me Tonight in Atlantic City,* there are moments where we see Jane reflecting on her past as well as her present and future. What role does Wongmom.com play in her exploration of time? How do these explorations into the present and future challenge the idea of memoir as something only based in memory/in the past? How does the nonlinear form of the book echo larger themes such as migration?

3. What role does New Jersey itself—in particular, Atlantic City and the Jersey shore—play in the memoir? In the context of this book and in your own life, how do you think the places where we grow up inform the people we become?

4. There are moments of humor throughout *Meet Me Tonight in Atlantic City,* such as trying to find "the grandma" to lead Jane and her mother to an illegal dentist in Chinatown. How does humor operate in a memoir that also carries the weight of trauma and loss?

5. Jane's memoir is unabashedly a poet's memoir, full of visceral description. What were some of your favorite moments of imagery?

6. In the chapter "The Object of Love," Jane writes about her experiences with intimate partner violence alongside the resilient power of friendship. Her friend Michelle repeatedly sends her a text message: "You are easy to love." She also includes quotes from bell hooks and Toni Morrison in this chapter, who guide her through moments of healing. What is the importance of returning to these quotes throughout the chapter? In your own life, has friendship aided you in similarly powerful ways?

7. There are numerous moments in Jane's memoir where she writes about nourishment and food, as a "restaurant baby" and as a grandchild of a family who experienced starvation and hunger during China's Great Leap Forward. How does Jane speak to both gluttony and hunger? What role does fruit play throughout the memoir? And what healing power does food have in your own life?

8. In chapters like "Astonished Enough?" Jane writes about her journey as an Asian American poet: "Maybe poetry was the portal through which my powers came alive." What is your

relationship to writing? What challenges and joys have you encountered? How does creativity and art impact your sense of self and
your communities?

9. Writer Sally Wen Mao praises the "tenderness and ferocity" of
Jane's prose. How did you see these two forces at play in the book,
both in terms of the language and in terms of the experiences Jane
is writing about?

10. In your own life, is there someone you'd like to share this book
with? Who do you think most needs to read this memoir?

JANE WONG is the author of the poetry collections *How to Not Be Afraid of Everything* and *Overpour*. An associate professor of creative writing at Western Washington University, she grew up in New Jersey and currently lives in Seattle, Washington.